SHOWTIME
AT THE APOLLO

SHOWTIME AT THE APOLLO

★ TED FOX ★

MILL ROAD ENTERPRISES • RHINEBECK, NEW YORK

ISBN: 0-9723700-1-3
Library of Congress Control Number: 2002114997

New Revised Edition 2003

This revised edition of *Showtime at the Apollo* is an unabridged reproduction
of the edition published in New York in 1983, with the substitution of a new
afterword for the original one. It is reprinted by arrangement with the author.

Published by
Mill Road Enterprises
P.O. Box 561
Rhinebeck NY 12572

Illustration Credits

For Gina, Jack, Olivia,
Reed and William
with all my love

Contents

· · · · · · · · · · ·

Acknowledgments   *xi*

Introduction   The World's Most Famous Theatre   1
1   Harlem's Early Years—The Apollo's Heritage   39
2   The Thirties   67
3   Amateur Night and the Apollo Audience   104
4   The Forties   132
5   The Fifties   167
6   Gospel and the Blues   214
7   The Sixties   239
8   The Struggling Seventies   285

AFTERWORD: How the Apollo Got Its Groove Back   310
Index   317

Acknowledgments

· · · · · · · · · · ·

I am most grateful to those who graciously allowed themselves to be interviewed for this book: Estrellita Brooks-Morse, Maxine Brown, Ruth Brown, John Bubbles, Benny Carter, Carol Carter, Deborah Chessler, Harold Cromer, Jimmy Cross, Sammy Davis, Jr., Billy Eckstine, Ahmet Ertegun, Little Anthony Gourdine, John Hammond, Lionel Hampton, Screamin' Jay Hawkins, Andy Kirk, Gladys Knight, Beverly Lee, David McCarthy, Herbie Mills, Scoey Mitchlll, Johnny Otis, Esther Phillips, St. Clair Pinckney, Dave Prater, Danny Ray, Leonard Reed, Timmie Rogers, Thurman Ruth, Bobby Schiffman, Sandman Sims, Percy Sutton, Doll Thomas, Big Joe Turner, Leslie Uggams, Eddie "Cleanhead" Vinson, Dionne Warwick, Tom Whaley, and Nancy Wilson. Their recollections and insights make this book what it is. My special thanks to Dionne Warwick for her help; to Lionel Hampton for opening his photo files to me; and to Harold Cromer for his advice and help.

To Dick Seaver, my editor, and Ronald Hobbs, my agent, thanks for taking a chance.

I'd like to acknowledge Trent Duffy, Kathie Gordon, Tom Noonan, Larry Jordan, and Simone Harris for their excellent editorial guidance.

A number of books proved invaluable in my research, especially the following: *Blues People* by LeRoi Jones (Imamu Amiri Baraka), *Honkers and Shouters* by Arnold Shaw, *The Gospel Sound* by Tony Heilbut, *The Sound of Soul* by Phyl Garland, *Jazz Dance* by Jean and Marshall Stearns, *This Was Harlem* by Jervis Anderson, and *Uptown, The Story of Harlem's Apollo Theatre* by Jack Schiffman. I'd like to thank the authors and recommend the books.

Thanks to Gordon "Doc" Anderson, Frank Driggs, and Dunc Butler for access to their splendid collections of photographs.

My very special thanks to Bobby Schiffman—my stepmother's twin sister's first husband—for the many hours he spent with me, the memories and memorabilia he made available, and for his honest appraisal of his family's years at the Apollo. "Write about the way the Apollo really was, the good and the bad," he told me. I hope I have.

Thanks to Eric Eiser, Arthur Leinoff and Joy Garber, Clarence Jones, Bonnie Ballard, Carole Wright, Debby Thomas at the Schomburg Collection, Loften Mitchell, the folks at D-A-Y, and Dick Godin for their help. Thanks also to Jerry Kupfer for keeping me up to date.

To my good friends in Manhattan and Owego, thank you.

Most of all, I'd like to thank my family for seeing me through the past three years. To my brother and best friend, Nick, and my father, Sol—also my earliest, most incisive, and most helpful editors—thank you. To my mother, and to Carol, thank you. I could not have done it without you.

I'd also like to thank all of the people who help to keep the Apollo thriving, especially those who worked most closely with me on this new edition: David Rodriguez, Jonelle Procope, Billy Mitchell, Dawn Frisby Byers and Randi Honig. Check out *www.apollotheater.com* for the latest information.

INTRODUCTION

· · · · · · · · · ·

THE WORLD'S MOST FAMOUS THEATRE

One crisp November evening in 1955, a cab rolled uptown from the RCA Victor offices in Rockefeller Center, down 125th Street in Harlem, and stopped between Seventh and Eighth avenues in front of the Apollo Theatre. After all he had heard about the fabulous Apollo, the passenger was surprised to discover that it was such an unimpressive edifice, just a drab, gray, three-story pile of bricks, the upper stories each fronted by four large plate-glass windows—giving the building the appearance of a typical garment-center shop rather than a theatre. But the marquee lit up the street. Projecting way out over the sidewalk along the left half of the theatre's façade, it was crowded with names framed in neon lights: "Dr. Jive's Rhythm and Blues Revue" starring top men Bo Diddley and Bill "Honky Tonk" Doggett, and featuring, in progressively smaller type, an impressive roster of "r and b" greats: The Four Jacks, The Flamingoes, The Harptones, The Heart Beats, Etta James, Dakota Staton, Willis Jackson, and Howlin' Wolf. Above the marquee, in a fifteen-foot vertical array, sequentially flashing purple letters on a white background spelled out: A-P-O-L-L-O. The passenger drawled "thaynk yew," paid his fare, stepped out, walked up to the box office, and plunked down a dollar for an orchestra seat.

As the sweet-faced twenty-year-old strolled through the long, narrow

1

The Apollo, 1951. ★ *After all he had heard about the fabulous Apollo, the passenger was surprised to discover that it was such an unimpressive edifice.*

lobby he drew little notice from the predominantly black crowd hanging around, checking each other out or waiting to buy candy, potato chips, and ice cream from Mary Johnson's concession stand. There were plenty of other white youngsters about, and even his perfectly sculpted, slicked-back pompadour, black pants, and pink shirt did not set him apart. The look that had seemed so bizarre in hometown Memphis was de rigueur in Harlem. The crowd may not have recognized him, but undoubtedly some in attendance must have heard deejay Tommy Smalls—Dr. Jive—spin the youngster's versions of Arthur "Big Boy" Crudup's "That's Alright Mama" or Junior Parker's "Mystery Train" on WWRL. But they probably thought Elvis Presley was a black man. He certainly sounded like one.

As he passed the snack concession, and just as he was about to enter the theatre, Elvis stopped to peruse the huge photo-montage panels to his left. Each panel was plastered with the figures and faces of hundreds of stars who had started at the Apollo or called it home: Ella Fitzgerald, Duke Ellington, Pearl Bailey, Jackie "Moms" Mabley, Lionel Hampton, Billy Eckstine, Bessie Smith, Redd Foxx, Cab Calloway, Billie Holiday, Lena Horne, Count Basie, Sarah Vaughan, Charlie Parker, Bill "Bojangles" Robinson, Sammy Davis, Jr., and so many others. Over the years, as they proved themselves worthy of inclusion in such an illustrious collection, portraits of new stars—James Brown, Dionne Warwick, Gladys Knight, Smokey Robinson, Diana Ross, Bill Cosby—would be added to the montages.

Suddenly, Reuben Phillips struck up the house band to signal the start of the show and summon the crowd's attention. Elvis moved into the theatre with the rest of the lobby loiterers. There, up front, were the oak boards of the legendary Apollo stage, bathed in red light and surrounded by eight Doric columns. He took his seat just in time to catch Dr. Jive announce: "It's Showtime at the Apollo!"

. . . . .

Elvis Presley, a young, still-raw hayseed, was making his first trip to the Big Apple to see his new record company, and the Apollo was where he wanted to be. Night after night in New York he sat in the Apollo, transfixed by the pounding rhythms, the dancing and prancing, the sexual spectacle of rhythm-and-blues masters like Bo Diddley. He had heard and emulated black singers all his life, but now he saw how black music affected the world's toughest audience. It was good medicine for him, and he repeated the dose often and to amazing effect.

In 1955, Elvis's stage presence was still rudimentary. But watching Bo Diddley charge up the Apollo crowd undoubtedly had a profound effect on him. When he returned to New York a few months later for his first national television appearance, on Tommy and Jimmy Dorsey's "Stage Show," he again spent hours at the Apollo after rehearsals. On the Dorsey show Elvis shocked the entire country with his outrageous hip-shaking performance, and the furor that followed made him an American sensation.

For more than four decades from its inception as a black theatre in 1934, the Apollo Theatre probably exerted a greater influence upon popular culture than any other entertainment venue in the world. It was primarily a black theatre presenting the finest black entertainers performing the most innovative material of their day. For blacks it was the most important cultural institution—not just the greatest black theatre, but a special place to come of age emotionally, professionally, socially, and politically.

"The curiosity that white musicians had about the Apollo is very simple," said Ahmet Ertegun, chairman of Atlantic Records, and a man who helped nurture the careers of Ray Charles, Big Joe Turner, and Aretha Franklin as well as Eric Clapton, the Allman Brothers, and the Rolling Stones. "When the Beatles and the Rolling Stones first came to America, they loved to hear the source of their inspiration, which was black music. The place to really hear the great black artists was the Apollo Theatre. They came to see whoever was there, and it was a great experience for them.

"The Apollo developed an aura of its own and myths of its own. It was the apex of black entertainment. It represented getting out of the limitations of being a black entertainer. If you're a black entertainer in Charlotte or Mississippi you have great constraints put upon you. But coming to Harlem and the Apollo—Harlem was an expression of the black spirit in America, it was a haven. The Apollo Theatre stood for the greatest—the castle that you reach when you finally make it."

"The Apollo was the top," said bandleader Andy Kirk. "It was *the* thing. You had to play the Apollo, and once you did play it, you had it made." As it was for Kirk in the thirties, so it was in the forties and fifties. "We knew that if you ever made it, you'd go to the Apollo," said Johnny Otis, the rhythm-and-blues pioneer. "If you went to the Apollo and they said, 'Yeah, that's good,' then that was it. That was the stamp. The postgraduate course." And in the sixties: "The Apollo will always be something special for us," said Beverly Lee of the Shirelles. "You'd hear the Reuben Phillips band hit their little warm-up, and you knew the show was beginning. It was the most beautiful feeling in the world. It was

Elvis Presley making his first national television appearance, with Tommy and Jimmy Dorsey, 1956. ★ *He was a young, still-raw hayseed, and the Apollo was where he wanted to be.*

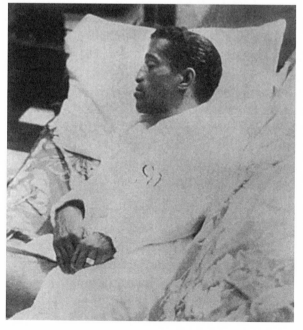

Sammy Davis, Jr., napping between shows, late 1950s. ★ Dave Prater: *"In the Apollo it was like you were home."*

Erskine Hawkins, the bandleader, back in the Apollo alley, late 1940s. ★
Ruth Brown: *"It was a place that was so well loved that even the performers who were not working there used to spend as much time there."*

the first major theatre we'd worked. We got our training there. I'm very grateful." In the words of Sammy Davis, Jr.: "It was like playing the Copa. You didn't go into the Copa lightweight: they'd break your legs. But at the Apollo they'd break your heart."

Nearly every black performer interviewed for this book has volunteered that "the Apollo was home." It was home to thousands of performers who over the years comprised the Apollo family. This was not a family in the phony, too-perfectly-harmonious-to-be-true sense of the word. No, it was a family that often scrapped, a family of sibling love and rivalry, but a family bound together by shared experiences, hopes, and ambitions. "Sam and I played all over New York before we played the Apollo," said Dave Prater of Sam and Dave. "But the Apollo was the number-one theatre on the map. In the Apollo it was like you were home." As the comedian Scoey Mitchlll put it: "If things weren't going well, you just stayed there—went into the dressing room and went to sleep. Backstage at the Apollo you could get anything you wanted: just put your order in. There wasn't much in the way of dope being sold there, and that was because there was a reverence for the Apollo. I'm not saying no dope ever got in there, but you were frowned upon because you were dirtying up the house. I guess that was home. It was home for a lot of acts, and it was the black Vegas. It was more meaningful than any other theatre on the circuit. I'm sure a lot of white performers wanted to know what it was that was so special about this place. It was a coming together, a community of what we all had there."

"It was a place that was so well loved that even the performers who were not working there used to spend as much time there," said Ruth Brown, one of the great rhythm-and-blues singers. "They would all get dressed up and come to the Apollo, and come backstage and spend the day back there. On any given day you would come backstage and find a celebrity just sitting in the wings watching the show. I remember a young Muhammad Ali, Sugar Ray Robinson, you name it."

It was a communications center, too. One of the main roots of the Harlem grapevine was anchored in the Apollo, and it was an excellent place to catch up on the latest show-biz gossip or hot Harlem news. The pay phone backstage was in constant use all day long, and scribbled on the wall surrounding the phone were hundreds of telephone numbers of agents, bookers, managers, nightclubs, and theatres from literally around the world. "The Apollo was the gathering spot," said Ruth Brown. "Entertainers would come there to receive their messages. I've known them to sit there all day and answer that pay phone."

7

Although it was actively discouraged by the management, one of the primary attractions and diversions backstage was the around-the-clock gambling scene. "There used to be all kinds of games going," said Sammy Davis, Jr. "If you wanted to play Tonk you went down to the rehearsal hall in the basement. [Tonk is a kind of gin game, with five cards.] There were always poker games in everybody's dressing room, or Bid Wist. It was so funny because you could hear the games when you went in, and if you lost your money in the Tonk game you could go up and play Bid Wist for nothing." Craps was also popular. "A lot of entertainers shot craps," said Howard "Sandman" Sims, a dancer, tale teller, and Apollo habitué. "They had games in the dressing rooms or in the basement. They had some guys who could really play those things. They made a living off it, especially on payday."

But Tonk was the main game at the Apollo. It was a big betting game normally played for two to five dollars a hand, but sometimes much more. "I've seen some guys like Count Basie, other bandleaders, singers, band members, Redd Foxx, damn near miss the show 'cause they didn't want to leave the table," claimed Sandman. "They'd say, 'Redd, you're on.' 'Be right there.' 'Five minutes, Redd.' 'I'll be right there.' Those guys would come out on the stage with half their costumes on. As long as the Old Man didn't see you, you could get away with it.

"Ray Charles used to play. He had a guy sitting on his shoulder telling him what he's got, and what the others played. He'd shoot dice, too, and win all the money. One time Ray Charles was playing Tonk with Willie Lewis, a very outstanding comedian at that time. Willie won all of Ray's money." According to Sandman, Ray replenished his stake, but continued to lose. Finally, he accused Willie of cheating. "So Ray gets mad and turns the table over and runs Willie Lewis out of the room," Sandman continued. "Ray said, 'Show me where he's at. Point me at him!' And continues this right up to the stage. They're holding Ray backstage. It's almost time for him to go on. Now, as he went out on-stage he's still talking back to the people backstage about what he's going to do to Willie Lewis when he comes off. It was funny, man. The audience thought he was doing comedy."

Occasionally, the backstage scene could get rough. "One time we were playing some poker in the dressing room," recalled Gladys Knight. "Somebody knocked on the door. Me, Miss Nice-Nice, I just get up and say, 'Oh, come in.' It was these three guys. One of them had a long knife and one of them had a gun. I said, 'Oh, Jesus, no!' One guy said, 'Well, you know what it is, all right.' They robbed us, and I was just glad they

Redd Foxx and Dizzy Gillespie in an Apollo dressing room, about
1955. ★ Sandman Sims: *"They'd say, 'Redd, you're on.' 'Be right
there.' 'Five minutes, Redd.' 'I'll be right there.'"*

didn't kill us. We got robbed two or three times at the Apollo." Yet despite her bad experiences, Gladys still has fond memories of the Apollo. "It was ninety percent more good happening at the Apollo than bad. It was something positive in the midst of all that negative stuff going on in Harlem in those days. There's good and bad in everything, and I think you have to have the bad sometimes to appreciate the good. It was a very, very positive thing in the midst of Harlem."

Even though the work was terribly difficult, the atmosphere sometimes threatening, and the physical condition of the theatre often atrocious—some called the theatre "the workhouse" or "the penitentiary"—performers always looked forward to returning to the Apollo, to coming home. "They didn't look forward to the five shows a day or the filthy dressing rooms," said Dionne Warwick. "But they did look forward to the feeling very much. The theatre was terrible: drafty, dirty, smelly— awful; and we loved every minute of it."

Leslie Uggams reminisced: "The Apollo was fascinating because there was always something going on. You had to keep your windows closed and locked; otherwise, when you came back the next day, you had no wardrobe. That happened numerous times. My mother would always put a roach bomb in the dressing room before we went in there for a week. And you always shook out your stuff, because you can bring home a lot of pets. People would come selling food—the greatest home cooking ever. Somebody always had a deal, 'You wanna buy a watch?' You had your numbers going. I worked on one show where they had two ladies they called exotic dancers, and the show backstage was better than the show out front because they worked their way right through whoever was performing back there. They were making it with everybody. It was incredible."

"The backstage atmosphere was great," said Gladys Knight. "There used to be a little [catwalk] that hung out over the stage up in the ceiling. And we used to play tricks on people up there while they were onstage— drop chicken bones and stuff down on their heads. Then there used to be a school right across the street in back of the Apollo. All the guys on the show, even the stars, nine times out of ten, they'd end up over there playing basketball. The ladies would end up sitting out there on the fire escape watching them play."

The Apollo had thirteen dressing rooms on four floors, and within their tacky, cold, painted-cement walls beat the heart of the Apollo Theatre. There Louis Armstrong entertained guests and well-wishers in his underwear. James Brown held court. Ella Fitzgerald set out her usual

Louis Armstrong and friend in an Apollo dressing room. ★ *Within the dressing rooms' tacky, cold, painted-cement walls beat the heart of the Apollo Theatre. There Louis Armstrong entertained guests and well-wishers in his underwear. . . .*

spread of fried chicken, cold drinks, and cut watermelon. There advice was given and lessons learned. Deals were made. Songs, dance steps, and comedy bits were created. There also a performer could measure his progress and status. "I don't care how big you thought you were, when you first came in the Apollo you were nobody," said Anthony Gourdine of Little Anthony of the Imperials. "I don't care if you had nine hit records, you stayed in the top dressing room on the fourth floor. Had to walk all the way downstairs." But once a performer proved himself, he would be moved downstairs, and ultimately to the bright red star's dressing room on the first level off the stage.

The stagehands controlled access to the dressing rooms, as well as the lights, sound, and scenery. Smart entertainers learned to keep the stagehands happy with polite smiles and occasional tips; otherwise, one's act could develop mysterious technical difficulties or one's guests would be kept cooling their heels in the basement waiting room. Especially important was a gruff character named William Spayne. "I remember the first time I saw that old mean Spayne," said Anthony. "He gave me the dirtiest look in the world. He would call me, 'Come here, Antnee, now here's the rules.' Like a drill sergeant; Spayne was the law. And Spayne could tell you everything about everybody. I used to sit as a boy and listen to him, just mesmerized at the things he told me. Things about the personal lives of some of the people. Philanderings that were going on. Some were oddballs, some were this, some were that, the good people and the bad. He was a newspaper, you could get all the news about the past, the present, and he would even predict the future." But Spayne's orneriness was accepted and respected, because everyone knew he had the best interests of the Apollo at heart. Like a crotchety old grandfather, he, too, was a part of the Apollo family.

"It was a real family feeling," said Ruth Brown. "I loved it because everybody worked for the good of the show. Whatever was best for the show; everyone went out and did their best." The performers at the Apollo generally pulled together and helped one another. "I didn't know anything about show business when I went in there," said Sandman Sims. "When I came out, I knew all about it. When I first went into the Apollo I danced with my back to the audience, watching the band. But the rest of the entertainers would be in the wings or out in the audience and they'd tell you what you were doing wrong, or what you should do. See, the entertainers made the acts. This is how the theatre was built—on self-help. We didn't have no critics."

In a community and race bereft of political power, housed in society's castoffs and denied access to many of its cultural and educational centers, the Apollo Theatre was a place of great pride, and it became a fabled institution of signal importance. The Apollo's black patrons faced the bitter reality of life daily—on the outside. But in the theatre, reality was beautiful women, strong men, and angelic children; the everyday street people portrayed by the Apollo comedians were characters to be laughed at or pitied. To the whites who ventured uptown, the Apollo was as close as they could come to the reality of the black experience. As Ahmet Ertegun said, the Apollo fostered a mythology of its own. The truth of the Apollo's great history is the stuff of which myths are made.

Thousands of performers crossed the Apollo's stage, and some of them achieved heroic stature. The black artists who made the Apollo great are heroes; the beauty they gave the world—their art—transcended the hatred, ignorance, and intolerance that often made their lives so difficult. Many, like Teddy Hale, the dancer, Willie Bryant, an all-around entertainer, or Little Willie John, the wonderful rhythm-and-blues singer, were virtually unknown outside the black community to whom they were stars. But like their better-known black colleagues, they were personal heroes to white entertainers who would readily acknowledge a great creative debt to them. The Apollo was the cylinder within which the spark of their genius ignited the imagination of the world to power most of the revolutions in popular culture and style in the past half century. The people who speak in this book are among those who made the Apollo what it was—an institution that had an extraordinary impact upon their lives and, perhaps more than we realize, upon our own as well.

The Apollo Theatre has been called many things: an "Uptown Met," a "black Grand Ole Opry," and "the black equivalent of the Palace." Surely it has been all of these, but more, too: few cultural institutions in the world have been so influential in so many different fields for so many years. Throughout the years, the Apollo led the way in the presentation of swing, bebop, rhythm and blues, modern jazz, commercially presented gospel, soul, and funk. And the Apollo always provided the latest in dance and comedy.

Yet it is not entirely accurate to say that the Apollo Theatre was a fomenter of cultural revolutions; rather, it was a legitimizer—the Apollo was the establishment. One Apollo legend tells of a group called the Orioles; out of nowhere they stormed the Apollo with a new look and sound that so excited the Apollo crowd that they leveled everything

Dinah Washington and Sam Cooke in an Apollo dressing room,
early 1960s. ★ Ruth Brown: *"It was a real family feeling."*

ABOVE: William Spayne (top) and another stagehand guarding the stage door for Moms Mabley. ★ Little Anthony: *"I remember the first time I saw that old mean Spayne. He gave me the dirtiest look in the world."* RIGHT: Fats Domino, a rhythm-and-blues revolutionary, knew the ultimate battle was to conquer the Apollo.

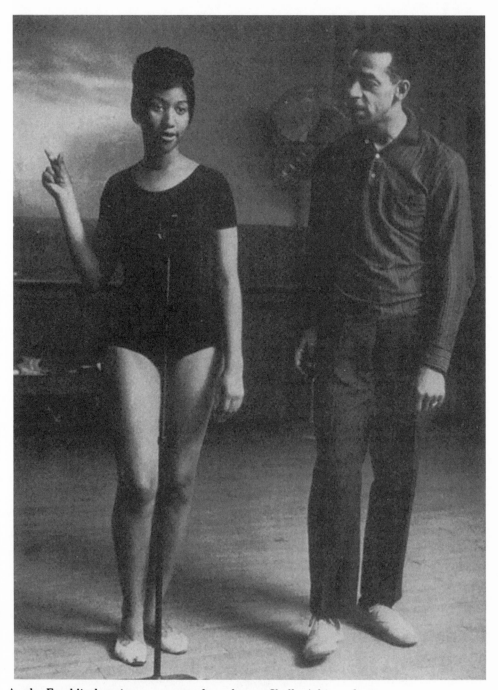

Aretha Franklin learning a new step from dancer Cholly Atkins, about 1960. ★ Sandman Sims: *"This is how the theatre was built—on self-help. We didn't have no critics."*

before them, and rhythm and blues was born. In fact, the Orioles had been shaking things up in Baltimore for at least a year before they made it at the Apollo. Likewise, other rhythm-and-blues revolutionaries were also active at the same time in other cities and other venues, among them bandleader Johnny Otis in the Barrel House in Los Angeles and pianist Fats Domino in the Hideaway Bar in New Orleans. As revolutionaries they fought in various places around the country, but they all knew the ultimate battle was to conquer the Apollo.

One of the keys to the Apollo's success was the theatre's adaptability. Like any establishment, the Apollo was sometimes slow to change, but as a black institution it adapted far more quickly than others. For, as Bobby Schiffman, son of Apollo patriarch Frank Schiffman, said, "Black people don't care what happened yesterday, they want to know what's going to happen tomorrow."

The theatre was run by a white Jewish family, the Schiffmans, but they were always up on the latest thing in black entertainment. As Ahmet Ertegun said, "All Bobby Schiffman had to do was stick his head out the door and there were three record shops on 125th Street blaring the new hit records. So he knew what the people were buying. He would check with the record companies to see who was hot and who was coming up." As something new came along, the Schiffmans seized it and brought it into their theatre. The ability to do this, while retaining their old clientele, for nearly fifty years is an achievement that has not been matched.

During any given season, the Apollo would offer all types of shows for all types of audiences. Modern jazz, gospel, big bands, rhythm and blues, star vocalists, traditional blues, and novelty acts would be interspersed. "The theatre had about 1,600 seats," said Bobby Schiffman. "If it did thirty shows a week that's 48,000 people. You had to try to nurture every market. One week you go after the Sarah Vaughan fans. One week you go after the Jackie Wilson fans. The next week the Dinah Washington fans. Then the sports fans with Joe Louis. Then the church people." This flexibility was another key to the Apollo's longevity and success. "People came there to see the artists," said singer Nancy Wilson. "It wasn't a jazz room or a soul room. They booked what was best. I think the beauty of it was the people just came to hear what they liked."

But the Apollo's flexibility was also a product of harsh economic realities, and a shrewd and calculated attempt by the Schiffmans to get the most out of the community. "There was one basic thing about the Apollo's box office that was different from any other," according to

Bobby Schiffman. "If you were selling five tickets to somebody for six dollars in a normal theatre, a guy would come up and drop a twenty-dollar bill and a ten to buy them. In the Apollo they would drop something like a ten-dollar bill, six dollars in quarters, ten dollars in dimes, because the people were scratching to get enough money to be able to come.

"You couldn't tap the same people every week; you would drain them dry. We used to schedule some of our shows with the payoff of the city employees every other week—and the welfare checks were very important. We knew when the welfare checks were coming out. We knew that a part of the welfare check was going to go for entertainment, and so if the welfare checks came out the first and third weeks of the month, that's when we would schedule the shows that required the welfare audience's money—the ones that the more elderly people would be interested in. We knew that young people will get the money anytime."

The main reason for the Apollo's success, however, was a firm belief in the old adage, "The show must go on"—good old-fashioned show-biz tenacity. "The policy at the Apollo," said Bobby Schiffman, "was that we were in business no matter what. We always did a show, some of them great, some of them fair, some of them lousy, but we did a show every week. We were outrageous promoters and we would often make outrageous productivity out of mediocre presentations because we really cared, and we used to do everything we could do to make the stage show as glamorous and as elevated as we possibly could. We knew that people would come to the Apollo to escape from reality. For the couple of hours they were there, they could fantasize that they were part of the elegant living they were seeing portrayed on the stage. The six-hundred-dollar mohair suits, the fancy shoes, fancy cars, and the beautiful women, all the other things that were part of the glamour of show business—we used to try to capitalize on that. We would spend hours and hours planning on a weekly basis how to glamorize the stage. We used to change scenery every week. No other theatre in the world would change scenery every week."

To insure that the show not only would go on, but keep going on in the future, the Apollo nurtured new and untried talents who would later become the stars who kept the theatre packed, generation after generation. The Apollo's Wednesday amateur-night show became world renowned. This showcase has been responsible for boosting the careers of hundreds of important stars from Bill Kenny of the Ink Spots to Sarah

Vaughan to the Clovers to the Isley Brothers. Also, the Schiffmans loaded their shows with new and unknown professional talent with promise.

"We had the golden opportunity to present a multitude of acts in every show," said Bobby Schiffman. "I used to do seven or eight acts on every show. The three or four acts at the top of the show were the ones that sold the tickets. Those at the bottom were the ones we were giving the opportunity to display their wares. James Brown was once the opening act for Little Willie John. Redd Foxx used to play the theatre all the time for $300, $400, $500. The same with Flip Wilson. Al Green was once an opening act in the Apollo. Gladys Knight would always be an opening act in the Apollo because she was so animated. The Spinners were another one. They were a local act, and every time we needed an opening act and couldn't think of someone to put in there, we'd go buy the Spinners. My brother Jack told me this story: One of the guys in the house band came out to get my brother and said, 'There's a young kid back there who's playing piano and singing up a storm between shows backstage.' So my brother said, 'Let's go listen.' There's this blind piano player off in the wings, the motion picture is on and he's singing, and he's so good. So they put him in a couple of numbers in the show, and that was Ray Charles."

In the days when vaudeville was popular, Frank Schiffman began his process of nurturing dancers, comedians, singers, even acrobats. He had a circle of acquaintances (some would say cronies) in nearby night-clubs and small theatres who broke in acts for the Apollo. "He would take you out and hold you awhile," said Sandman Sims. "Groom you and work you around till you got a real good act. Then he'd work you into the Apollo, build your act up, and bring it back."

All this talent did not go unnoticed. Every talent and booking agency—William Morris, GAC, Universal, Associated Booking—had representatives in the audience for the first show of the week on Friday. Oscar Cohen, head of Associated Booking, told Arnold Shaw, in his book *Honkers and Shouters*, how the company's founder, Joe Glaser, one of the top *machers* in black show business, used to pick him up to go to the Apollo: "We did that for twenty years. We caught the Apollo bill twice a week: The first show on Friday and the first show on Sunday. Regardless of who was playing there, we went. And, we saw every show for twenty years."

Harold Cromer, the "Stumpy" half of the comedy team of Stump

The Apollo lineup for the week of November 9, 1962. ★
Bobby Schiffman: *"We had the golden opportunity to present a
multitude of acts in every show."*

ONE WEEK ONLY BEG. FRIDAY, APRIL 24

LITTLE WILLIE JOHN

JAMES BROWN and the FLAMES

The UPSETTERS

BUTTERBEANS & SUSIE | VI KEMP

Apollo handbill for the week of April 24, 1959, with James Brown backing up his friend and mentor, Little Willie John.

The Spinners, early 1970s. ★ Bobby Schiffman: *"They were a local act, and every time we needed an opening act and couldn't think of someone to put in there, we'd go buy the Spinners."*

and Stumpy, recalled the scene: "The agents and managers would talk to Mr. Schiffman to find out who the agent was, or who was handling you. Sometimes they would come backstage and approach an artist to find out if he had an agent or manager. They would say, 'I'd like to handle you, and I think we can go places.' Sometimes the artist ended up on the other side of the stick. But the most important thing was to get on the stage and perform. Hopefully, they could make a lot of money, and some of them did; but most of them just made a couple of bucks and that was it."

Son Bobby built upon his father's system, and established a rapport, and often friendships, with performers that ultimately paid off for the Apollo. "We gave performers a showcase where, for a dollar return, they could nurture their talent and popularity. And they owed us," said Bobby. "The first time I played Gladys Knight and the Pips I paid them $800 for thirty-one shows over seven days. The last time I paid them $80,000 for sixteen shows. Now there was no way, based upon a long-standing personal relationship I had with them, that they could say no to me if I said I need you. Because I was involved in incubating their careers. . . . When they came into the theatre we did everything to make them comfortable. We talked to them, and we kidded with them and socialized with them. Smokey Robinson and I used to play golf together, and Marvin Gaye and I were good friends. We used to go out together."

Gladys Knight confirms this. "They were some of the first people to give us the opportunity," she said. "They were *fair* people. They always kept faith in us and they always kept bringing us back. They were as interested in your act as you were—sometimes more. And they would give people the encouragement they needed. They are so much a part of what we are today, I cannot tell you. People may think, 'Okay, this is an interview about the Apollo and for the Apollo,' but they cannot really know what the Apollo has meant to so many people in this business— especially black people."

Although the Apollo family was black, it did have an almost mystical allure for whites. Perhaps the white mystique derived from a reverse of Groucho Marx's famous quip: "I wouldn't want to join any club that would have me as a member." The Apollo club was black, and so inherently difficult for whites to join; and on top of that, to make it in you had to be the best.

"John Lennon was the most curious about the Apollo," said Esther Phillips, the rhythm-and-blues prodigy whom the Beatles invited to appear on their November 1965 BBC-TV show. "He asked me, was it as hard to go up and see as he had heard. They were curious as to why it was so hard to play. They were making quite a bit of money, and I guess it really came easy to them. They'd heard so many stories about the Apollo—I think it was a mystique to them. They really wanted to see what the Apollo was about. And the Animals' Eric Burden; he was not only curious, he was ready to come on over here and go do the Apollo."

The Apollo was a shrine for all types of popular performers and headhunters eager to taste at the wellspring of inspiration. The first place the Beatles wanted to see when they came to America was the Apollo Theatre, according to legendary record producer Phil Spector, who accompanied them on their first trip to America. Ed Sullivan used to frequent the Apollo weekly, scouting new talent for his television show. Milton Berle and Joey Adams were regulars during the glory days of black comedians like Dewey "Pigmeat" Markham and Dusty Fletcher. Mick Jagger and Janis Joplin always made a point of stopping at the Apollo whenever they were in town. More recently, the top rock group the Police headed for the Apollo when they first hit New York.

Many of the white entertainers who played the Apollo were honored to be allowed to perform there. White rhythm-and-bluesman Wayne Cochran, after difficult negotiations, was booked into the Apollo. "I was standing backstage with him," said Bobby Schiffman. "He was very, very nervous and he turned around and said, 'You know I can't believe I'm about to go out on the stage that Bessie Smith, and Billie Holiday, Otis Redding, Fats Domino, and Harry Belafonte played. I want you to know that in the end I would have paid *you* to allow me to have this opportunity to appear on your stage.' " As Ahmet Ertegun said, "It was like going to Mecca."

Dionne Warwick told how she came to introduce heartthrob Tom Jones to the Apollo: "I'm coming out of Scepter Records on the corner of Fifty-fourth and Broadway. And there's a guy with a T-shirt and a pair of jeans and a leather jacket and a pigtail and a very crooked nose and super blue eyes. And he called my name and I turned around and it's Tom Jones. Tom had just come over to do a tour with Dick Clark. I asked him what he was doing standing on the corner of Fifty-fourth and Broadway and he says, 'I'm just looking around.' I mean he's just a new kid in town and he's walking up and down the streets looking at the lights. He asked where I was going and I said, 'I'm going to the Apollo.' He grabbed my arm and said, 'Can I—I—I—go with you?' So I said, 'Of course you can go with me,' and that was his first exposure to the Apollo

Theatre. That night he sang at the Apollo. Chuck Jackson was starring and Chuck pulled him right up onstage and he *killed* the audience. It was amazing. It was wonderful. I think *that* was the beginning of his career. He said in his entire life he'd never felt anything like that before." Other white stars—Harry James, Bunny Berigan, Charlie Barnet, Buddy Rich, Dave Brubeck, Bobby Darin, Buddy Holly, the Four Seasons—also bowled over audiences at the Apollo.

For white performers, acceptance at the Apollo was an added stamp of approval from a special audience. For black artists it could be everything, or the beginning of everything. Show business was one of the few ways for blacks to make it. As Paul Robeson once said, "I knew a Negro lawyer could only go so high, no matter how good he was. On the stage, it was different. Only the sky, I felt, could be my roof." The Apollo represented the pinnacle of achievement in black show business, and for most it was as high as black artists would ever go. But if the emotional motivation for playing the Apollo was the pride of doing one's best before one's own people, the implicit hope was that the Apollo would launch one into the higher trajectory of popular success in the white world. As the black newspaper the *New York Age* said in 1934: "Everything the Negro does on the stage or the screen is done with an idea of selling it to white people."

Nevertheless, until the civil-rights movement and the rock-and-roll revolution changed things by the late sixties, only a handful of black stars went on to make it in the white world: Louis Armstrong, Duke Ellington, Pearl Bailey, Sammy Davis, Jr., Sidney Poitier (who appeared at the Apollo in 1951 in the stage play *Detective Story*), and a few others. Throughout most of the Apollo's history it was nearly impossible for even its top stars to gain access to or acceptance in the American popular culture represented by movies, radio, television, "downtown" theatres, magazines, newspapers, and recordings. Still, however embittered, however mistreated, black artists wanted to make it in the white world—not to become part of it, but to get the respect and wide audience that all artists desire. Yet it is ironic that if segregation had not existed, black culture, so deeply inspired by injustice, hate, and inequality, might never have developed into the vital cultural force it became—and neither would the Apollo Theatre.

As the civil-rights movement began to alter the nation's consciousness, other areas of opportunity became available at last to black performers. The system the Apollo was forced to work within for so many years began to collapse. The general acceptance of black culture into American popular culture was the beginning of something brand new, but it was also the beginning of the end for the Apollo Theatre. For it is the final irony that the ultimate casualty of this revolution was the Apollo itself.

· · · · ·

When the Apollo Theatre was christened in 1934, the area around it on West 125th Street was a transitional neighborhood. For over two decades before, the theatre had been operated as a music hall, vaudeville house, and burlesque joint, presenting white shows to white audiences. While many think of "Uptown" as always having been a black community, the history of blacks in New York actually begins at the extreme opposite end of the island of Manhattan, where the first Africans worked as slaves. Only gradually, over more than two hundred years, did blacks migrate uptown to ultimately make Harlem the world's greatest black neighborhood.

Around the turn of the century, blacks were forced out of Manhattan's middle West Side, then the primary black district. Some began moving to Harlem—a white middle- and upper-middle-class community—as a refuge. Speculators who had eagerly built apartments in anticipation of the opening of the Lenox Avenue elevated subway in 1904 found that supply outpaced white demand. They turned to blacks to fill in, usually at exorbitant rents. By 1914 Harlem was the fashionable place for blacks who couldn't afford Brooklyn. The black community grew quickly. What in 1919 was a relatively isolated section of blacks from 130th Street to 143rd Street and from about Seventh Avenue to Madison grew, by 1930, to include a major part of present-day Harlem.

To a large degree, the entertainment scene in the changing Harlem community was controlled by two men: Frank Schiffman and Leo Brecher—although they would not control the new Apollo Theatre until 1935. Brecher was there first. The Austrian immigrant owned and operated a number of theatres around Manhattan, and he was the money man behind all the Schiffman-Brecher operations. But he was content to remain a silent partner until his death in 1980 at the age of ninety. Schiffman, a former schoolteacher who had grown up on the Lower East Side, managed the theatres, and eventually became part owner of the Apollo. Their power uptown became indomitable when they assumed control of the granddaddy of all black theatres, the Lafayette. When they took it over in May 1925 they inherited a theatre with more than a decade's tradition as the "cradle of stars." But by this time they had already developed an impressive theatrical reputation of their own.

"They had all the theatres in Harlem," said Francis "Doll" Thomas, former film projectionist, spotlight operator, and general backstage factotum at the Apollo. "I went to work for Mr. Leo Brecher in 1914, long before he tied up with Mr. Schiffman. Leo Brecher was a very nice, very shrewd, and a very smart individual." Sitting in his apartment right above the Apollo, the man known as "Mr. Apollo" continued, "Up here he owned the Odeon on 145th Street. Then the business was so good he opened one down the street called the Odeon Annex. These were primarily movie theatres. He owned the Roosevelt at 145th and Fifth, the Douglas at 142nd and Lenox, and of course the Lafayette at 132nd and Seventh. In the upstairs lobby over the Douglas Theatre was the Cotton Club. He was not only the landlord for the Cotton Club, but he was the landlord for all the show business the colored talent had up here in New York City. And there was no competition—or they wouldn't allow any competition."

Brecher met Schiffman when the latter helped the former out of a sticky situation involving Brecher's movie theatres. "In those days the projectionist went downtown and got the films before the show," said Doll Thomas. "You took the film back after the show. And if you had booked a film a rival movie-house exhibitor wanted, he had a gang waiting to take the film away from you. They'd take the film out of the box and roll it up and down the street. So through some knack of genius or something, Mr. Schiffman created a film-delivery service, the first one in New York City. And through the film-delivery service he met Mr. Brecher. That formed one of the most airtight and one of the most successful theatre combinations that there was, especially in black show business. It gave them an absolute monopoly."

In 1922 they took over the Harlem Opera House on 125th Street, just down the block from the Apollo, and developed a successful format of stage comedies and musicals featuring stars and stars-to-be, among them Al Jolson, the Four Marx Brothers, and a stock company presenting Ann Harding. For a time, their operations also included running girlie shows at the Loew's Seventh Avenue on 124th Street and operating Harlem's Lincoln Theatre. However, the Lafayette became the capital of their theatrical empire, and Frank Schiffman devoted himself to the development of black entertainment.

There were pragmatic reasons for this. Broadway and Forty-second

Street were giving the 125th Street burlesque houses—including Schiff-man and Brecher's Harlem Opera House—a run for their money. The top draws were beginning to be lured away by the greater financial rewards and prestige of the downtown theatres. Schiffman and Brecher saw the writing on the wall and decided to diversify into an area that was not being fully exploited—black entertainment in the new black commu-nity centered around the Lafayette on upper Seventh Avenue. Black talent could be had much more cheaply than white. Also, the black community could always be counted on wholeheartedly to support enter-tainment ventures that appealed to them. At the height of the Depression a conference of movie exhibitors found that, as the *New York Age* wrote, "In all New York, Harlem was the last to show signs of business falling off. . . . This goes to prove that Harlemites will not allow hard times to make hermits and recluses out of them, but will scrape up enough to take in their amusements."

Frank Schiffman emerged as a controversial figure in Harlem and remained so long after he and Brecher took over the Apollo. He was, as we will see, a vicious competitor who would do nearly anything to eliminate anyone invading his turf. He was loved and hated, hailed as a progressive genius, and denigrated as a lucky opportunist.

"I got to say this for Frank Schiffman," said Harold Cromer. "He was marvelous. I knew what he was doing. He had to show a profit, but at the same time he was making these elaborate shows available to the immediate area. They could come see a show for a reasonable price that they could afford. What he was trying to do was maintain the prices at the box office, and also hopefully pay the entertainers at a certain figure. He had a community idea of thought, and an awareness of community problems."

"Anyone would like these people," Frank Schiffman told a New York newspaper in 1937. "I'm the largest employer of colored theatrical help in the country." In fact, for many years the Apollo was the *only* theatre in New York that would hire blacks. Virtually everyone in the Apollo except Schiffman was black, including his stage manager, Jimmy Marshall, who started with him at the Lafayette; Tom Whaley, the rehearsal band conductor and musical director; Doll Thomas, the techni-cal director; and Norman Miller (alias Porto Rico), the number-one stagehand in charge of sound.

"I learned more from Frank Schiffman in two years about show business than I learned in twenty years of knocking around theatres," said Leonard Reed, who once had a dance team with Willie Bryant,

Frank Schiffman (second from left), with Mayor La
Guardia and black community leaders in the early
1940s. ★   *"Anyone would like these people,"* he
told a New York newspaper in 1937.

became a producer, formed a comedy act around his pal Joe Louis, and served a stint as manager of the Apollo. "He was the smartest theatre operator I ever knew. Everybody used to talk about him: 'Cheap son of a bitch. He won't do this and he won't do that.' I said, 'The man's not cheap, he's a businessman.' Only two white men I know knew black show business. Frank Schiffman was the best, Lew Leslie [the impresario] was next. He was a genius." Estrellita Brooks-Morse, who formed the popular comedy team of Apus and Estrellita with her husband Apus Brooks, remembers a man who was kind but firm. "Some people say he was a little rough, but he was 'Pops' to me. Pop Schiffman was a nice man. He gave many performers breaks to come in to play, even though the money was poor. He'd always give you a draw, he'd never say no. On opening day they'd bug him all day: 'Pop, can I have a draw?' "

Others saw Frank Schiffman in a less virtuous light. John Hammond, a friend of the Schiffmans who produced and popularized Billie Holiday and Count Basie as well as Bob Dylan and Bruce Springsteen, said the Apollo was just "a way of making money. Frank had no artistic taste whatever. He looked at a singer as to would she draw or wouldn't she. Could he make a decent profit off her." He said Frank was "not at all" enlightened. As for his community spirit, Hammond feels, "that was just a way for a white man to stay in business in Harlem. I can remember him talking about Negroes and using the word *schvartzer*."

Some performers were skeptical, too. "Schiffman didn't know much about how to handle the people, he was just lucky," said John Bubbles, the great dancer. "He was just lucky to get a theatre and have Negro entertainment. You can't get luckier than that. What did he know? Only thing he knew was how to get people as cheap as he could, and work them as long as he could. He misused the people. People wanted to work, and he wouldn't give them a job. He knew they were good acts."

Andy Kirk, for one, was blackballed by Schiffman. "RKO took over the [Alhambra] ballroom on 126th Street," said Kirk. "They were trying to give the Apollo some competition. So I went in there—the big-band era was just about over at this time. He came backstage there to tell me he thought I was an enemy of his because I was playing for the opposition. . . . So that was the last time I played the Apollo with my band. I said, 'Okay, I won't starve without you.' But you know something, to me it was a laugh. I laugh now and I laughed then. It was kind of childish, to my way of thinking." Furthermore, according to John Hammond, "The Apollo had a working arrangement with the Howard Theatre in Washington, the Royal in Baltimore, and the Earle in Philly.

If [a performer] wanted to play the Apollo, you had to get booked for the lower price at the other theatres."

Whatever his true motives, Frank Schiffman was a key factor in the development of the Apollo's shows. Many credit him with maintaining the Apollo's consistently high standard of performance. He had strong ideas about the way the acts should run. Said Estrellita Brooks-Morse: "The morning before the show, Thursday morning, he'd be standing in the back leaning up against the wall. He would look at the show [rehearsal] and whatever was in that show he didn't like, he'd take out. Or he'd say, 'Look, do it this way.' He was never a dancer and he was never a comedian, but being in the business he was in, he was trying to be everything. When you did a joke he could tell you, 'It's not going to go over. But if you turn it around and do it this way it's going to click.' He was right."

Schiffman used to say that he could predict the weekly gross of any show within $200 after the first Friday-night performance. He kept meticulous notes on file cards of every performer and every performance, sometimes using a little penlight to write in the darkened theatre. He had plenty of opportunity to sign new acts to personal contracts—he passed on signing Ella Fitzgerald, to the great relief of bandleader Chick Webb—but he preferred to concentrate all his efforts on the Apollo. In the late forties and early fifties he and his elder son, Jack, would usually rope off a section in the center orchestra as an observation post and from there, or anywhere in the theatre, could communicate via a sort of closed-circuit walkie-talkie to the stagehands and light operators. "If he didn't like an act," said Estrellita, "that was it. I don't care how good you were. If he didn't like the act, you didn't play the theatre."

There used to be a saying backstage: "Don't send out your laundry until after the first show." When he came backstage after the show he'd be greeted with, "Hey, Mr. Schiffman. Should we send out our laundry?" He'd laugh—or fire them.

Once he had conquered the uptown scene, and vanquished his serious competitors, Frank Schiffman seemed to mellow, or at least internalize his combativeness. He was impatient when things were not running smoothly, and he still maintained an iron grip on the controls in his theatre, but his demeanor was even-tempered, restrained, even placid. "He was a very courteous man," said Johnny Otis. "He was highly opinionated about decorum, timing, stagemanship, and these things. He overdid it a little bit as far as I'm concerned. Because when you become regimented and preoccupied with should you have a black tie on, not a red one, or turn to the left stage when there's a singer, and all these show-business rules, it tends to take away from the spontaneity. Instead of having fun you tighten up; you're more concerned with standing in a straight line than groovin'. He was almost like a little tyrant, but a benevolent one. He was really a good-hearted man and a sweet guy."

Sandman Sims remembers a man whose occasional displays of affection could be the kiss of death: "He was a very educated man, and very quiet. You hardly heard him, and when he was around, you would never know he was there. If you did a bad act, he would never embarrass you, he would always come and put his arms around you. You knew when he came and put his arms around you, you weren't going to work anymore. He'd say, 'Oh, Mr. Sims, your act didn't go over too well. You better go back and try again. You're not on the next show. I'm sorry.' He'd come over just so soft and nice and you'd see him do that huggin', and you knew that act was through."

But Schiffman didn't always have his way. The great Bessie Smith was on the skids when she played the Apollo in 1935. In fact, her four weeks' work at the theatre that year represented the sum total of her professional engagements in 1935, and her salary had dropped from a stellar $3,500 to a mere $250 per week. Yet she was a legend, perhaps the greatest black performer of her time. After watching a rehearsal of her act, Schiffman waited for Bessie's own chorus girls to leave, and approached her tentatively. He complained that the girls were too dark, and appeared gray under the lights. Summoning all her stature, Bessie calmly replied, "If you don't want my girls, you don't want me." Schiffman was contrite, but she continued to lambaste him, and he was forced to give in.

Later, during the engagement, Bessie went to ask for a draw against her salary and was refused. Furious and humiliated, she stormed out into the lobby and threw herself to the ground. Rolling on the floor, kicking wildly, she screamed at the top of her powerful lungs, "Folks, I'm the star of the show. I'm Bessie Smith, and they won't let me have no money!"As a crowd gathered, she continued, "All I asked for is a little bit of money, and they won't give it to me!" Chastened and chagrined, Frank Schiffman gave her the money.

One management device that Frank, and later his younger son, Bobby, used was to insert a black manager between themselves and the performers—Jimmy Marshall in the early years, Leonard Reed in the fifties, or Honi Coles (the renowned dancer) in later years. And while Bobby was still his father's assistant, he too acted as a barrier between

31

Bessie Smith, early 1930s. ★ *Rolling on the floor, kicking wildly, she screamed, "Folks, I'm the star of the show. I'm Bessie Smith, and they won't let me have no money!" Schiffman gave her the money.*

Frank Schiffman with Cab Calloway, early 1970s. ★ *In Harlem show-business circles Schiffman was God—a five-foot-nine-inch, white, Jewish, balding, bespectacled deity.*

the performers and Frank. "Forget the Old Man," said Dionne Warwick. "Bobby was his buff. Old Man Schiffman was too busy counting his dollars in that cruddy old office. Honi Coles was the buff between Bobby and us, because Bobby represented the white man. So when we had any real complaints we would say, 'Hey, Honi...,' and he would say, 'Bobby...,' and by the time it got to Old Man Schiffman it was another story altogether. I had the good fortune of knowing Old Man Schiffman, and he was a gruff, arrogant, but shrewd businessman who cared first primarily about the Apollo structure, then the entertainers. The compassion he should have shown to the entertainers should have been first, I think. Bobby showed more compassion for the entertainers. He is still one of the nicest people I've known."

Even those who disliked him respected or feared Frank Schiffman. In Harlem show-business circles he was God—a five-foot-nine-inch, white, Jewish, balding, bespectacled deity. Frank's brand of personality and drive was what was needed to make the Apollo Theatre great. His son Bobby's friendlier, more laid-back style was what was needed to keep it going through changing times. "My father was godlike as far as I and a lot of other people were concerned," said Bobby Schiffman. "What he did was create a great legend. My father was a fantastic theatre operator who taught me and taught everybody else whatever there was to be taught."

From boyhood, Bobby spent a great deal of time in his family's theatre. When he wasn't getting underfoot and giving the stagehands *tsuris,* he learned. "I worked with a half day off every other week. From ten in the morning till midnight. My father paid me the grand sum of thirty-five dollars a week and made me learn every single facet of the business. My dad made sure I was exposed, as my brother was before me, to every facet of the business, so that in years to come when I took over responsibility for the whole operation, there was no job that I hadn't performed."

Bobby's older brother, Jack, was involved in helping his father run the theatre for a few years in the late forties and early fifties. He, too, had the Schiffman knack, but he soon moved on, eventually settling in Florida to raise cattle. Bobby learned from him as well. "My brother had been on the job four or five years, and I used to listen with my mouth open to the manner in which he and my dad dealt with some of the performers." Leslie Uggams remembers both brothers: "I always had a crush on Jack. He always looked like the button that didn't belong there. He was so chic, and I used to think, 'What the heck is he doing with us

33

crazy people back here?' He just never seemed like he belonged there, to me. He looked like a banker. But Bobby was one of the people. He hung out with everybody. He had a good rapport with everybody. He could deal with this person who's strung out on drugs—he still got them to the show—or deal with this person with a drinking problem so everything's happening. He saw the changes coming in the business—I mean the business of rock and roll. He was into that. He kept up with what was happening, so after a while he ran the place. He ran it very well. He could communicate with everybody."

Bobby became active in running the Apollo in the early fifties, and in 1961 he persuaded his father to let him take over. "My father's time had come," said Bobby. "I knew what the people in the street were thinking and what they liked because I made it my business to find out. I would go into bars and listen to the jukeboxes. I would go to record companies and find out what was selling. I, and the people who worked for me, would find out—as my father had before. I knew my job and I knew my business, and I went in and said to him, 'Hey, Dad, I think it's time we changed chairs. You be my assistant. Let me run the theatre.' He told me, 'I've been waiting for you to tell me that, and I'll be glad to do it.' Which is something fathers are not prone to do."

Frank may have known for a while that it was time for a change, and this knowledge may have affected him. As Johnny Otis suggested, "What happened, I think, was that Frank's whole posture was a defense mechanism. He saw the world changing around him, and to keep his regimentation and ideas intact he put on this whole attitude." After Bobby took over, Frank went into semi-retirement, but constantly kept an eye on things until his death in 1974 at the age of eighty.

"Fortunately for me," said Bobby, "the legend of the Apollo was already there when I took over. I felt I was important, but the reason the Apollo succeeded was the people of the community, the Joe on the street who came in and plunked down his money. The Apollo had its ear to those people, and fortunately we were able to find out what they wanted and give it to them, but it was the community of Harlem that made the Apollo flourish."

Whether out of altruism or economic pragmatism or a combination of both, the Apollo catered to the black community, and they packed the place. "We were in the business of pleasing the black community," said Bobby. "If white folks came as an ancillary benefit, that was fine. But the basic motto was: 'To bring the people of the community entertainment they wanted at a price they could afford to pay.' When I first went

Bobby Schiffman, mid-1970s. ★ *"I knew what the people in the street were thinking and what they liked because I made it my business to find out."*

334 Auburn Ave., N.E.
Atlanta, Georgia 30303
Telephone 522-1420

Southern Christian Leadership Conference

Martin Luther King Jr., *President*   Ralph Abernathy, *Treasurer*   Andrew J. Young, *Executive Director*

September 21, 1965

Mr. Frank Schiffman
253 West 125th Street
New York, New York

Dear Mr. Schiffman:

This is a rather belated note to express my deep personal gratitude
to you and our wonderful friends, Dr. and Mrs. Arthur Logan and
Mr. and Mrs. Jackie Robinson, for providing the opportunity for a
check in the amount of $5500.00 to be presented by Mrs. Marion
Logan at the SCLC convention to start the "Martin Luther King
Freedom Fleet."

There are some experiences that we have in life that cannot be
adequately explained by those symbols called words. They can
only be articulated by the inaudible language of the heart. Such
was the experience that came to us when you demonstrated such a
marvelous expression of support for our work. Needless to say,
your great contribution will go a long, long way in helping us to
carry out the herculean task ahead to double the number of Negro
registered voters in the South. We presently have some four
hundred staff members working in more than one hundred counties
in six southern states. They must often cover whole counties within
a matter of days. So it is easy to see how important it is to have
the necessary transportation to meet the trememdous challenge
of moving around the various counties. Your contribution will be
of invaluable help in aiding us to purchase the automobiles that
are necessary to carry on our work.

Again, let me thank you for your genuine good will and your
uncommon magnanimity. The "Tribute" that our dedicated friends
had for you was certainly well deserved. Your bigness of heart in giving
the funds for such an important cause will never be forgotten. When
the bright day of freedom emerges, and the tragic expression of man's
inhumanity to man is cast into unending limbo, your name will certainly
shine as one of those individuals who had the vision, courage and dedi-
cation to work for a reign of justice and a rule of love.

Very sincerely yours,

Martin Luther King, Jr.

*A letter of appreciation from Martin Luther King, Jr.,
proudly hung in the Apollo office.*

to the Apollo we were charging seventy cents to see a show and a movie. The highest price I ever charged was six dollars. I tried seven for Redd Foxx once, and they stayed away in droves. Affordability was very important—so that a guy could go out with his girlfriend to the Apollo and go for a hamburger or dinner after and spend less than any other place he could go to. Aside from that, when people came into the Apollo there was a cordial, friendly come-in-and-have-a-good-time atmosphere. So the Apollo became the thing to do."

According to some, not every element of the community was satisfied with the Apollo's reasonable pricing policy, and some attempted to grab a little bit more. "Colored gangsters tried to move into the Apollo," said Doll Thomas. "They were called the five percenters. It cost the Apollo anywhere from one to five thousand dollars a week to stay open. You had to pay that much graft or you'd have a very unhappy theatre. There would be no peace in the theatre and there would be fights, arguments, disruptions of shows; the house would get bombed." Sandman Sims concurred, "They'd extort money out of Schiffman. They'd tell him, 'If you don't give us some money, that show ain't going on.' They'd picket the theatre and have people scared to come to it. One time they closed it. Schiffman wouldn't pay off. Then, after he paid—you could tell, the theatre would open and the shows would go on. When Schiffman called the leaders up, they would have a conference. Then you'd see them take the barriers down and people going in buying tickets and you'd know he done paid someone off. This is in everything in Harlem. Graft."

In every way the Apollo Theatre was a vital part of the Harlem community. Since 125th Street was Harlem's main commercial artery, the merchants greatly depended on the Apollo to draw crowds to the street and generate traffic in their stores. A hot show at the Apollo meant money in the bank for everyone on 125th Street.

Local legend has it that Frank was personally responsible for breaking down the color barrier that existed in many of the stores and restaurants on 125th Street well into the 1940s. As the story goes, he and black film producer Oscar Micheaux went into Frank's Restaurant, a well-known Greek-run steak house, and ordered two steaks. When Micheaux's came smothered with pepper, Schiffman exchanged dishes with him, ordered another, and told the waiter if he ever tried that again, he'd have a hell of a fight on his hands. Soon after, blacks began working and eating there, and segregated policies elsewhere on the street slowly began to change.

The Schiffmans supported a host of organizations such as the NAACP, CORE, the Urban League, SNCC, the local YM and YWCA, and many others, and Frank Schiffman was one of the founders of the Freedom National Bank. A letter of appreciation from Martin Luther King, Jr., proudly hung in the Apollo office. The theatre was always available for special benefit shows, and the Apollo hosted dozens of them, including a 1971 benefit for the families of the Attica dead, when John Lennon finally realized his wish and appeared on the Apollo stage, along with his wife, Yoko.

The Schiffmans made a conscious effort to make the Apollo a part of the community. "I want them to feel bad when a performer gives us the shaft," Bobby Schiffman has said. "I want them to feel bad when the roof leaks. I want them to feel bad when we can't get a first-run film. . . ." They did feel bad when the Apollo had troubles. But more often they had reason to feel good. For years the theatre was billed as "Harlem's High Spot"—and that it was.

HARLEM'S EARLY YEARS – THE APOLLO'S HERITAGE

· · · · · · · · · · ·

Apollo was the Greek god of music, poetry, and the arts, and his temple at Delphi was a place of purification, as was the temple that bears his name at 253 West 125th Street, Harlem, New York City. Harlem's Apollo would become as famous as the temple at Delphi, but not until it emerged as the sole survivor of a vicious theatrical war waged during the tumultuous early years of black Harlem. Frank Schiffman, the man who guided the Apollo to greatness, was not the original owner of the theatre, and the Apollo was not the theatre's original name. It began as an all-white music hall and burlesque theatre, and was famous in the twenties and early thirties as Hurtig and Seamon's Burlesque. Not until January 1934 did it open as the 125th Street Apollo Theatre, featuring mainly black entertainment. It was originally owned by Sidney Cohen, who took the Apollo name from a little neighboring theatre he owned that was, ironically, located directly above the foyer of Schiffman and Brecher's Harlem Opera House.

By the time the Apollo opened as a black theatre in 1934, Harlem had passed through its greatest period—the Harlem Renaissance—a term used to distinguish an impressive group of black writers, musicians, and artists who gathered in Harlem in the 1920s from the masses of poor blacks who streamed into the black Promised Land on earth. During that period of Harlem's high life, blacks and Harlem became fashionable. No smart New York party would have been considered complete without a smattering of Harlem Renaissance intellectuals, and one could imagine no more exciting evening than a raucous crawl through several of Harlem's swankest clubs. Or, to enjoy an authentic slice of black culture, visitors to Harlem might venture into one of the theatres presenting black vaudeville and revues, such as the Lincoln, Alhambra, or Brecher and Schiffman's Lafayette Theatre. The fabulous Harlem Renaissance continued for more than a decade—until the Great Depression and, finally, a bloody riot on March 19, 1935, marked the end of white infatuation with Harlem. The events of Harlem's early years made the Apollo possible, and in a sense, the Apollo until its demise was the only institution in Harlem to keep alive the hope and promise of these years.

The 1920s were the Jazz Age. Stride piano players like James P. Johnson, Willie "the Lion" Smith, Luckey Roberts, and their protégé, Fats Waller, were at the height of their popularity and influence in the early twenties. These men took the basic ragtime tunes popular since the turn of the century, separated the ragtime beat with a steady left hand, and jazzed up the melody with the dexterous digits of the other hand. It was modern, sophisticated, and wild—nearly everything Prohibition-era hedonists desired. The final ingredient, sensuality, was provided by the classic women blues singers who gained national popularity after the smashing success of Mamie Smith's historic 1920 recording, "Crazy Blues."

Like the stride pianists, classic blues singers such as Mamie Smith, the young Bessie Smith, and Ida Cox had been stars in the black community before World War I. However, when "Crazy Blues" began selling eight thousand records a week and continued to do so for months, a blues craze began. The music itself was not new, but its availability on recordings was. Mamie Smith's recording of the Perry Bradford tune has been called the first recording of an "actual blues performance by a Negro artist with Negro accompaniment."

The astounding success of "Crazy Blues" was the first concrete commercial example of the power of black music as a visceral emotional force as well as a readily exploitable commodity. Could Sophie Tucker (who had to turn over that 1920 recording session to Mamie Smith because she was too ill to perform) have elicited the same response from these lines?

I can't sleep at night
I can't eat a bite
'Cause the man I love
He didn't treat me right

Smith's record no doubt helped pave the way for the first recording of a black jazz band, Kid Ory's Sunshine Orchestra, in Los Angeles in 1921. Jazz was invented by blacks, yet it was a white group from New Orleans, the Original Dixieland Jazz Band, that had made the first jazz recording four years earlier with "Tiger Rag." Their New York debut generated nationwide headlines and helped popularize jazz. Meanwhile, the black jazz originators like trumpeter Bunny Bolden; the Eagle Band; the Original Creole Band; and Joseph Petite, Freddie Keppard, and Joseph "King" Oliver of the Olympians—all from New Orleans—worked in relative obscurity. Legend has it that the Original Creole Band, then headed by Keppard, had the opportunity to do the first jazz recording, but Keppard turned down the offer because he was afraid a record would only encourage imitators.

At any rate, the Original Dixieland Jazz Band's records sold millions. As Marshall Stearns wrote in *The Story of Jazz*, "almost overnight, the word 'jazz' entered the American vocabulary to describe a rackety musical novelty with barnyard—or worse—antecedents. Thus—the same year that Storyville [the black section that was the crucible of jazz] was closed by the Navy in New Orleans—New York, then Chicago, and then most of the cities of the North opened their doors to the new music."

In Harlem in the early twenties, this led to a strange dichotomy. Although jazz was an idiom pioneered by black artists, the music that Harlemites heard on their radios was a white dilution of black jazz. Paul Whiteman had been crowned the "King of Jazz," and his and another white band, the Mound City Blue Blowers, were tops in the field. Until records by black jazz bands reached the black ghetto in the mid-twenties, most blacks may not even have realized that the roots of the music sweeping the country were anchored in their own creative heritage.

Harlem's black masses had to content themselves with recordings of some of the hottest and most influential black orchestras. The best of the bands were booked for lengthy engagements, almost as soon as they arrived in town, at some of the top high-class spots in the heart of Harlem and on Broadway, many of which were not open to blacks. In 1923, Duke Ellington, newly arrived in Harlem, began a five-year stint

CRAZY BLUES

By PERRY BRADFORD

MAMIE SMITH AND HER JAZZ HOUNDS

Get this number for your phonograph on Okeh Record No. 4169

Published by
PERRY BRADFORD
MUSIC PUB. CO.
1547 Broadway, N. Y. C

When "Crazy Blues" began selling eight thousand records a week and continued to do so for months, a blues craze began. The astounding success of "Crazy Blues" was the first concrete commercial example of the power of black music as visceral emotional force as well as a readily exploitable commodity.

The Fletcher Henderson Orchestra at the Apollo in February 1942. ★ *For seven years, beginning in 1924, the Fletcher Henderson Orchestra, perhaps the greatest hot-jazz big band of all time, was entrenched in the white Roseland Ballroom.*

at the Kentucky Club with his small group, and then moved on to become the house band at the fabulous Cotton Club, until Cab Calloway took over in 1931. For seven years, beginning in 1924, the Fletcher Henderson Orchestra, perhaps the greatest hot-jazz big band of all time, was entrenched in the white Roseland Ballroom.

The recordings they made reached not only into the black community, but across the sea, to influence, along with bands like Claude Hopkins that toured the Continent, the musical scene in Europe. When the French composer Darius Milhaud arrived in New York in 1922 he remarked upon the great influence American music was exerting on European composers. Reporters questioning him were shocked to learn that the American music he referred to was a type they considered undignified and unworthy—black jazz. Milhaud said that when in New York he "never missed the slightest opportunity of visiting Harlem."

Most of the white swells who frequented Harlem's myriad nightclubs were hardly astute cultural explorers like Milhaud. They were the glitterati of their day, a combination of high-society aristocrats, nouveau riche entrepreneurs, and celebrities looking for the peculiar exhilaration the rich find in excitements tinged with danger. For them, the attraction of Harlem was much the same as today's Beautiful People for the latest and most outrageous gay disco. In 1935 a local journalist reminisced: "Harlem became the playground of the Park avenues, Broadwayites, and out-of-town visitors. The hey day of Harlem's night life, attracting people from all over the world and all walks of life, was a prosperous era for Harlem. People wanted enjoyment, pleasure, hot entertainment. They wanted something that was different, something that was new. Harlem was the place and they came. They loved our entertainment, and they kept coming, night after night. They still come, but the big thrill is not what it used to be."

Certainly the biggest thrill of all was a visit to the Cotton Club, the "Aristocrat of Harlem," located at 142nd Street and Lenox Avenue. Along with Connie's Inn, Smalls' Paradise, and Barron Wilkins's club, it was one of Harlem's Big Four nightclubs. Gangster Owney Madden, backed by Al Capone, took over fighter Jack Johnson's failing Club Deluxe, and reopened it as the Cotton Club for white customers only in 1923. Madden helped provide the requisite menace for free-spending thrill seekers, and his thugs were on hand to keep out interracial couples and the black throngs who lined up to gawk as welcomed patrons like Mayor Jimmy Walker, George Raft, Eddy Duchin, and Emily Vanderbilt spilled out of their Rolls-Royces, Dusenbergs, and Stutzes. The stage was decorated to represent the Old South, replete with cotton plants and slaves' cabins, and the shows were written and produced by Harold Arlen, Dorothy Fields, Jimmy McHugh, Ted Kohler, and Lew Leslie.

Lena Horne, who began her career there as a sixteen-year-old chorine, has said, "The shows had a primitive naked quality that was supposed to make a civilized audience lose its inhibitions." Many of the era's top black stars rose to national prominence at the Cotton Club. Bill "Bojangles" Robinson, Ethel Waters, and the Nicholas Brothers were featured attractions. Duke Ellington provided his sophisticated sonorities, as he might have put it, and when he hit with "Black and Tan Fantasy," gained tremendous attention for himself and the club. His replacement, Cab Calloway, created an even bigger stir yodeling his trademark "hi-de-hi-de-ho" while Madden's patrons tossed back bootlegged hooch.

Connie's Inn, located in the basement next to the Lafayette Theatre, was the Cotton Club's prime competitor, and some felt its shows superior to the other club's. Perhaps its greatest revue, Andy Razaf and Fats Waller's "Hot Chocolates," featured Louis Armstrong, and, when it moved to Broadway, made songs like "Ain't Misbehavin' " and "Can't We Get Together" national favorites. Connie and George Immerman were Harlemites who had emigrated from Germany and once ran a delicatessen where Fats Waller worked as a delivery boy. Their club was located on "The Corner," 131st Street and Seventh Avenue, a favorite after-hours meeting place for black entertainers. Directly above the bandstand of Connie's Inn was The Barbeque, a popular musicians' hangout said to have had the first jukebox in Harlem. Across the street, the Band Box Club was run by a musician, Addington Major, and although he never provided entertainment, his bar became one of the most popular places for impromptu jam sessions where the patrons were more than happy to entertain themselves.

Much as Minton's, Monroe's, and other clubs in the 1940s, the after-hours musicians' hangouts of the twenties and early thirties provided a test-tube atmosphere for experimentation by musicians employed in the show orchestras of the day. Another important feature of the scene was the weekly Sunday-night–Monday-morning breakfast dances upstairs at the Lenox Club, next door to the Cotton Club. As the *Daily News* reported, "Here the crowd is usually about 90 percent colored and the seven o'clock whistles that call the faithful back to work on Monday

A 1932 Cotton Club program. ★ *The biggest thrill of all was a visit to the Cotton Club, the "Aristocrat of Harlem." Lena Horne has said, "The shows had a primitive naked quality that was supposed to make a civilized audience lose its inhibitions."*

Smalls' Paradise in 1929. ★ *Of the Big Four nightclubs it was considered the most authentic Harlem night spot by white cognoscenti who thrilled to listening to real Negro music.*

morning find the boys and girls of both races drinking briskly, with an hour or two to go. . . . You will not enjoy the Lenox if you object to dancing shoulder to shoulder with colored couples."

Barron Wilkins's club, two blocks up from Connie's Inn, was known as the "rich man's black and white" cabaret. Duke Ellington, one of the many top black pianists Wilkins hired over the years, said that in 1923 it was the "*top* spot" in Harlem, a place "where they catered to big spenders, gamblers, sportsmen, and women, all at the peak of their various professions." Wilkins and his club might have become even better known, if the "Night Life King" had not been murdered by a junkie and gambler called Yellow Charleston, in 1926.

Smalls' Paradise, on Seventh Avenue and 135th Street, run by the well-liked Ed Smalls, offered hot big-band jam sessions, exciting floor shows, and nimble waiters who danced the Charleston while busing trays of food and drink. Of the Big Four it was considered the most authentic Harlem night spot by white cognoscenti who thrilled to listening to real Negro music, surrounded by real Negroes.

All of the joints on "Jungle Alley," a strip of West 133rd Street between Lenox and Seventh avenues, were black clubs frequented by whites. Celebrities and locals crowded into Pod's & Jerry's to hear the great stride pianist Willie "the Lion" Smith. Tillie's Chicken Shack was so popular with patrons, who gorged themselves on fried chicken and sweet-potato pie, that Tillie had to move to larger quarters on 120th Street, and ultimately downtown. The Clam House was most popular with whites drawn by the perverse charms of Gladys Bentley, who dressed like a man and sang her famous double-entendre lyrics. The club also featured a female impersonator who called himself Gloria Swanson. Hot new musicians out to make their reputations and established greats in town for an engagement might well make Mexico's a required stop. There, in the early hours, furious "cutting contests" would ensue between younger hopefuls testing their chops against jazz greats like Ben Webster, Don Byas, and the man everyone wanted to beat, Coleman Hawkins. As white reedman Milton "Mezz" Mezzrow said, "These contests taught the musicians never to rest on their laurels."

Although some top clubs like Barron Wilkins's and Smalls' Paradise were more lenient in their admission policies, their prices proved exclusionary for most Harlemites. But none of the fine black entertainment at the top two clubs was available to black customers at any price. As the music of his progeny soothed and stimulated the white revelers inside, W. C. Handy, "the Father of the Blues," was once turned away by the Cotton Club's manager, George "Big Frenchy" Demange. Connie's Inn also barred blacks, while the outraged *New York Age* charged that the Immermans admitted the " 'slummers,' sports, 'coke addicts,' and high rollers of the white race who came to Harlem to indulge in illicit and illegal recreations." But the Immermans were somewhat more amenable and socially attuned than Owney Madden at the Cotton Club, and they began opening their club to black musicians in the wee hours of the morning after they had finished their stints at other clubs—and after most of the Immermans' white patrons had gone home.

The clubs brought Harlem fame and attention, but for the masses of Harlem, the place to really let loose was at a rent party in someone's apartment, with the lights down low, the soul food piled high, and one of Harlem's top stride pianists flailing at the keys of a dilapidated upright. The rent-party tradition began in the South with church socials designed to raise money. In Harlem, the concept was refined.

Willie "the Lion" Smith was intimately involved with many of these affairs. He remembers them vividly in his memoir, *Music on My Mind*: "An entire family would work for days preparing for one of these socials: there'd be piles of hog maws, pickled pigs' tails, pigs' feet, southern-fried chicken, mashed potatoes, chitterlings, potato salad, corn bread, red beans and rice, crab soup, and sometimes they'd even come up with a Chinese dinner with piles of chop suey. . . . When Prohibition days came along they had another excuse to have a party. Gallons of gin, beer, wine, whiskey, eggnog, and brandy were made available to wash down all those vittles. . . . Then even before the Depression, Harlem citizens having a hard time meeting their rents latched onto the gimmick of having a party and charging anywhere from twenty-five cents to a dollar for admission. . . . They would crowd a hundred or more people into a seven-room railroad flat and the walls would bulge—some of the parties spread to the halls and all over the building. All the furniture was stashed in another apartment except the chairs and beds. When there wasn't a crap game, or poker, going in the back bedroom, they'd use it for a place to rest up, or sleep off, or make love. The rent party was the place to go to pick up on all the latest jokes, jive and uptown news. . . . It got to be a big business. They would advertise a house-rent party for a month in advance. . . . They even built up mailing lists. . . ."

A night that ended in a hot club or a wild rent party might well have begun, for society swells, gangsters, show people, taxicab drivers, laun-

Hollywood's 1936 version of an uptown rent party in
Dancing Feet. ★ *For the masses of Harlem, the place to
really let loose was at a rent party in someone's apartment,
with the lights down low, the soul food piled high, and one of
Harlem's top stride pianists flailing at the keys of a
dilapidated upright.*

dry workers, and shoe-shine boys alike at one of Harlem's great black theatres. "I started going to Harlem theatres in the twenties when I was at Hotchkiss," said John Hammond. "When I was twelve or thirteen years old I would stand outside the Lincoln Theatre. I would listen outside because Fats Waller was playing organ there. [He played for the silent movies, often injecting his own offbeat riffs, to the amusement of the audience.] I didn't have enough guts to go into the theatre on my own, but I started going very regularly to the Lafayette Theatre, then to the Alhambra. I preferred the Alhambra to the Lafayette because I would usually hear better music there. It was the first time that I heard Bessie Smith in the flesh; it was in 1927. A man by the name of Milton Gosdorfer owned the Alhambra. Gosdorfer was not the best businessman in the world, but there was a wonderful spirit in his theatre."

Young John Hammond was afraid to enter the Lincoln Theatre because it was in the heart of black Harlem and until about 1914 was one of only two theatres in the city mainly for blacks, the other being the neighboring Crescent. Harlem theatres were segregated, often until the 1930s, even though black entertainment was featured. "There were no blacks on 125th Street," said Doll Thomas. "That was all Irish. It was in the twenties that the switch really started to colored. Even when I was in the Alhambra back in 1927, all of this neighborhood was strictly white. If [a black person] wanted to go into the Alhambra, or the theatre that's now the Apollo, you entered from 126th Street. Up the back stairs. The Alhambra was pretty tough. They just wouldn't sell [blacks] an orchestra seat. They were either sold out or they'd flatly refuse. Also on 125th Street, Frank's Lunchroom—you couldn't get served in there. Across the street was Childs. You couldn't get served in there. Next door was Loft's Candy Shop. Couldn't get served in there. Right down the street was Fabian's Seafood Shop. Couldn't get served in there. All the bars here and everything else was the same way."

Generally, the first theatres to change their segregationist policies were the first theatres that fell within the advance of the black community. One of the earliest to do so, and the most important theatre of its time, was the Lafayette. At first, blacks were admitted there only grudgingly, out of economic necessity, and they were relegated to the balcony, or "nigger heaven," as it came to be known. Blacks were not openly admitted at the Lafayette until the Schiffman-Brecher regime began in 1925.

The Lafayette, even while it maintained a restricted or segregation-

The Lafayette Theatre in the 1920s. In front is the Tree of Hope, with out-of-work entertainers gathered around it. To the right is Connie's Inn. ★ *The Lafayette became the theatre in Harlem to see top black stars. A Lafayette debut was as important as an Apollo debut would later become.*

FACING PAGE: Two views of 125th Street, in 1927 (top) and 1934 (bottom); the Apollo is shown (at left) before and after it became the Apollo. ★ Doll Thomas: *"There were no blacks on 125th Street. That was all Irish. If [a black person] wanted to go into the theatre that's now the Apollo, you entered from 126th Street. Up the back stairs."*

ist admissions policy, was the first theatre to introduce black syncopated dancing and music to white New Yorkers. In 1913 the world-famous black comedian Bert Williams prevailed upon impresario Flo Ziegfeld to see a performance of "Darktown Follies" at the Lafayette. Ziegfeld was particularly impressed with a number called "At the Ball" in which Ethel Williams and the cast balled the jack "every which way you could think of." He bought the rights to this sexually suggestive part of the show to use in his downtown Ziegfeld Follies. This Lafayette show, Harlem Renaissance writer James Weldon Johnson later wrote, "drew space, headlines and cartoons in the New York papers; and consequently it became the vogue to go to Harlem to see it . . . the beginning of the nightly migration to Harlem in search of entertainment began."

The Lafayette quickly became *the* theatre in Harlem to see top black stars like Bessie Smith, Bill "Bojangles" Robinson, Louis Armstrong, Buck and Bubbles, and the Mills Brothers—well before Schiffman and Brecher took over. A Lafayette debut was as important as an Apollo debut would later become. "During that winter [1918]," Ethel Waters wrote in her autobiography, "I made my first appearance on Seventh Avenue when I was asked to appear at one of the special Sunday-night shows at the Lafayette Theatre, the Uptown Palace. Those Sunday shows were events. Harlem's dictys got their first gander at my work that evening. They knew performers and they decided that I had a future bigger than my present or my past." From the Lafayette, Miss Waters went on to become one of the top black singing, dancing, stage, and screen stars, and an Apollo favorite, too.

When the song-and-dance team of Ford Lee "Buck" Washington and John "Bubbles" Sublett came into the Lafayette, they had already established themselves as stars—the first blacks to play the most famous vaudeville theatre in the world, the Palace, on Broadway. "At that time," said John Bubbles (he had his name officially changed to Bubbles), according to most whites "the most important things in the Negro world were a crap game, a bottle of gin, and a pair of dice—understand? Anything concerning an appreciation of life or your mother or father could not occur to the mind of the Negro. Well, I went on the stage of the Palace and sang a song written by a colored composer called 'Mammy o' Mine.' We had started out with colored gags, then my manager says, 'Bubbles, tell the audience about that letter you got from your mother.' So then the orchestra hit the keynote and I recited the verse: 'I read your letter, mammy of mine. And I feel much better, mammy of mine. . . .'

And I'm singing, man. I gotta have a voice, and my partner could play, too. When I sang that verse you could hear a pin drop. Theatre was packed. Now, the story of this song is telling how I feel right now. [He and Buck were, in fact, teenagers away from hometown Louisville for the first time, burdened with the pressures of antiblack sentiment.] When I got to the part, 'Mammy of mine, I long to kiss you, I miss you all the time,' the tears are just pouring down my cheeks, man, 'cause I'm heartbroken from what I'm going through, I was really overloaded. The manager came running down after the show: 'Where's the two colored boys?' They locked us in our dressing room so we wouldn't go away. We were such a hit, man."

Most of the black performers who made it to the Lafayette, including Ethel Waters and Buck and Bubbles, had first to learn the ropes and prove themselves by playing a string of motley theatres around the country known as the Theatre Owners' Booking Association circuit— T.O.B.A., or Toby Time. Among black performers those initials came to stand for "tough on black asses." With the T.O.B.A. serving as its farm system, the Lafayette thrived.

Leonard Reed started playing the circuit in 1923 as a Charleston-style dancer. "The Grand Theatre was the first on the T.O.B.A. circuit," he said. "That's where they started: Chicago. Then they went to the Globe in St. Louis. From the Globe they went to the Lincoln in Kansas City, then Oklahoma City, Muskogee, and the Ella B. Moore Theatre in Dallas. From Dallas to Houston, Galveston, Shreveport, and then to Mobile and Birmingham. It went all the way down to Atlanta. Most of the theatre owners were white, except for three women who owned theatres in Oklahoma City, Tulsa, and Dallas. The T.O.B.A. circuit ended in Washington, D.C., at the Mid-City, Blue Mouse, and the Four Acres Theatres—that was a split week. Then you could also go to Baltimore, to another theatre called the Lincoln."

From the T.O.B.A. circuit, black performers moved up to the big league in black entertainment, which included the Lafayette, the Royal Theatre in Baltimore, the Howard in Washington, D.C., and the Earle in Philadelphia. The shrewd owners of these theatres got together and worked out an arrangement to assure them a steady supply of top-quality shows at fixed rates. In New York, Frank Schiffman would hire leading black producers like Leonard Harper, Clarence Robinson, and Addison Carey to put together new shows every week for the Lafayette and the other Big Four theatres. Leonard Reed explained how it worked: "Next

First telegram:

CHARGE TO THE ACCOUNT OF   APOLLO THEATRE   3/24/39   DAY LETTER

CHECK SERVICE DESIRED OTHERWISE MESSAGE WILL BE SENT AT FULL RATE	
DOMESTIC	FOREIGN
FULL RATE	FULL RATE
DAY LETTER	CDE RATE
NIGHT LETTER	URGENT
SERIAL	DEFERRED
RESERVATION	NIGHT LETTER
TOUR-RATE	SHIP RADIO

Send the following message, subject to the Company's rules, regulations and rates set forth in its tariffs and on file with regulatory authorities

ABE LITCHMAN   HOWARD THEATRE   7th and T STREET WASHINGTON D C

TOLD SCOTCHMEN YOU WOULDN'T PAY MORE THAN TWO HUNDRED
AND SEVENTY FIVE. HOW IS HARTLEY TOOTS BAND? HOW IS
DANDRIDGE SISTERS? THANKS IN ADVANCE

FRANK SCHIFFMAN.

Second telegram:

CHARGE TO THE ACCOUNT OF   APOLLO-THEATRE   4/8/39   DAY LETTER

Postal Telegraph
Mackay Radio   All America Cables
Commercial Cables   Canadian Pacific Telegraphs

CHECK SERVICE DESIRED OTHERWISE MESSAGE WILL BE SENT AT FULL RATE	
DOMESTIC	FOREIGN
FULL RATE	FULL RATE
DAY LETTER	CDE RATE
NIGHT LETTER	URGENT
SERIAL	DEFERRED
RESERVATION	NIGHT LETTER
TOUR-RATE	SHIP RADIO

Send the following message, subject to the Company's rules, regulations and rates set forth in its tariffs and on file with regulatory authorities

ABE LIGHTMAN   HOWARD THEATRE   WASHINGTON D C

WE ARE WELL INTO APRIL AND YOU ARE HOLDING UP MY DISTRIBUTION
ON BIG FELLA. HAVE MADE DEAL WITH DISTRIBUTOR WHO WANTS TO
COMPLETE BALANCE OF TERRITORY. WOULD APPRECIATE IT IMMENSELY
IF YOU WOULD WORK OUT DATES FOR ME. PLEASE WIRE ME WHAT CAN
EXPECT. HOPE BUSINESS IS GOOD.

FRANK SCHIFFMAN.

Two 1939 telegrams from the owner of the Apollo to the owner of the Howard Theatre in Washington, D.C. ★ *The shrewd owners of these theatres got together and worked out an arrangement to assure them a steady supply of top-quality shows at fixed rates.*

door to the Lafayette, two floors above Connie's Inn, was a rehearsal hall. While one show was playing in the theatre, another show was rehearsing next door—that would be Leonard Harper, or whoever was producing, preparing to open the Lafayette next week. The attraction—the band or whoever—the chorus line, and the comics would all be there rehearsing. The show that's coming out of the Lafayette would close Thursday night, get on a bus that night, and drive to Philly to open the next morning. The show that was in Philly would move to Baltimore, the Baltimore show would move to Washington, and the Washington show would come and go into rehearsal to go back into the Lafayette. 'Round the World' is what they'd call it."

Schiffman, the savvy manager of the Lafayette, soon developed a reputation as a tough businessman and a cutthroat competitor. "I can remember Gosdorfer at the Alhambra back in the early thirties saying that Schiffman was impossible to compete with," said John Hammond. "Schiffman with his contracts saying $1,000 a week to a player. He'd pay them $300, but as long as they could show that piece of paper around, that's really all some of these performers did."

"Yes, that's true," said Doll Thomas, who worked at the Alhambra from 1927 to 1931. "Sometimes he'd give a performer a contract that said $1,000, but it was just his way of competing with us at the Alhambra—see, then a performer could come to us and say, 'If you give me more, I'll go to you.' These contracts were just Schiffman's way of hiking the costs to his competitors. He had all kinds of tricks. If a performer thought he was getting $1,000, Frank would charge him for things. He'd charge the cost of renting the films they played between shows to the performers."

"Once in a while they caught up with him," said Hammond. "There was a tap dancer named Eddie Rector and he had one of these pieces of paper that said $1,000. He had drawn half of it, I guess, but when he came for the rest of it, it wasn't there, and he chased Schiffman around the Lafayette with a gun. Schiffman had to call the police. Usually Schiffman could sweet-talk these people, and Frank was actually a pretty nice guy. I got to realize that later on."

"Performers worked for Schiffman at the Lafayette or they worked for nobody," Doll Thomas said. "Whatever his price was, that was the best they could do, and they had to take it. If they worked in the Alhambra, they couldn't work for Schiffman again. And then he put up a blacklist and they *had* to work at the Alhambra. They had to wait until

Eddie Rector, late 1920s. ★ John Hammond: *"There was a tap dancer named Eddie Rector and he had one of these pieces of paper that said $1,000. He had drawn half of it, I guess, but when he came for the rest of it, it wasn't there, and he chased Schiffman around the Lafayette with a gun. Schiffman had to call the police."*

they got really hungry until they could get another job [at the Lafayette]." John Hammond concurs: "Bessie Smith played the Lafayette just once after she played the Alhambra. I think she had to crawl to do it. They had all the action. There was no place else for the performers to go. If you wanted to work black theatres in general, you had to deal with Schiffman. This is how fierce a competitor he was: Gosdorfer was having a rough time, but finally he pulled in Cab Calloway's band and paid a lot of money for them. Schiffman got hold of Blanche Calloway, Cab's sister, and put her in front of a band—this is back in 1931. While poor Gosdorfer has Cab Calloway, Schiffman was able to have the name Calloway, with Blanche so small you could hardly read it. Of course, poor old Gosdorfer suffered. Frank had to claw his way up. Show business was rough in the old days. There was nothing he wouldn't do to annihilate his competition." By the end of 1931 the Alhambra had folded, but with one major competitor out of the way, Schiffman's greatest battle still lay ahead.

· · · · ·

Sidney Cohen was another powerful theatrical landlord who owned a number of downtown burlesque houses, most notably the Gaiety and the Roxy. He also held the mortgage on Hurtig and Seamon's Burlesque—the showplace that would become world famous as the Apollo Theatre. In 1914, Benjamin Hurtig offered singers and other light entertainment for his customers, who could order a quart bottle of Mumm's for four dollars, an absinthe for twenty cents, or a glass of Pabst for a nickel. When burlesque came in, Hurtig and Seamon's Burlesque featured top names such as George Jessel and Fannie Brice.

John Hammond recalled: "I can remember bringing Charles Laughton up to see midnight shows, raunchy strippers, and the rest, but a terrible white band. In those days, 125th Street was white. I understand the Apollo actually had Joe Ward's Coconut Grove, which was a white club, in the basement—that's where Louis Armstrong had his first New York gig." When Joe Ward's closed about 1930, it became the Rathskeller; and when that closed, the space was converted into a rehearsal hall for the Apollo.

Estrellita Brooks-Morse was on the other side of the footlights: "I played the Apollo when it was Hurtig and Seamon's, as a child, really—a child stripper. I guess I was about fifteen. When they found out I was so young and everything, they pulled me out of it. [In the early thirties] the

A 1914 program from Hurtig and Seamon's Music Hall; twenty years later it became the Apollo Theatre. ★ *Benjamin Hurtig offered singers and other light entertainment for his customers, who could order a quart bottle of Mumm's for four dollars, an absinthe for twenty cents, or a glass of Pabst for a nickel.*

HURTIG & SEAMON'S MUSIC HALL WINE LIST.

Champagne.

	PT.	QT.
Moet & Chandon White Seal	$2.00	$4.00
Pommery Sec	2.00	4.00
G. H. Mumm Extra Dry	2.00	4.00
Pipe Heidsieck Sec	2.00	4.00

Liquors.

Dreadnought Scotch Whiskey	.15
Burke's Irish Whiskey	.15
Burke's Scotch Whiskey	.15
Hennessey Brandy	.30
Hennessey Brandy, pony	.20
Maryland Club	.20
Antediluvian Whiskey, in decanters only	.20
Old Pepper	.20
Mount Vernon	.20
Old Crow	.20
Canadian Club	.20
Holland Swan Gin	.15
Old Tom Gin	.15
Jamaica Rum	.15
Usher's Scotch Whiskey	.15

Bitters.

Orange	.15
Boonekamp	.15
Angostura	.15

Ales and Porter.

Burke's Bass Ale	.30
Burke's Guinness Stout	.30
Bass's Ale, White Label	.30
Dog's Head	.30
Guinness' Stout	.30

Wines.

	GLASS
Sherry	.15
Rhine	.15
Claret	.15
Port	.15
Blackberry	.15

	QT.
Laubenheimer	$1.00
Niersteiner	1.50
Hochheimer	2.00
Oppenheimer Goldberg	2.50
Rhine Wine, cup	1.50
Liebfraumilch	3.00

Clarets.

	QT.
Medoc	$1.00
St. Emilion	1.50
Pontet Canet	2.00
Chateau Larose	3.00

Cordials.

Absinthe	.20
Creme Yvette	.20
" de Cacao	.20
" de Menthe	.20
" de Vanilla	.20
" de Maraschino	.20
" de Curacao	.20
" de Chartreuse, yellow or green	.20
Kummel	.20
Benedictine	.20
Pousse Cafe	.25
French Vermouth	.25
Tom Collins	.25
Genuine Westphalian Steinhaeger	.15

Mixed Drinks.

Gin Fizz	.15
" Cocktail	.15
" Rickey	.20
Sherry Cobbler	.20
" Punch	.20
" Flip	.20
Milk Punch	.20
" with Brandy	.20
Brandy Cocktail	.15
Manhattan "	.15
Martini "	.15
Whiskey Sour	.20
Claret Punch	.20
Silver Fizz	.20
Gold Fizz	.20
Brandy Sour	.30
Brandy Smash	.30
Whiskey Cocktail	.15
American Beauty	.25
Horse's Neck	.25
Queen Charlotte	.20
Gin High Ball	.15
Whiskey High Ball	.15
Absinthe Cocktail	.20

Mixed Drinks—Continued.

Brandy Flip	.15
Absinthe Frappe	.25
Mint Julep	.20
Rhine Wine and Seltzer	.15
Claret and Seltzer	.15
Japanese Cocktail	.20
Dewey	.20
Sarsaparilla Sangaree	.20
Ginger Ale	.20
Hurtig & Seamon Cocktail	.20
Star Cocktail	.20

Mineral Waters.

	PT.	QT.
Apollinaris	.25	.40
Seltzer, per siphon		.25
White Rock	.25	

Soft Drinks.

Soda	.10
Ginger Ale	.10
Sarsaparilla	.10
Cap Soda, bottle	.15
Cap Sarsaparilla, bottle	.15
Lemonade	.15
Seltzer Lemonade	.20
Club Soda	.15
Imported Ginger Ale	.25

Beer.

	GLASS
Pabst Milwaukee Beer	.05

Bottled Beer.

Pabst Milwaukee Beer	.15

Kindly report to the management any inattention or overcharge on the part of employees.

CIGARS ARE DELIVERED IN SEALED WRAPPERS, WITH PRICES THEREON.

BALCONY

PARQUETTE

first part of the show would be all white, but then they'd have maybe ten to twenty-five people working the second half of the show when there would be a black chorus line and a black comedian and a black singer, and then they'd have a black stripper. You'd have to do auditions to see if yours is the kind of body that could be shown. You weren't nude, you were really covered. You had your G-strings on—the G-strings were so gorgeous with beads and everything—and your bust covers were all rhinestones and beads. Your body was just beautiful. I wore a mesh leotard from the neckline down to the ankle, and over that I had my regalia, then I had this gorgeous gown that would be taken off in pieces. You take one sleeve off at a time and walk. You'd get big applause. Throw the other sleeve off. Then you'd probably drop the front—tease a little bit. It wasn't vulgar or anything like that. We were working to beautiful music, and taking off pieces beautifully. Very artistic. It wasn't anything that was demoralizing to a person's personality or making her look like she was a low-down woman or something. This is what people think, you know."

Another Hurtig and Seamon's venture, also owned by Sidney Cohen, was a small but elegant 900-seat theatre with a huge stage, located in a space above the foyer of Schiffman and Brecher's Harlem Opera House just down 125th Street. From 1918 until it closed in 1933, this little theatre was run as a burlesque house by bump-and-grind impresario Herbert Kay Minsky and his partner Joseph Weinstock. Through the years the theatre was known variously as Hammerstein's Music Hall, Minsky's Burlesque, and Apollo Burlesque—this was where the Apollo name first appeared on 125th Street.

By 1930 New York's burlesque theatres were in trouble. As a ribald form of entertainment, burlesque was considered passé and was increasingly threatened by Broadway musical-comedy revues that often blatantly emphasized nudity, daring to feature chorus girls displaying naked limbs, bereft of the traditional tights. When that happened, burlesque took off its gloves and its tights and fought back with bare knuckles and knees and more and more bare skin. But soon the city fathers felt it had gone too far, and in 1933 newly elected Mayor Fiorello La Guardia began his campaign against burlesque in New York City. Lessees Hurtig and Seamon were driven out of business, and Sidney Cohen was left $60,000 in arrears, with two empty burlesque theatres on his hands. He closed the little 900-seat theatre over the Harlem Opera House, borrowed its name, and reopened the larger Hurtig and Seamon's Burlesque as the new 125th Street Apollo Theatre.

An unusual ad appeared in the Theatricals section of the *New York Age*. It read:

MESSAGE TO HARLEM THEATRE-GOERS

Dear Friends and Patrons,

The opening of the 125th Street Apollo Theatre next Friday night will mark a revolutionary step in the presentation of stage shows. The most lavish and colorful extravaganzas produced under the expert direction of Clarence Robinson, internationally known creator of original revues, will be a weekly feature.

The phrase "the finest theatre in Harlem" can be aptly applied to this redecorated and refurnished temple of amusement.

Courtesy and consideration will be the watchword of the management, truly a resort for the better people.

High-Fidelity RCA sound equipment, the same as used by Radio City Music Hall, and an innovation in public address systems, has been installed, and we feel certain that the 125th Street Apollo Theatre will be an entertainment edifice that Harlem will take pride in showing off to neighborhood communities.

The Apollo's inaugural show Friday, January 26, 1934, was billed as "Jazz a la Carte" and featured Harlem showman Ralph Cooper, Aida Ward, Benny Carter and his Orchestra, sixteen "Gorgeous Hot Steppers," the Three Rhythm Kings, Norton and Margot, Troy Brown, Mabel Scott, and the Three Palmer Brothers. The film feature was *Criminal at Large*. All the proceeds of the opening-night performance went to the Harlem Children's Fresh Air Fund. As if the lavish show and clever charity pitch were not enough, Cohen and his manager, Morris Sussman, invited representatives of various New York and out-of-town black newspapers to schmooze and "crack a quart of whiskey" at the Renaissance Casino.

The emergence of Cohen and Sussman's Apollo—a wily new competitor—hit Schiffman and Brecher at a poor time. Some seven months earlier, "in a further effort to meet existing economic conditions," Schiffman had announced a "substantial reduction in prices" at the Lafayette. Early admission, from 10:00 A.M. until noon, was dropped to

61

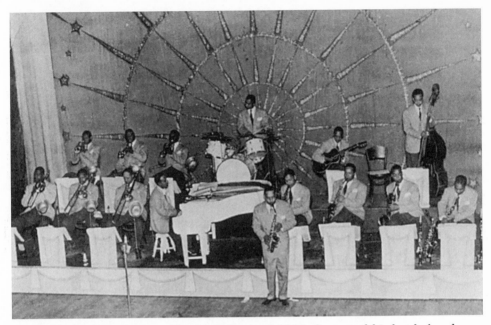

The Benny Carter Orchestra at the Apollo in April 1942. Carter and his band played the Apollo's inaugural show, "Jazz A La Carte" on Friday, January 26, 1934.

A 1934 Harlem Opera House handbill. Note the minuscule billing for Ella Fitzgerald (above) and Lena Horne (below). ★ *Just down the street from the Apollo, the Harlem Opera House was the perfect base from which to do battle with the interlopers.*

just a dime, the afternoon price to twenty cents, and the evening charge to thirty cents. Schiffman tried everything to bolster the Lafayette's sagging box office, from a free buffet breakfast served in the balcony foyer, "an idea which is widespread in Europe," to the establishment, with m.c. Ralph Cooper, of "Wednesday Auditions"—the famed Amateur Night. But nothing helped.

Schiffman probably felt out of it at the Lafayette way up Seventh Avenue at 132nd Street. Until the early thirties, this stretch of Seventh Avenue had been known as "Black Broadway," and was in the heart of the new black Harlem community, while 125th Street was still all white. However, by the time Sidney Cohen rechristened the Apollo Theatre in 1934, 125th Street had become Harlem's show-business and commercial center. Now, at the Lafayette, Schiffman, the leader of the pack, had been left behind for the moment.

Schiffman's boss, Leo Brecher, owned a theatre on 125th Street— the Harlem Opera House—that he had leased to another operator. Since it was just down the street from Cohen and Sussman's Apollo Theatre, it was the perfect base from which to do battle with these interlopers. The tenant was ousted and the Schiffman-Brecher team moved in on June 9, 1934. They halted live shows at the Lafayette, except for a brief reprise at the end of 1934.

With Cohen and Sussman operating the Apollo, and Schiffman and Brecher at the Harlem Opera House, one of New York's most hard-fought theatrical struggles was under way. In Harlem, the smart money was on Schiffman and Brecher, because in the black entertainment world, they were the team to beat.

A can-you-top-this billing war had begun while Schiffman and Brecher still operated the Lafayette. Sussman advertised the Apollo as "America's Finest Colored Theatre," with the "Biggest Shows at the Lowest Prices." The Lafayette's management countered with "America's Leading Colored Theatre" and also claimed to offer the "Biggest Shows at the Lowest Prices." The Apollo then shifted to "America's Smartest Colored Theatre" for its tag, with the "Only Stage Show on 125th Street." When Schiffman and Brecher's operations shifted to the Harlem Opera House, they advertised "The Finest Screen and Stage Shows on 125th Street," and in a Depression-wracked community, claimed the Harlem Opera House was the "Greatest Show Value in Harlem."

With the demise of the Lafayette, the Apollo and the Harlem Opera House were the only black houses left in Harlem. "Each one was trying to out-attraction the other," said Leonard Reed. "The difference between Schiffman and Sussman was Sussman played big bands religiously. Schiffman stuck mostly with revues and the comics and the bits and the local bands like Tiny Bradshaw, Edgar Hayes, and Don Redman. They both had chorus lines. The Apollo against Schiffman used to have two bands, one big and one not so. They had a bandstand with the setup for another band behind it. As one band finished and played their theme song, the bandstand would move around and the other band would play their theme."

Sometimes a band would get caught in a revolving door between the two theatres. In November 1934, the Harlem Opera House accused Turner's Arcadians of "skipping over by intrigue to the Apollo Theatre." Apparently Turner booked himself into the Apollo while promoter Moe Gale (also booker for the Savoy Ballroom) pledged Turner to Schiffman at the Harlem Opera House. Crying foul, Schiffman threatened to sue, charging that Turner was "sold to the Apollo for a bigger consideration as an inducement."

Schiffman also watched miserably as Ralph Cooper took his Wednesday Amateur Night to Cohen and Sussman's Apollo. Schiffman countered with his own Tuesday Amateur Night. When Cooper began to broadcast "Amateur Night in Harlem" over WMCA early in 1935, Schiffman again fought back with his own identically titled program on WNEW. Not to be outdone, Sussman's Apollo ran special ads touting "Amateur Nite [sic] in Harlem with the one and only Ralph Cooper direct from the stage of the 125th Street Apollo Theatre—Originators of This Broadcast."

However, Sidney Cohen didn't have the stomach for this kind of battle. He was essentially a real-estate man, not an impresario. He turned to an old family friend, John Hammond, one of the most knowledgeable men about black music and the Harlem theatrical scene. "I knew Sidney Cohen because he lived in Armonk, very close to my family's place in Mt. Kisco," said Hammond. "I was very friendly with Sidney and he wanted to have somebody who loved show business and knew musicians and knew artists. It was quite logical for us to get together. I would book the shows, he would put up the capital, and I would have a percentage of the profits. It was an agreement very much to his advantage rather than mine." But, at the last moment, the deal went tragically awry. "Sidney had an office on Forty-fourth Street next to the Algonquin Hotel, and this is where we had all our talks and did all our business. On the way to sign

John Hammond, 1940. ★ *"Sidney wanted to have somebody who loved show business and knew musicians and knew artists. I would book the shows, he would put up the capital, and I would have a percentage of the profits. It was an arrangement very much to his advantage rather than mine."*

the papers, I called up the office to confirm the appointment. They said, 'We're terribly sorry to tell you, but Mr. Cohen has just had a heart attack and is dead.' Just like that."

According to Doll Thomas, "Sidney actually didn't want the Apollo. He just didn't want to close it and didn't want Schiffman to have it. He hated the way colored performers were treated by Schiffman. He hated that monopoly." Yet Sussman, the surviving competitor, seemed friendly, or at least pragmatic enough to work out a deal. After Cohen's death, Hammond was, as he himself said, "really in no position to take over the theatre because I'm not that good a businessman." So Schiffman and Sussman got together. "After all," said Doll, "they were just two Jewish kids. They're the best of friends. 'Maybe we can get together and talk over what's happening. I'm paying them money and they're using me to run up the salaries to you. We can get together and talk this over.' "

At first, following a conference on May 13, 1935, between Schiffman and Sussman, it was announced that the Apollo and the Harlem Opera House would merge. But the merger was, in fact, a takeover. Schiffman and Brecher turned over the Harlem Opera House to movies and moved their operation to the Apollo.

According to Hammond, the Harlem Opera House was not nearly as good a theatre as the Apollo. "The Harlem Opera House had perhaps the most dangerous second balcony in the world—practically perpendicular. When [Schiffman and Brecher] had a chance to get in the Apollo, they stopped the stage shows completely at the Harlem Opera House. When they took over the Apollo it was a far better deal for everybody. They were about 300 seats larger, the acoustics were better, the equipment was much better, and they had a first-class stage."

Leo Brecher was so pleased that, according to his daughter, Vivian Pack, he "gave" Schiffman a half interest in the Apollo because he had been "a good and faithful manager." That made Frank Schiffman the big winner. He was now an owner, undisputed king of the uptown scene. He had vanquished the last of his serious challengers. And he was in the finest theatre in Harlem. The Apollo changed its billing to "The Only Stage Show in Harlem," and the legend began.

THE THIRTIES

· · · · · · · · · ·

The Apollo became practically the only show uptown after Schiffman vanquished the other black theatres, and the Harlem cabaret scene greatly subsided. Word soon spread uptown and downtown that something hot was happening on 125th Street. For, with a virtual monopoly, the Apollo could attract and feature the finest entertainment. Its audiences came to expect the best, and generally their wild enthusiasm inspired the best. Their displeasure with those who didn't meet their expectations produced a reaction few performers who experienced it would ever forget. The Apollo quickly became an integral part of the city's hip social scene. The media soon caught on, and in January 1937 the *New York World-Telegram* provided its curious readers with a condescending "inside view" of the "Harlem Stompers" at the Apollo:

> The Apollo is a sort of uptown Met dedicated to furious jazz, coffee-colored chorus girls and grinning, drawling comedians. . . . [It is] the first stand and last jump-off for the large caravanserai of Harlem entertainers. . . . The theatre stands behind a gaudy neon sign on West 125th Street, between a haberdashery and a leather goods store. The sidewalk outside

LEFT: The Apollo Theatre in 1934. ★
*Word soon spread uptown and downtown
that something hot was happening on
125th Street.*
BELOW: On line in the lobby in 1947.
★ *Making the scene at the Apollo was
the ultimate night on the town.*

is a favored location for old men lugging sandwich signs and pitchmen unloading razor blades and patent medicines. You buy your ticket at a sidewalk booth (from fifteen cents mornings to a fifty-cent top Wednesday and Saturday nights) and enter through a narrow lobby lined with bathroom tiles, glistening mirrors and photographs of such Harlem idols as Ethel Waters and Louis Armstrong, all affectionately inscribed to the Apollo. At a candy counter you can buy chocolate bars and peanuts, but no gum. That is to protect the seats. In the lobby, three or four colored boys generally are waiting for their dates to show up.

Until a few years ago the Apollo was a burlesque house, and its interior decorations still bear numerous mementos to that colorful era of its history. On the rear wall hang three large oil paintings in ponderous frames, each featuring several square feet of female flesh. "They're genuine originals," an usher will inform you. "The center one is supposed to be Cleopatra. Picturesque, ain't she?" The wallpaper has a recurring motif of a nude young woman.

The house seats 1,750 people in the parterre and two balconies. Adjacent to the stage on both sides are several roomy boxes, generally inhabited by young men who appreciate the less flagrant charms of the chorus line. The stage itself is edged with applied pilasters of imitation marble, well chipped along the corners and tinted red, gilt and blue. The curtain is a startling crimson.

Making the scene at the Apollo was the ultimate night on the town, especially on Saturday nights and at the annual Easter and Christmas shows, when the crowds really "showed out." The men appeared in tight-belted, high-waisted coats with freshly marcelled hair "conked" into beautifully rippling waves. The women, fragrantly scented, gracefully glided through the lobby in tight slinky dresses, high heels, and veils. But every night was special, for the Apollo was becoming the center of Harlem's cultural and social life. Stump and Stumpy (Jimmy Cross and Harold Cromer), the popular comedy team, were a part of the early Apollo social scene:

"They used to have the *Amsterdam News* Christmas Show, and Saturday nights a lot of celebrities and entertainers used to come up for the midnight show," said Harold Cromer. "They would watch the show and then they'd get up on stage, and everybody's up there doing things, and the show would last until about four or five in the morning. After that they would go to Eddie Green's barbecue."

"On 126th Street," Jimmy Cross chimed in.

"Yeah, and you had all of the biggies just standing outside, waiting for ribs after you leave the Apollo Theatre. All the white people tried to make reservations, but there's no reservations, man, you just walk on in. If you get in, you get in."

"Talking about Franchot Tone, Burgess Meredith . . ."

"Betty Grable . . . a lot of them, they were there . . ."

"Dorothy Kilgallen."

"Walter Winchell and his crew."

"Well, Walter Winchell, naturally . . ."

"Mark Hellinger . . . then you'd go to an after-hours place. . . . Damon Runyon . . . and drink and laugh, and the musicians would be playing some more . . . the Rhythm Club . . ."

". . . Into the next day, and the next day you'd wind up in the Apollo doing the first show."

As downtown came uptown, so too did at least one segment of Harlem take part in the white entertainment scene downtown. The Palace, Paramount, and Roxy, the downtown theatres that featured stage-and-screen shows, were in the same borough of the same city as the Apollo, but they might as well have been in Chicago or Philadelphia, for the Apollo was no competition for them and they did not compete with the Apollo. At first, only white-oriented black acts like the Mills Brothers and Buck and Bubbles, or the top black bands could play the white houses, but as more black acts showed they could draw white audiences, they were booked into the Broadway citadels in increasing numbers.

"Very few of the people who were up in Harlem would come down to the Paramount," said Herbert Mills of the Mills Brothers. "It was a different clientele altogether. No competition whatsoever." Some performers would play the Apollo and one of the downtown theatres simultaneously, a practice known as doubling. John Bubbles recalled: "We'd do a matinee uptown and a night show downtown. Do the same act, if you do it right you didn't have to change the act neither place. Keep the same material."

In Cab Calloway's autobiography, Benny Payne, his piano player, reminisced about the way the doubling routine worked for the Calloway band when they played the Apollo and the Paramount simultaneously: "We were already playing five shows a day at the Apollo. . . . For four days we played eight shows a day. I never will forget that. We played two shows at the Apollo, got taxicabs downtown to the Paramount, ran back uptown just in time for the next show at the Apollo, jumped in cabs again to get downtown for the second Paramount show, came back uptown, then downtown again, then back uptown for the midnight show at the Apollo."

"Everybody'd work different places," said Harold Cromer. "You'd work the Apollo and you'd work the Cotton Club when it moved downtown. And the shit that went on . . . There was this nutty cabdriver, Calvin, would get you there."

"Six minutes from 125th Street to Broadway," added Jimmy Cross.

"Guaranteed, guaranteed," said Harold. "Yes, he was dependable. But how he made the trip! And you're wet and you're changing in the cab into your dry clothes, and they're all standing in front of the theatre waiting for you to come back. Schiffman's there, the manager is running up and down the place yelling, 'Where the hell are they?' The show is on and they can't even see ya. Now they're trying to make adjustments, just in case. . . . You can see why Schiffman lost most of his hair. . . . And they're switching music on the bandstand."

"Before Harold, I worked with my first partner, Eddie Hartman, and we worked with the Ink Spots at the Paramount," said Jimmy Cross. "We had to come from the Paramount to the Apollo in an ambulance."

"You got one costume there, one here," Harold said. "How do you breathe? Who breathes! You just went out there and did the show for the love of it. . . . And Calvin: you would get in his cab, and he's driving through Central Park and he knew every curve, he knew the lights, and boom, boom, boom, he'd get to the club. And he'd say, 'Don't worry, I'm coming back.' And he'd go do another act and come back and catch you in time. A phenomenal man."

. . . . .

As a showcase for the best and the newest in black entertainment, a supplier of talent for white venues, and a source of creative inspiration, the Apollo began to exert a great deal of influence upon American culture. Through Ralph Cooper's Wednesday "Amateur Night in Harlem" show, broadcast live from the Apollo over WMCA and twenty-one of its affiliated stations around the country, the Apollo became nationally known. For many whites around the country the Apollo radio broadcasts were their first exposure to the new sounds of black swing music.

The pioneering sounds of the black big bands soon began to

influence white musicians. This development, and the Apollo's contribution to it, had tremendous cultural significance. As Imamu Amiri Baraka, formerly LeRoi Jones, put it: "Afro-American music did not become a completely American expression until the white man could play it," and furthermore: "The big colored dance bands of the thirties . . . were also the strongest influence on American popular music and entertainment for twenty years."

Sometimes the inspiration white performers found at the Apollo bordered on larceny. Honi Coles, the Apollo's longtime production manager, has said he remembers seeing Martha Raye and her arranger in the theatre "night after night" watching June Richmond perform "Mr. Paganini," a song that soon became, in a close cover version, a Martha Raye trademark. It has also been said that Milton Berle used to come to the Apollo accompanied by a stenographer. "That is true," said Harold Cromer. "He was searching for material and he used to come up here on Wednesday night and on Saturday night when they had the midnight show. And if he wasn't performing downtown, he'd come and sit back here and listen to the jokes and sort of turn them around. But Milton Berle didn't need a stenographer. He's still the kind of guy who can listen to a joke and remember it, twist it around, and make it work. He was fantastic."

Dewey "Pigmeat" Markham, a paragon among Apollo comedians for forty years, concurs: "We used to have a midnight show every Saturday night, and you couldn't get in there for the white comedians—Milton Berle, Joey Adams—all the guys came to Harlem. They'd have a girl with a pencil and shorthand paper, and steal comedy from all us boys. They stole it and carried it into burlesque and kept it for years."

But, as Frank Schiffman has observed, the exchange of material was also a "two-way street," with some material, especially in the early days, converted from white vaudeville and burlesque routines into black-oriented comedy skits. The Apollo was a black theatre, but as Schiffman said, he did not "draw the color line," and white performers also played the Apollo as entertainers. In the thirties and forties some of the top white bandleaders brought their orchestras into the theatre, including: Harry James, Bunny Berigan, Woody Herman, and Charlie Barnet.

One of the greatest Apollo attractions was Barnet. He so appreciated the response he got at the Apollo that he chose the theatre as the place to announce his retirement in 1950, and when he tried a comeback a year later it was also at the Apollo.

The Paramount Theatre in 1945. ★ *The downtown theatres that featured stage-and-screen shows were in the same borough of the same city as the Apollo, but they might as well have been in Chicago or Philadelphia, for the Apollo was no competition for them and they did not compete with the Apollo.*

Milton Berle in the late 1930s. ★ *It has been said that he used to come to the Apollo accompanied by a stenographer.*

"I think Frank had a lot of guts," said John Hammond. "In the first place, Frank used to book white artists. Charlie Barnet's band was the first [band led by a white man] that had black musicians, and Frank booked them. They couldn't get booked on the regular vaudeville circuits. He always wanted Benny Goodman's orchestra, but Benny would never play the Apollo. He felt it would hurt his box-office image or something. I've always been very proud of Frank booking white acts. It was fine."

. . . . .

For the first two decades of its existence, the Apollo Theatre presented shows based upon the tried-and-true vaudeville variety format. The shows were designed to appeal to the common folk of Harlem, who relied on the Apollo to provide a little elegance to offset their dreary lives, convey compassion for their plight and solidarity with their struggle, and to generate some excitement. This did not always sit too well with middle-class blacks, to whom the Apollo's shows, sometimes justifiably, were an embarrassment. Throughout the Apollo's early years, the *New York Age* railed against the "vulgarity, suggestive dancing and black-face comedy" of the Apollo. They pleaded for "wholesome presentations of acts and revues that can be enjoyed by all members of the family. Songs with catchy tunes and words that mean something sung by people who can sing; comedy that's funny yet clean and with enough wit in it to cause it to stick in the mind long afterwards; dancing that is interpretive of something and nòt just so some girl can show what she has to arouse the lustful passions of the men in the audience and perhaps get her a hot date after the show."

Despite the *Age*'s admonishments, the Apollo apparently was doing something right. As another newspaper of the day reported, "The Apollo is nearly jammed at every performance." Many feel that this was the Apollo's Golden Age—although this would be disputed by rhythm-and-blues connoisseurs in the fifties and soul-music fans in the sixties. The Apollo opened its doors at 10:00 A.M., and night workers, housewives, and hooky-playing schoolchildren would dig deep for their nickels and dimes and enter a dream world where they were welcome to stay all day if they liked.

Many, especially the kids, *would* stay all day, packing sandwiches or cold chicken from home, catching three, four, or five shows a day and taking catnaps between performances. It didn't even matter who was playing, for the shows were always basically the same. First a short film, perhaps a Betty Boop cartoon. Next, a newsreel, followed by the feature film. Then a pause. Silence. And at the last the master of ceremonies would announce, to the rising applause and screams from the audience: "Ladies and gentlemen, it's showtime at the Apollo!" Ba-ba-boom, the band would break into the Apollo theme song, "I May Be Wrong (But I Think You're Wonderful)," and the show was rolling. The band would do a number with the chorus, then the m.c. would bring on a "sight act" such as a tap dancer, acrobat, or animal act, followed by a singer, the chorus again, a comedy act, and finally the featured attraction or band in the finale.

The shows, or revues, as they were usually known, loosely revolved around a theme and were given titles such as "Modern Rhythm," "Hill Billy Revue," "Harlem Goes Hollywood," "Ebony Showboat," or "Voo-doo Drums." The bill changed every week, and there were usually thirty-one performances—four a day, plus an extra show on Wednesday, Saturday, and Sunday. Most shows ran sixty to ninety minutes, and performers often complained that by the time they came offstage from one show, the "half" for the next show would already "be in"—in other words, the backstage bell signaling thirty minutes to the next show had already rung.

"The Golliwog Revue," presented the week of May 18, 1934, was typical. It featured at least seven different acts, plus the film *Blonde Crazy* with Jimmy Cagney. The headline act was the band of Don Redman, one of the finest arrangers and leaders. Clarence Robinson's chorus wore ostrich feathers and opened the "Golliwog Revue" in a woodland setting. The Jack Storm Company, a white act, performed acrobatic stunts in luminous costumes against a dark backdrop. Myra Johnson sang torch and blues songs. The Four Bobs tapped up a frenzy, followed by dancer "Jazz Lips" Richardson, whose ridiculous painted-on white lips, while disconcerting some, nevertheless dazzled the audience. Leroy and Edith, winners of the Apollo's Lindy Hop contest, also were on the bill. Throughout, comedians Pigmeat Markham and Johnny Lee Long cavorted with master of ceremonies Ralph Cooper. Quite a good value for fifteen cents.

The weekly revues were created and coordinated by a handful of black producers who worked with the acts Frank Schiffman booked. "The producers put the shows together," explained Leonard Reed. "Schiffman would have whom he had for his attractions. The producers

Bandleader Charlie Barnet with photographer Gordon Anderson in the late 1940s. ★ John Hammond: *"Charlie Barnet's band was the first [band led by a white man] that had black musicians, and Frank booked them. They couldn't get booked on the regular vaudeville circuits."*

Producer Clarence Robinson with his top dancers in the late 1920s. ★ *The weekly revues were created and coordinated by a handful of black producers who worked with the acts Schiffman booked.*

had nothing to do with hiring or firing. More or less the producers were choreographers." Estrellita Brooks-Morse, who worked as a chorus girl for a number of producers, said, "All these producers—Charlie Davis, Addison Carey, Leonard Harper, Teddie Blackman, Clarence Robinson—had their own chorus lines. Because they used to go 'Around the World' from the Apollo to Philly, Baltimore, and Washington, those lines stayed intact." Leonard Reed continued: "They staged the dances with the girls—those producers who could dance. Clarence Robinson couldn't dance, so he had Ristina Banks and another girl to do that. He'd say, 'Do that step. I like that. Let's put that in.' They did nothing except have ideas for the opener. Most of the shows consisted of a regular format. You could almost close your eyes and know what each one was going to do."

The Apollo chorus girls were considered to be the best line in New York, although the Cotton Club's chorus was more prestigious and better paid. "I was astounded at the dancing ability that most of these young ladies had," Honi Coles has said. "A dancing act could come into the Apollo with all original material and when they left at the end of the week, the chorus lines would have stolen many of the outstanding things that they did. For example, in a group that was called the Number One Chorus, there were all exceptional dancers, and mostly tall girls. Three of them were truly great dancers, Ristina Banks, Bertie-Lou Woods and Yak Taylor. These three young ladies were capable of doing anything that any male tap dancer did. As a result most acts used to try and load their steps up to the point that they couldn't be stolen."

The life of an Apollo chorus girl was difficult, according to Carol Carter, who was an Apollo chorus girl before she gained attention as a member of the Fontaine Trio. "These poor girls would do a show, go downstairs to the rehearsal hall, learn the new numbers, get fitted for costumes [which were made in the Apollo's own tailor shop], and, by the time they had finished rehearsal, they only had five or ten minutes to go upstairs. There was a little exit in the rehearsal hall so you wouldn't have to go out on 125th Street. Just go in the back and up the little steps and go through the alley, which would take you to 126th Street. Then the girls would take a left turn toward Eighth Avenue, run through the stage door and upstairs to the big dressing room, and get into their costumes real fast for the next show." The pay was poor, too. John Hammond remembers dealing with Addison Carey at Hammond's Public Theatre in the early thirties, where: "Chorus girls he paid $16 a week, from which they had to buy their shoes; and everybody had to kick back."

These conditions ultimately brought on discord. "AGVA [the American Guild of Variety Artists] was organized about 1937," said Jimmy Cross. "The chorus girls at the Apollo were getting $20 a week, and they wanted $22. So they went on strike for $22.50, because then the Cotton Club girls and the Connie's Inn girls were getting $25 a week. And the Apollo girls could outdance them by far. The Apollo girls were real street dancers, never studied ballet or nothing. So Ristina got them together and said, 'We're going to get $22.50 or we're not going to work.' They struck, and marched up and down in front of the theatre with signs. It was a great routine. They had the music of the horns and the trolley cars clanging up 125th Street as their beat. They settled it in about two weeks." But the regular Apollo chorus did not last much longer. By the early forties, Frank Schiffman had phased it out to cut costs.

. . . . .

While the producers devised a continual series of new revues, and Frank Schiffman stood watch over all, it was the masters of ceremonies, especially Ralph Cooper and Willie Bryant, who kept the shows moving and lively, performance after performance, week after week. Some have credited Schiffman and the Apollo with originating the modern-day concept of the master of ceremonies.

Soon after the Apollo opened, Ralph Cooper became one of Harlem's leading celebrities, thanks largely to the success of his weekly live radio show from the theatre. Yet all of Harlem seemed to know how Frank Schiffman resented Cooper for abandoning him to go to Cohen and Sussman's new Apollo in 1934. When Schiffman took over the theatre the following year, the *Age* speculated that "one of Frank Schiffman's first official acts will be, of all things, to fire Ralph Cooper!" But the *Age* was wrong; Schiffman was far too smart to sacrifice a good attraction like Cooper out of personal pique.

"The Cooper personality infests both the audience and the performers," a local newspaper reported in 1935. Cooper was a versatile performer. He had a dance act with Eddie Rector, and led two bands, the San Domingans, then the Kongo Knights. After he left the Apollo he made movies, such as *The Duke Is Tops* (featuring Lena Horne's first notable screen appearance), worked in radio, and had his own television show, "Spotlight on Harlem." Loften Mitchell, the playwright, reminiscing in the *Amsterdam News*, said of Cooper: "He served as an idol when black children had precious few. And he was one who would eternally encourage and offer you his hand. The greatest comment about Ralph is

The Apollo chorus line, about 1940. They were considered to be the best line in New York. ★ Honi Coles: *"A dancing act could come into the Apollo with all original material and when they left at the end of the week, the chorus lines would have stolen many of the outstanding things that they did."*

Frank Schiffman, Willie Bryant, and Ralph Cooper in the late 1930s. ★ *It was the masters of ceremonies, especially Ralph Cooper and Willie Bryant, who kept the shows moving and lively, performance after performance, week after week. Some have credited Schiffman and the Apollo with originating the modern-day concept of the master of ceremonies.*

that he used to write out passes for us. We kept the passes for his autograph, then paid our way into the show. And in the depression that was really something!"

Ralph Cooper was idolized and respected in Harlem, but Willie Bryant was loved by all who knew him. However, his is ultimately a sad story. "Willie Bryant was very fair-skinned," said Harold Cromer. "He was like an octoroon. He had 'white' hair, but he knew of his heritage, so he stayed in Harlem, basically around the Apollo Theatre. He had an opportunity to perform as white—in other words, to forget he was black, and go out and make money. But it didn't work; it just couldn't work."

Leonard Reed, who also has a very light complexion, was an early dance partner of Willie's, and together they worked the Lafayette and the Harlem Opera House. "He was a great showman," said Reed. "He could do it all. He was a good actor. I learned a lot from him. This man's mind was . . . [he snaps his fingers]. He was on the ball, but bitter, and he had a right to be. Willie was as good as, if not better than, [a major white comic] ever dared to be. But they knew he was part Negro, and downtown they wouldn't let him work. Willie was made to stay in Harlem. He never got the chance to work in places that, say, Bob Hope did—and Bob was, and I don't care who says it, he was never as good as Willie Bryant. Never. In his wildest dreams. But Willie was Negro, and he never did get the chance. It embittered me, too, but I didn't let it bother me because I went white. Willie didn't. I played all the white places by myself. . . . Willie was a genius. He was one of the greats in show business that never got anywhere, because of his color. The white man only lets a few Negroes through. At the time there was no room for five; maybe one or two." But uptown Willie was so well loved that when he asked a Harlem audience in 1934 to forgive him for arriving late without rehearsal time, he was cheered.

. . . . .

In the swing era, bands were an integral part of any Apollo show. Not only were the bands on hand to showcase their own talents and play their hit tunes, but they also played for all the acts on the bill. One week, the Nicholas Brothers might dance to the sounds of Jimmie Lunceford's orchestra, while the next time they played the Apollo it could be to the accompaniment of Duke Ellington or Claude Hopkins or Count Basie.

"We had to play for the acts, and I enjoyed the performers that I backed up," said bandleader Andy Kirk, who was born in the nineteenth century, lives in the twentieth century, and looks as if he is going to be with us in the twenty-first. "They gave me their music. Like, Bojangles [Bill Robinson], he had his own beautiful arrangement on 'In the Still of the Night.' Boy, it just killed me. You could hear every little step. He was something else. I loved him. Playing the Apollo was different from playing a dance hall, because in a dance hall the dancers had to dance to your music. At the Apollo, with a star like Bojangles, we had to play music for *him* to dance to. Instead of injecting yourself, you'd soften down, so you could hear every one of his steps. The people could hear this beautiful music, but they could also hear what he was doing. What he was doing was the important thing. Same way for the acts, when we played background music for them we wouldn't show off. But then, when we did *our* thing, that was when we'd feature our music. We always had regard for the artist, whatever he was doing, and our music was background. We wanted to play it right—the way he wanted it."

For the first few years, all except the mightiest big-band attractions played in a pit immediately in front of the stage. From there they would play for the chorus and the opening acts. Then the curtain would come down; and, while the comics did their bits out front, the band members picked up their instruments and headed backstage and another bandstand was set up onstage, where the band would do their specialty number. As the bands grew into bigger and more important attractions, however, this arrangement, which many bandleaders found degrading, was eliminated. By the late thirties, all the bands played onstage, and the stage was built out over the old pit.

Earl Hines tells how he reacted to working in the pit, in Stanley Dance's book *The World of Earl Hines*: "The producer came and said, 'Now, look, you're going to play in the pit.' We had white suits that were very pretty, and we had some heavy fellows in the band, like Darnell Howard. The pit was so small and so difficult to get in and out of, I was afraid we were going to get our clothes dirty. We had to play the show from the pit and then go up onstage for our specialty. I had written three weeks before we got there that we wanted to wear the white suits and be onstage all the time, and they had agreed. 'I'm not going in the pit,' I said, getting salty. The producer called the manager, and he came and said, 'You *are* going in the pit!' I told all the guys to pack up then, and we left the show standing there. Next morning I went to the theatre and said, 'Well, what about it?' The stage manager said, 'We've got you set up on the stage.' Then the owner of the theatre, Frank Schiffman, came by. He had a fit. . . . Anyway, we didn't go in the pit, and from then on any number of bands started working on the stage."

Big bands had been the main force behind the jazz years since the early twenties. But a new musical form with a pulsing, unaccented, 4/4 rhythm began to emerge by the time Duke Ellington hit in 1932 with "It Don't Mean a Thing If It Ain't Got That Swing"—the tune that gave the new sound a name. Although white bandleaders like Benny Goodman, the Dorseys, Artie Shaw, and many others soon adopted, refined, and popularized the swing sound, once again it was the black musicians of the seminal black orchestras like Ellington's, Fletcher Henderson's, Cab Calloway's, Chick Webb's, Andy Kirk's, Jimmie Lunceford's, and later Count Basie's, who created the new music.

Like all new musical forms, swing was, at first, misunderstood, and it was routinely denigrated by critics and audiences alike. As Fletcher Henderson said ruefully in the late thirties: "The objections to [swing] are still too numerous: it is too brassy, it is not music, it is cheap." The notable difference between swing and earlier jazz forms was the emphasis on rhythm instead of the melody. This was the basis of the moralist's displeasure, for a melody could soothe the soul and inspire the intellect, but a swinging rhythm could only incite passion.

No more passionate swing fans could be found anywhere than in Harlem. From the beginning, the Lindy Hoppers at the Apollo's dance contests, and especially at the Savoy Ballroom—"the Track"—delighted in devising furious steps to the jumpingest bands. The clubs swelled with the sound, and the Lafayette, Harlem Opera House, and the Apollo became the main theatrical outlets for swing music in the early thirties. Ralph Cooper's Apollo radio broadcasts help spread the sound across the nation.

Frank Schiffman appreciated swing music, and was one of its earliest purveyors, but he worried that its popularity might threaten the viability of his treasured variety format. However, after an experiment of offering a show without an "outstanding" big-band attraction failed at the box office, his business acumen won out. By the time he took over the Apollo, swing had arrived. As *Downbeat* magazine put it, "In the early thirties swing was creeping up on the American citizen, and in 1935 it struck him so forcibly that he didn't know what had happened."

Each of the dozens of bands that played the Apollo in the thirties and forties strove to become identified with its own particular style. None succeeded better than the Duke Ellington band. The Duke was an Apollo favorite throughout the swing era, and he and Count Basie were the only ones to continue as Apollo royalty for decades after the big bands faded. Ellington had been developing and honing his sound for ten years by the time swing became a national phenomenon, and he, more than anyone else, had a right to be discouraged when the music became identified with white stars. Yet, even in disappointment, the Duke was the most dignified of men. "I took the energy it took to pout," he said, "and wrote some blues." Ellington was the epitome of black urban sophistication— he was what men dreamed of becoming, and women dreamed of possessing. This, as much as his music, captivated the Apollo audience.

Ellington was, of course, a fine composer and pianist in his own right, but in 1939 he brought in Billy Strayhorn—the man who has been called his alter ego—as arranger and alternate pianist. Their unique collaboration lasted for almost thirty years and produced such outstanding compositions as "Take the A Train" and "Chelsea Bridge." In 1941, Ellington hired Tom Whaley, also a talented arranger, who had been working as the Apollo Theatre's musical director.

Ellington's pride helped make him the Duke, and after he bought out his share of his contract from Irving Mills in 1939 he was completely in control of his own destiny. Frank's son Bobby Schiffman found this out the hard way in the late fifties. "Ernestine Anderson was an interesting lady and a wonderful singer," said Bobby. "But she had the misfortune of being written up in *Time* magazine during the early phase of her career, and the writer said she was the next Sarah Vaughan and Ella Fitzgerald combined. Duke Ellington was on the show. After this story appeared, we talked Ellington into paying Ernestine Anderson for being part of the show. She was going to be the closing act." Ellington was not really comfortable with the arrangement—he already had a singer, Lil Greenwood—but he realized that Ernestine Anderson could add to his band's drawing power. "Now, Duke had this most gracious way about him," said Bobby, "and he could really get to an audience. In the show Duke did an introduction of Lil Greenwood—you would think she was Jesus Christ. When Lil came out to sing, and she was a fine singer, Duke stayed on the stage and conducted the band, and he did everything he could to make Lil Greenwood sound like twelve million dollars. But, when it came time for Ernestine Anderson to perform, Duke introduced her by saying, 'and now Ernestine Anderson,' and walked off the stage. He was a real egotist, but the world loved him, and I loved him too."

While Duke Ellington appealed to Harlemites' sense of style, it was

WEEK BEGINNING FRIDAY, SEPTEMBER 27th

HOT CHOCOLATES of 1936

AMERICA'S GREATEST ROAD SHOW

GLADYS PALMER | LeROY SMITH and BAND | RADCLIFFE and ROGERS

ONE WEEK ONLY—BEGINNING FRIDAY, OCTOBER 4th

Meeres and Meeres

Eddie Green

3 Dukes

Ivy Anderson

DUKE ELLINGTON

AND HIS FAMOUS ORCHESTRA

LEFT: Handbill for Duke Ellington's Apollo engagement in the fall of 1936. ★ *Each of the dozens of bands that played the Apollo in the thirties and forties strove to become identified with its own particular style. None succeeded better than the Duke Ellington band.*

BELOW: Count Basie at the Apollo, 1938, a year after his Apollo debut. ★ John Hammond: *"Basie was scared because he realized that unless he went over, it would take him a much longer time to make it."*

ABOVE: Andy Kirk conducting his Clouds of Joy, with Mary Lou Williams, 1937.
RIGHT: Billie Holiday taking a bow at the Apollo, 1938. ★
A local review: *"When the rhythm-wise redhead swings 'I Cried for You' and sings of her 'Last Affair,' the Apollo, the audience, and all the fixtures truly belong to her."*

Count Basie who more than anyone else, appealed to their sense of excitement. Bill Basie was from New Jersey. He was greatly influenced by listening to Fats Waller play at the Lincoln Theatre. He played the Lafayette in 1931 with Bennie Moten's band, and his special talent caught the attention of John Hammond. However, on a road trip Basie became stranded in the Midwest and he settled into the Kansas City scene. It wasn't until four years later that Hammond again heard Basie, over his car radio in Chicago on a live broadcast from the Reno Club in Kansas City.

Basie's band was powered by jazz greats: Hot Lips Page on trumpet, Buster Smith and Lester Young on saxes, Walter Page on bass, Jo Jones on drums, and the blues shouting of Jimmy Rushing. Hammond was overwhelmed and began writing about the band, but he was too late to sign them. Decca records had signed Basie to a contract that gave the Count only $750 without royalties for twenty-four sides. Hammond was able to get the contract terms improved somewhat, and more important he got his friend Willard Alexander of the MCA agency to book Basie into the Grand Terrace in Chicago, where there was a national radio wire. The band was a hit, and their national exposure carried them to New York, where they did a six-week stand at the Roseland Ballroom downtown. But what really made the band was its debut at the Apollo on March 19, 1937.

"From Roseland Basie went to the Apollo," John Hammond wrote in his autobiography, "a crucial test because untried bands were made or broken by Apollo audiences. For a Negro band, making it at the Apollo guaranteed acceptance by blacks everywhere. . . . The Apollo was family territory to me and I had enough influence to get a place in the stage show for any act that particularly interested me. Although Basie was no big name when he opened at the Apollo, Willard Alexander insisted on and got good money for him. Willard also persuaded the Apollo to spend extra money to promote Basie's debut. Nobody in Harlem will ever forget the opening."

In an interview for this book, Hammond said, "Basie was scared because he realized that unless he went over, it would take him a much longer time to make it. I was there for the first show, which went on about 12:45, and as soon as [Basie's band] played the Apollo theme song, 'I May Be Wrong,' I knew Basie was in." From the Apollo, the Basie band went on to become one of the most popular outfits in jazz, greatly influencing the jazz revolutionaries of the 1940s and continuing as a musical legend into the 1980s.

While a local review was generally kind to Basie, the reviewer raved about Basie's co-star, Billie Holiday. "The nicest thing at the Apollo this week isn't the rocking rhythm of that noble of rhythm—Count Basie," he began. "It isn't the slim, graceful bronze Jeni Le Gon. Nor is it even the swing-shouting of Jimmy Rushing, despite the fact that he hung 'em from the rafters. The sensation of the show is the statuesque and effervescent Billie Holiday and braving controversy we dare to place her in a superior position to Ella Fitzgerald. When the rhythm-wise redhead swings 'I Cried for You' and sings of her 'Last Affair,' the Apollo, the audience, and all the fixtures truly belong to her."

The Apollo was instrumental in nurturing Billie Holiday's career and propelling her to stardom. By 1935, Billie had been scuffling around various Harlem dives for a couple of years, and had made an unsuccessful record for John Hammond. One day Ralph Cooper stopped in at the Hot-Cha Bar and Grill on 134th Street and Seventh Avenue, and was completely captivated as Billie entertained. He touted her on to Frank Schiffman, saying, "You never heard singing so slow, so lazy, with such a drawl. . . . It ain't the blues—I don't know what it is, but you got to hear her." Schiffman knew that Cooper, m.c. of so many amateur shows, had a shrewd sense for talent, and booked her for the week of April 19, 1935, on a show headlined by Cooper and his orchestra.

Billie thought the booking was a gift from God and couldn't believe her luck. Her father, Clarence Holiday, a musician, told her how important an Apollo engagement was. She was nervous and unsure of herself, and not wanting to capitalize on her father's name, had herself billed as Billie Halliday. Cooper bought her an evening gown and slippers and put the band through its paces, familiarizing them with Billie's arrangements of "Them There Eyes" and "If the Moon Turns Green." At her debut, Billie was nearly overcome by stage fright, and had to be gently shoved from the wings by comedian Pigmeat Markham. Once the spotlight hit her, she regained her composure and to her surprise and delight, won the Apollo crowd. They would not let her go without an encore, and she cemented her love affair with the Apollo with "The Man I Love." She left the stage to thunderous applause. She returned four months later, with a number of important recordings behind her, as an Apollo favorite; and her work with Basie ensured her fame.

Andy Kirk's Clouds of Joy was another Kansas City outfit. Unlike Basie's, it also appealed to the softer side of the Apollo audience. Kirk's 1936 recording of "Till the Real Thing Comes Along," a ballad, was a big hit. Based on the success of that tune, the band was introduced to the

Apollo. But the Clouds of Joy could really swing, too. Out of the practical experience of having to gather his roving musicians for the next set in the clubs of Fifty-second Street and elsewhere, Kirk developed a routine that he used at the Apollo. "I used to have a law about being on time," said Kirk, "because if I have a contract for ten, I don't want to hit at five minutes after ten. If we had a fifteen- or twenty-minute intermission, Ben Thigpen would look at his watch and, on time, he would get up on the bandstand and make a roll on that drum. Of course I'd be there. When Dick Wilson [Kirk's fine saxophone player] heard him make that drum roll, if Dick was up at the bar or whatever, he would come and start playing, and from that we developed a head arrangement that used to break up the show. Then everybody would fall in, and pretty soon we'd have the whole band. So we used this and called it a Battle of the Saxes, and that would be our showstopper in the theatre."

Kirk's most popular showstopper was his pianist-arranger, Mary Lou Williams, who left the Clouds of Joy in 1942 and went on to a stunning jazz career of her own. "Mary Lou was a princess," said Kirk. "I'd always feature her at the Apollo. She'd do something that she'd done on the recordings that people had heard. I'd cut the band out while she was playing, and just come in at certain places to put a little phrasing behind her. She came with me when she was nineteen. Died on my birthday, twenty-eighth of May—my eighty-third birthday. She did a lot for the band. There wasn't nothing that you'd ask of her that she didn't do."

Women were an important part of the swing era, although they did not really come into their own until the big bands began to fade in the forties. Life in the male world of the big bands was tough for women. Despite their important contributions, they were often underappreciated and underpaid. Billie Holiday earned only about seventy dollars a week with Count Basie, out of which she also had to maintain her wardrobe.

One stunning woman who did better was Lena Horne—although she had to wait more than four decades for the full appreciation due her. She began as a sixteen-year-old chorus girl, chaperoned by her mother, at the Cotton Club. Encouraged by Ethel Waters, who heard her singing "Stormy Weather" in her dressing room, she left the Cotton Club, despite pressure from the Owney Madden mob, and joined the Noble Sissle orchestra. Later, she became a primary attraction in the integrated band of Charlie Barnet.

Her presence easily overwhelmed her bandleaders. "Mr. Sissle is a satisfactory leading man," wrote a 1936 reviewer of an Apollo show, "and a springboard par excellence for launching the Lena Horne numbers. . . . Lena Horne, (Body by Fisher and face by Michael Angelo), sings well enough, in fact quite well. But she gets the boys to gurgling when she begins to put her wardrobe on exhibition. She finally stands them on their chairs when her feature number comes up, a brilliantly executed routine in radium effect outlined from a backdrop of pitch blackness. Flanked by singing bandmen, she does a toy turn that ends in a tantalizing truck." Lena was often compared to the great white beauties, but as the same reviewer said, "It seems to me that Miss Lena Horne has enough on the ball to stand on her own. Why must she be advertised as the sepia Eleanor Powell. . . . Why be an echo, sepia or otherwise?"

The nonpareil was Ella Fitzgerald, who was compared to no one, but against whom others were measured. The story of her early days as a nervous amateur has frequently been recounted—usually erroneously stating that she got her start at the Apollo's Amateur Night. In fact, she was discovered by friends of Chick Webb at an amateur-night performance at Schiffman's Harlem Opera House in 1934, although she had made the rounds of the Amateur Nights at the Apollo, and probably the Lafayette and Loew's Seventh Avenue, too.

"I was sitting right there in the audience [at the Harlem Opera House]," said comedian Timmie Rogers. "She was a Lindy Hopper at the Savoy Ballroom who could sing. She sang 'Judy' and 'The Object of My Affection Could Change My Complexion from White to Rosy Red.' She didn't know that she could sing that well. She stopped the show cold. They made her take an encore. Bardu Ali [the bandleader and later manager of Redd Foxx] rushed backstage and grabbed her immediately and said come to the Savoy tomorrow for rehearsal and meet Chick Webb. He asked her where she lived and she told him. The next day, he didn't trust her; he went and got her. I was there. She broke the mother up."

Ella's talent had a great impact on Chick Webb's band. Webb was already tremendously popular in Harlem, especially at the Savoy Ballroom, where he held court for years. He so totally captivated the dancers there that no one could topple him, although both Count Basie and Benny Goodman faced him in battles of the bands. He was a superb drummer whose thundering solos attracted a large serious jazz audience, and he is still cited as a major influence by many.

LEFT: Lena Horne, 1936. ★
An Apollo review: *"Body
by Fisher and face by
Michael Angelo."*
BELOW: Ella Fitzgerald singing
with the Chick Webb band at
the Apollo in 1937. ★ *Ella
and Chick may have been two
ugly ducklings, but they were
blessed with abundant talent,
and they were drawn together in
a bond of love, respect, and
support.*

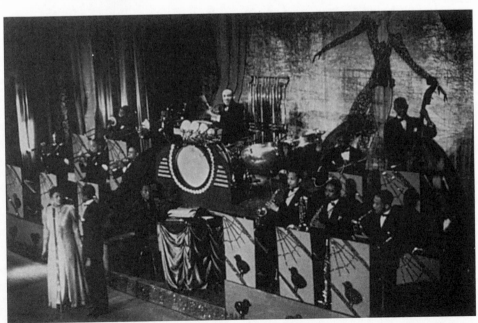

Chick was a most unlikely-looking bandleader. Victim of an ongoing bout with tuberculosis, he was small and frail and his deformed spine caused him to sit hunchbacked behind his massive drum set. Ella, on the other hand, was large, gawky, and plain-looking. They may have been two ugly ducklings, but they were blessed with abundant talent, and they were drawn together in a bond of love, respect, and support.

Ella brought Chick national prominence through her popularity, and she remained loyal to him even when Benny Goodman and others tried to lure her away. When Webb died in 1939, she couldn't bear the thought of the band breaking up, so she took over the lead and kept the unit together for another three years. Jack Schiffman recalled in his memoir of the Apollo that when Webb died, "Dad was home that night, and they called him from the theatre to tell him that Chick Webb had died. Dad said later that the most moving thing he ever heard was Ella Fitzgerald singing 'My Buddy' over Webb's casket. Even those who barely knew the man wept."

· · · · ·

Today it seems surprising that the music of the swing era could have caused such consternation within certain segments of the sophisticated Harlem community. Yet to a black middle class concerned above all with fitting in to white society, swing was often an anathema—for the very characteristics that made swing great, and even important, were so different from and at least subliminally hostile to the white world. As a local newspaper put it: "Every time a white person wants to learn something about colored people he comes to Harlem and visits one of our theatres. And, my friends, I shudder as I think of the impression he must take back downtown with him."

If the black middle class was upset with the state of black music, the black comedy of this period could send them into total apoplexy. "I am told that there should be a racial flavor preserved in our comedy so as to make it definitely recognizable as belonging to the Negro race," said the same writer. "But when that comedy remains absolutely in the sewer and seldom ever rises to the level of the gutter, I wonder how many of what kind of people will be content to have it reflect their lives, thoughts and actions to the outside world?"

In fact, there was a subtle message behind the outrageous routines of the black comedians who kept Apollo audiences in stitches. As Clayton Riley wrote in a *New York Times Magazine* article, "The laughter that cascaded out of the seats was directed parenthetically toward those in

America who allowed themselves to imagine that such 'nigger' showtiming was in any way respective of the way we lived or thought about ourselves in the real world."

Butterbeans and Susie's comedy song "I Want a Hot Dog for My Roll" was typical of the type of material frowned on by the moralists. Joe and Susie Edwards were stars on the black vaudeville circuit for years before the Apollo opened. They were famous for double-entendre gags, but this tune proved to be a bit too much and was rejected by Okeh records. It was Susie's vehicle. "Here come 'da hot dog man!" she'd squeal, then croon, "I want a hot dog without bread you see. 'Cause I carry my bread with me. . . . I want it hot I don't want it cold. I want it so it will fit my roll." Just in case anybody missed the point, Butterbeans answered, "My dog's never cold!" Then Susie continued, "I sure will be disgusted, if it don't have a lot of mustard. . . . Don't want no excuse, it's got to have a lot of juice!"

But Butterbeans and Susie could be topical, too, before it became acceptable for black humor to be so. Andy Kirk remembers the team fondly: "They were wonderful, and well seasoned. They used to do a thing at the Apollo where she said, 'I'm ready to go down South.' He says, 'I ain't going with you, Sue.' 'Why ain't you going with me, Butter?' 'Cause there's too many ups down South.' 'What you mean ups, Butter?' 'Well, early in the mornin' you got to wake up. Then you got to get up. Then you go out on the farm, and if you didn't do the work like the boss said, the boss would beat you up!' "

From the early thirties until the late forties most of the comedy at the Apollo was presented in sketches or skits involving up to a half-dozen people or more. Frank Schiffman liked to call these *lebenspilder*, or pictures of life. The skits were performed in front of a scenic backdrop while the stagehands set up the bandstand or changed scenery on the stage behind it. Almost all the black male comics wore burnt-cork "blackface" makeup and huge white painted-on lips, despite protests from the NAACP and others that this tradition was degrading. But most comedians said they felt naked without it, and they prevailed until the argument reached a climax in the late forties. The Apollo could boast a virtual stock company of the finest black comedians in the country, including Pigmeat Markham, Dusty Fletcher, Sandy Burns, Johnny Lee Long, John "Spider Bruce" Mason, Tim "Kingfish" Moore, Spo-Dee-O-Dee, and Jimmy Baskette (Uncle Remus in Disney's *Song of the South*).

In a typical Apollo routine of the period, Johnny Lee Long is a

Butterbeans and Susie in the early 1930s. ★ *"I want a hot dog without bread you see. 'Cause I carry my bread with me. . . . I want it hot I don't want it cold. I want it so it will fit my roll."*

LEFT: Dewey "Pigmeat" Markham in 1946. ★ *He probably played the Apollo more often than any other performer.* BELOW: Apollo comedians John "Spider Bruce" Mason, John "Ashcan" LaRue, and John Vigal in the late 1930s. ★ *Almost all the black male comics wore burnt-cork "blackface" makeup and huge white painted-on lips, despite protests that this tradition was degrading.*

preacher of the sleaziest kind, lustful and swearing. The scene is a decrepit hotel. After making shameless advances to the hotel manager, played by Edith Wilson, the preacher is given a room. Pigmeat then appears with a pretty chorus girl and asks for a room. The manager says they must be married first, so the preacher is called, and he performs the "ceremony" in suitably lewd fashion. As the couple retires, a cop, played by Charlie Ray, enters and arrests the preacher as a "confidence crook." In a hypocritical snit, the manager calls Pigmeat, and he and his girlfriend appear in night clothes.

"You two have to get your clothes and get out of here," says the manager. "You aren't married!"

"Not married," says Pigmeat. "But didn't the reverend just marry us?"

"He was no reverend. Just an old confidence man. The cop just took him away."

"Then you mean we're not married?" said the girl.

"No, and you've got to get out!"

"Well, it's too damn late now," says Pigmeat, obviously experiencing the most painful kind of sexual frustration. "C'mon, gal!"

The lights black out.

Dewey "Pigmeat" Markham probably played the Apollo more often than any other performer. During the middle thirties he was on the bill every week for four years. He acquired his moniker in a Georgia carnival where, in a comedy skit, he uttered the immortal lines: "Sweet Papa Pigmeat, with the River Jordan at my hips, and all the women is just run up to be baptized."

He is most famous for the "Heah Come de Judge" routine, introduced at the Alhambra Theatre in 1929, and made nationally famous by Sammy Davis, Jr., on the "Laugh-In" television show in the late sixties. In appreciation, Davis signed Pigmeat for a two-month tour of Lake Tahoe and Las Vegas at $5,000 per week—big money considering that Markham earned $75 a week at the Apollo in the beginning.

His other great claim to fame, although some have challenged it, is the invention of "truckin'." This bizarre comical dance took Harlem by storm in the thirties. Pigmeat says it was stolen from him and introduced at the Cotton Club and on film. "It was the biggest thing in the country," he has said. "I tried to keep it to myself. Then one day I saw an Al Jolson movie, and there in a big colored sequence was Cab Calloway and his band trucking all over heaven. There was my truck gone down the drain, just like 'Heah Come de Judge.' "

Markham played the consummate clown, the buffoon who could rarely get a break. The key to his success and longevity was his ability to reach audiences of any era. During the depths of the Great Depression he performed a routine that always killed them at the Apollo. He and Ralph Cooper would walk onstage counting rolls of bills. Tens and twenties were flipped. Then suddenly Pigmeat would yell, "What the hell is this one-dollar bill doing in here?" and rip the bill to shreds. Cooper would admonish him, "Man, as long as you hang around with me, don't ever be seen with no damn one-dollar bill!"

Another of the classic comedians of this era was Dusty Fletcher, who was best known for a bit called "Open the Door, Richard." In this routine, Fletcher appeared onstage alone, with a ladder his only prop. Staggering drunk, dressed in ill-fitting rags, a battered top hat and ridiculous, oversized, pointy-toed shoes, Fletcher would plant the ladder in the middle of nowhere, climb up a couple of steps and naturally fall flat on his face, after futilely screeching "Open the door, Richard!" In frustration he would mutter, "I met old Zeke standin' on the corner the other day. That cat sure was booted with liquid. He was abnoxicated. He was inebriated. Well, he was just plain drunk. He sure was salty with the bartender. The bartender's trying to make him buy another drink. See, he said there ain't no reason for me to buy drinks when everybody else is buyin' them. I'm goin' to drink to everybody's health till I ruin my own." Then he'd try the ladder again, and beseech Richard to "open the dooooor!" Another crash and another monologue, "Why he don't know who he's throwing out of that joint. Why I'll go back to that joint and take a short stick and bust it down to the ground! Open the doooooooor, Richard! I hate to be caught out on the street like this 'cause it makes you look so common. . . . Hey, Richard, open the door! Now, look at that old woman across the street stickin' her head out the window. . . . 'Ain't that him?' Yeah, it's me and drunk as hell! Open the door, Richard! I know he's in there 'cause I got on the clothes. They can't throw him out 'cause I owe just as much back rent as he does. . . . Open the door, Richard!!!" And as he shuffled offstage the audience would once more hear Dusty bellow, "Richard, why don't you open that door?!"

But of all the early comedians, probably the most beloved and most successful was Jackie "Moms" Mabley. She began on the T.O.B.A. circuit, was a regular for years at Connie's Inn during the Harlem Renaissance, started at the Apollo at $85 a week, became a headliner in black theatres and white nightclubs, and by the early seventies commanded a salary of $8,500 at the Apollo. Her real name was Loretta Mary Aiken, but to everyone she was "Moms." She dressed in old-timey cotton print dresses, clodhoppers, and dowdy hats like a backwoods mammy and addressed her audience as "my children." One of the early monologuists, she would delight the crowds at the Apollo with folksy tales that brought cries of identification.

As Lawrence W. Levine reported in *Black Culture and Black Consciousness*, she used to describe how her Southern relatives sent her those special items one could only get in the South at hog-killing time: "They shipped me some of that meat, you understand what I me-e-ean. They shipped me some of them neckbones with a whole lot of meat on it. Not like the neckbones you get up here. When they say neckbones, they mean neck *bones*. . . . Nothin' on 'em but the *bones*. Baby, I had the meat on, I put it on with a pot of cabba-a-age. . . . And I made some cracklin' bread. . . . Went down to the board and got me two quarts of butter-mil-l-lk. . . . Then I cooked me some gre-e-eens, you understand what I me-e-ean . . . and corn on the cob."

She played many roles for her "children"; the silly old bat whose "Moms' shuffle" was almost as well known as Pigmeat's truckin'; the old sage who said, "My slogan is: by all means do what you want to do, but know what you're doin' "; or the randy granny who feels that an "old man can't do nothin' for me but bring me a message from a young one."

Like all great comedians, her routines sought to touch her audience's sense of recognition, to create a sense of community that insulated the theatre from the injustices of the outside world. She told a story of a black man and a white man who robbed a bank, killed three tellers, two policemen, and wounded a bystander, and were sentenced to be hanged. As they were about to be executed, the white man pleaded, "I don't want to be hung. I don't want to be hung." The black man reproved him, "Oh, man, we done killed up all them people and you talk about you don't want to be hung. . . . They gonna hang you, so why don't you face it like a man?" "That's easy for you to say," the white replied, "you're used to it."

. . . . .

"At one time in the world of show business the tap dancer, or hoofer, as he was called by fellow dancers, was probably the most important act on the average bill," Honi Coles wrote in the *Amsterdam News*. "Not because

97

of any terrific drawing power, unless it was a Bill Robinson, a Buck and Bubbles, or an act of similar stature, but because he could open the show, close it, or fill any spot, especially the trouble spots. He was the best dressed, the best conditioned, the most conscientious performer on any bill, and in spite of being the least paid, he was the act to 'stop the show.' "

Over the years, Honi Coles became the most ardent historian of dance at the Apollo. He was there from the beginning and actually made his New York debut with the Three Millers at Schiffman's Lafayette Theatre in 1931. In the early thirties he developed a style of dance known as "high-speed rhythm tap."

Coles played the Apollo as part of various acts, most notably with the Lucky Seven Trio and in a comedy act with Bert Howell. While traveling with Cab Calloway's band between 1940 and 1943 he met Cholly Atkins, and after the war the two formed the team of Coles and Atkins. But by that time the golden era of the dancers and the big bands had passed, making the duo "the last of the class acts"—as Marshall and Jean Stearns dubbed them in their definitive book *Jazz Dance*. Frank Schiffman, who first booked the act sight unseen, was a tremendous fan of Coles. The team danced with the last of the big bands, on Broadway and in Las Vegas, and through the fifties they traditionally reopened the Apollo, with Billy Eckstine, in August after its summer break for renovations. In the early sixties Coles became the Apollo's production manager, although he can still throw a tap with the best of them.

During the big-band era there were as many as fifty top dance acts that played regularly at the Apollo and other black theatres. Often there would be three different dance acts on one Apollo bill—one to get things off to a fast start, a second to keep the middle from sagging, and a third right before the headliner to build excitement. Despite all the competition, the good acts had little trouble finding work on the string of theatres that made up the B. F. Keith's circuit, the Sun Time circuit, or the Apollo's own little "Around the World" circuit. Also, every big-band road show carried at least one dance act. But, as a matter of professional pride, every dancer kept on his toes, inventing new steps and keeping a watchful eye on the competition.

"When big-name dancers played the Apollo, there was nothing in the audience but dancers with their shoes," said Sandman Sims. "Up in the balcony, dancers, and the first six rows, you saw nothing but tap dancers, wanta-be tap dancers, gonna-be tap dancers, tried-to-be tap

98

ABOVE: Jackie "Moms" Mabley and Dusty Fletcher onstage in the late 1930s or early 1940s. LEFT: Coles and Atkins at the Apollo in the early 1940s (Cholly Atkins is on the left, Honi Coles the right). ★ *They were dubbed "the last of the class acts."*

dancers. That's the reason a guy would want to dance at the Apollo. But he would be scared to death; he'd do most of his dancing backstage, trembling. You look out in the audience and see all these faces, man. And they had a tendency to acknowledge the fact that so and so's here. When you heard those names, man, my goodness the cold chills would run through you 'cause you really got to be on your best. . . . A lot of dancers have been challenged right there onstage. Just got up and say, 'Hey, man, I want to dance against you. You ain't doing anything for the public. Let me come up there and see what you can really do.' They'd come right up onstage 'cause the steps is right there. And Ole Man Schiffman, he wouldn't care. Boy, this was a big thing for him. He loved it."

By the time the Apollo opened, the competition on the dancing scene was forcing dancers into more and more acrobatic stunts, as each act tried to outdo the others. Often the strenuous routines resulted in debilitating injuries that shortened careers and left dancers nearly crippled. Some acts, like the Three Little Words, lulled the Apollo's audience with a sweet soft-shoe number, and then, just as the crowd began to lose interest, they would inject a wild challenge dance with each Little Word trying to top the other. Tip, Tap and Toe were a top trio who worked with Eddie Cantor and made a splash in 1936 in *George White's Scandals.* They were the top act for several years and were among the first to tap in line, to the same music, each dancer producing the same sounds with different steps. They also invented the slide, a maneuver that Bob Fosse used in his film *All That Jazz.* The Four Step Brothers began with Duke Ellington in the late twenties. They incorporated all types of acrobatics in their act, but their forte became comedy. As the group began their challenge dance, the quartet's clown, Maceo Anderson, would wickedly taunt his colleagues, to the delight of the audience. Pops and Louie had a similarly loose act. Their trademark was improvisation, and they supposedly never performed the same routine twice—quite an achievement when doing thirty shows a week. Son and Sonny may have had the ultimate acrobatic act. Their routine was so fast that it lasted only four minutes. As a finale, the duo executed incredible flying flips from a standing position, landed in excruciating splits, snapped back into position on the beat, and repeated the stunt again and again.

Perhaps the greatest dance acts of all time were the Berry Brothers and the Nicholas Brothers. They were known as flash acts because of their blinding speed and fancy steps, and were among only a handful of dance acts that could carry an Apollo show as headliners. The Berry Brothers' star was Ananias Berry. Once, to top the Nicholas Brothers in a 1936 Cotton Club challenge meet, he devised a finale where he and brother Jimmy leaped from the bandstand and, as the band played its final note, crashed twelve feet down into tendon-ripping splits on both sides of brother Warren, who also did a split after completing a twisting back somersault. The Berry Brothers began with Ellington, toured abroad, helped open Radio City Music Hall in 1932, and also worked in Hollywood. Ananias, weakened by years of bodily abuse in pursuit of his art, died in 1951 at the age of thirty-nine.

Harold and Fayard Nicholas started as a juvenile act. Aged eight and fourteen, respectively, when they opened at the Cotton Club, the boys, clad in top hats and evening clothes, became the darlings of Harlem. When they came into the Apollo they had already made the film *Kid Millions* with Eddie Cantor and starred in the Ziegfeld Follies on Broadway. The Nicholas Brothers were an all-around act, combining wild airborn splits with tasty tapping and singing, and Harold also did imitations of Cab Calloway and Louis Armstrong. When they appeared in the Broadway version of *Babes in Arms*, choreographer George Balanchine devised a routine for them where they did cartwheels and flips over a line of chorus girls. Then, while the girls lined up with their legs apart, the boys would slide between their legs in splits and snap back up in front of them.

Great as these acts were, the men to whom all the Apollo's dancers owe the greatest debt are Bill "Bojangles" Robinson and John Bubbles. For thirty years, Bill Robinson fought for stardom. He began his career as a "pick"—from pickaninny—for white vaudevillians. It was customary in the early days of vaudeville for white stars to employ these fast-stepping black children as surefire showstoppers to aid the star's lackluster act. Many of the early dance greats began as picks. Bojangles attracted little notice in New York until the early 1920s, when he was fifty years old. Stardom didn't come until the smash hit 1928 stage production of Lew Leslie's *Blackbirds*. Suddenly, Ethel Waters wrote, "Harlem was crazy about Bojangles. They would yell, 'Bo, Bo!' whenever they saw him. . . . Everybody in Harlem said Bojangles was a magnificent dancer and they were certainly right."

As the Apollo was taken over by Schiffman, Bojangles achieved his greatest fame starring with and coaching Shirley Temple in the film *The Little Colonel*. The "Mayor of Harlem" then became a national star.

The great Bill "Bojangles" Robinson in 1941. ★ Ethel Waters: *"They would yell, 'Bo, Bo!' whenever they saw him. . . . Everybody in Harlem said Bojangles was a magnificent dancer and they were certainly right."*

Buck and Bubbles in the late 1930s (John Bubbles is standing, Buck Washington is reaching up from the floor). ★ *"It was an 'aw.' We walked on the stage uptown in a downtown style, and that's where the 'aw' comes in. They looked at us and said 'aw.'"*

Although Bill Robinson was popular with the public, his private persona was often dark and moody. Perhaps embittered by his long wait for stardom, he had little patience for young dancers and was notoriously egotistical. In fact, despite the cheerful sound of the name Bojangles, some have speculated, it may have come from a contraction of a countrified pronunciation of boar—"bo"—and a slang word for quarrel—"jangle"; so Bojangles would mean boarlike quarreler.

Finally, there is the great John Bubbles, inventor of rhythm tap, a style Honi Coles later mastered and speeded up. By the time Bubbles and partner Buck Washington played the Apollo, they were headliners. In 1935 Bubbles was George Gershwin's personal choice to play Sportin' Life in *Porgy and Bess*. As Bubbles said, Buck and Bubbles was "a white act" or a downtown act. "It was an 'aw,' " he recalled. "We walked on the stage uptown in a downtown style, and that's where the 'aw' comes in. They looked at us and said 'aw.' " Dancer Paul Draper recalled in the Stearnses' book: "Bubbles has a casual approach to the complicated steps he executes. His nonchalant manner contradicts the incredible things his feet are doing. You think he is just going to stroll around the stage, when presto, he'll toss off a burst of sight and sound that you just can't believe. At the same time, Buck plays stop-time on the piano in the laziest manner imaginable. He falls off the stool, remembering to reach up from the floor just in time to plunk one note every sixteen bars."

In the sixties Bubbles was "rediscovered," and until he suffered a stroke in 1967, was a popular attraction on "The Tonight Show." Still consulted for advice and information, he is the dancer old-timers at the Apollo most admire—and the respected old sage that hopeful newcomers look up to.

AMATEUR NIGHT AND THE APOLLO AUDIENCE

· · · · · · · · · · ·

The ghettos, factory towns, and dusty crossroads of America are filled with dreamers. Little could these communities offer to stimulate those with imagination, and—dare they hope it—talent. While star-struck white kids traditionally headed for Hollywood or Broadway, their black counterparts bucked the odds and beat a path for Harlem and the Wednesday-night amateur show at the Apollo. They knew they would face the toughest and most demanding audience in the world, a crowd notorious, especially on Amateur Nights, for its vocal and sometimes physical demonstrations of displeasure. They knew about Porto Rico, the crazy stagehand who served as the audience's hitman on Amateur Night. They knew they might not even pass the preshow audition, much less win the contest.

Yet they showed up and tried—an estimated fifteen thousand in just the first twenty years of Amateur Night at the Apollo. They had faith in themselves, and they knew the Apollo audience was the most astute judge of talent and the most appreciative audience in the world. If they could please the people at the Apollo, they could please any crowd. They also knew that four first-place wins guaranteed a week's professional engagement at the theatre. And they knew that the theatre's Amateur Nights had launched many careers. Apollo Amateur Night winners included Billy Kenny of the Ink Spots, Sarah Vaughan, Pearl Bailey, Billy Ward of the Dominoes, Frankie Lymon, Leslie Uggams, James Brown, King Curtis, Wilson Pickett, Ruth Brown, Screamin' Jay Hawkins, Dionne Warwick, and Gladys Knight. In 1975, Bobby Schiffman claimed that 30 to 40 percent of the "major black attractions that are working today" were launched at the Apollo's Amateur Night.

Joe Arrington, Jr., took a chance. He arrived in New York in the spring of 1955 from Baytown, Texas, and settled in a dingy rooming house in Hempstead, Long Island. He got a thirty-five-dollar-a-week job in a clothes store, and to fill his evenings began singing on street corners with his buddies. They were impressed with his talent and urged him to give the Apollo a try. Joe didn't think he had the stuff, but his friends prevailed and he went down to the Apollo's basement rehearsal hall on a Wednesday night to sign up for Amateur Night.

Twenty-five years before, the rehearsal hall, once Joe Ward's Coconut Grove, had been the Rathskeller, a white club, and it still bore the fake stone buttresses, exposed wood beams, and Germanic cityscapes left over from its previous incarnation. All around him hopeful contestants practiced, primped, fixed their costumes, and waited anxiously. Joe walked up to the desk and the man in charge asked who he was. Joe told him and said, "All I want is a chance." The man explained that there was a three- or four-month waiting list and told him to come back the following Monday to sign up.

Joe sat down dejectedly to watch the amateurs who were to go on that night. Bobby Schiffman sat down beside him to direct the proceedings and determine the order of performances. Joe struck up a conversation with him, and soon found himself pouring out his story to Bobby. Touched by his tale, Schiffman arranged for Joe Arrington, Jr., to appear that night. Joe selected an Arthur Prysock tune, "Woke Up This Morning," quickly rehearsed it with pianist Frankie Owens, and dashed out into the streets excitedly proclaiming his imminent appearance to everyone he passed.

Joe returned to the theatre at ten. As he stood in the wings waiting to go on, he could barely contain his pounding heart and shaking body. He looked out on stage and spotted a short polished tree stump sitting on a pedestal in front of and just to the left of the bandstand, near the wing where the amateurs entered. It was the remains of the fabled Tree of Hope—a chestnut tree that had once stood outside the Lafayette Theatre. Until the tree was cut down in 1933, it had been a favorite gathering place for out-of-work performers. Since booking agents soon realized that it was a good informal hiring hall, many jobs were landed there and the tree became a lucky charm for entertainers, many of whom got a piece of it when it was cut down. The largest chunk found its way to the Apollo, and Amateur Night tradition required all amateurs to touch the stump before going on.

When the master of ceremonies announced him, Joe dashed blindly to the microphone. The crowd was laughing at him. "Wait just a minute, young man," the m.c. said. "You forgot to touch the Tree of Hope." Frozen with confusion, Joe finally comprehended his mistake. After correcting his faux pas, he walked to the mike, and when he mentioned his hometown to the inquiring m.c. it got a round of applause, as usual, from the Wednesday night crowd. He announced his song, the m.c. wished him luck, Joe clutched the mike stand, and began to sing. Convinced that the audience hated him, he was overwhelmed when he completed his song and was greeted with tumultuous applause. He won the twenty-five-dollar first prize that night, then three more times, and was awarded a week's professional booking. Henry Glover of King Records saw him and signed him, and he went on to become one of the top stars of soul music in the sixties: Joe Tex.

The Apollo crowd wasn't infallible in its choice of winners and losers. Roy Hamilton was a good-looking youngster whose confidence could not be shaken, despite repeated tirades from Porto Rico when his amateur specialty, "You'll Never Walk Alone," consistently fell flat in the last few bars whenever he appeared on Amateur Night. Bobby Schiffman, sympathetic to his ambitions, reluctantly told Hamilton he didn't have what it takes.

Finally, one Wednesday night, Roy won "a poor third," according to Leonard Reed, who had emceed. "A few weeks later Frank Schiffman came to me, and asked, 'What have you got on the amateur hour, male, to open the show for us?' I said we had a good-looking boy that just barely made third, Roy Hamilton." Hamilton's manager had cut a record of "You'll Never Walk Alone," and he arranged to have the record store across from the Apollo play the disc constantly over its outdoor speaker. "We put him on," said Reed. "And when he finished singing—on his knees—they screamed. He stopped the show cold everyday." Soon afterward, Hamilton returned, as a headliner.

Another great star, Anthony Gourdine, leader of Little Anthony and the Imperials, was so awed by the prospect of an Apollo Amateur Night appearance that he blew the initial audition with Bobby Schiffman. Nearly two years before his 1958 professional debut at the Apollo with the Imperials, Anthony was with a group called the Duponts. Their manager arranged for them to audition for Amateur Night. "When I found out we were going to play the Apollo, my heart went up in my mouth," said Anthony. "Because all these years the thing I had created in my mind about the Apollo, and what I had heard from my parents, was that the Apollo was the big time. I used to walk past the Apollo as a boy and see the pictures, the murals, of all these people I heard on the radio or on records; I started to build an impression in my mind as to who I wanted to be and what I wanted to do from that. So when I walked into the Apollo it was like going into a holy sanctuary.

"There is a feeling, that humanistic feeling, I think John Glenn got it when he went around the Earth, there's an experience like—tah dah!—and you know where he was. I was in the cellar of the Apollo. That's a heck of a place to have an experience like that, but every board, every dirt corner, every little hole in the wall of that basement was hallowed ground to me. I knew all these people—Sammy Davis and Ella Fitzgerald—rehearsed down there. I just sat mesmerized. I was so nervous at the audition that I sang very badly. We were just very bad, and Bobby Schiffman said, 'Well, they're nice. Let them try and practice some more, maybe come back, they're not ready.' I was blown out when we got turned down, I was depressed. Now Bobby always hits me with that. He says, 'I turned you down! And you end up being a big star!' "

. . . . .

The original Harlem Amateur Hour was presented by Ralph Cooper and Frank Schiffman at the Lafayette Theatre in April 1933. When Cooper took his show to Sidney Cohen's rival Apollo a few months later, similar shows began cropping up in theatres and movie houses all over Harlem. At one point late in 1934, the Lafayette had an amateur night on Wednesday, the Harlem Opera House on Tuesday, and the Apollo on both Monday and Wednesday, with Cooper's "Harlem Amateur Hour" on WMCA. The radio show, later taken over by a white announcer, Joe O'Brien, brought the Apollo's Amateur Night into homes all over the country through a syndicated network of twenty-one stations.

Every Wednesday night from eleven to midnight, "Harlem Amateur Hour" presented the regular Amateur Night at the Apollo show—seven or eight hopeful amateurs plus a couple of numbers from the theatre's featured attraction. At the end of the show, the m.c. brought out all the contestants, and as he held his hand over each of their heads, the audience applause determined the winner. But the people listening in on

Little Anthony and the Imperials, about 1960. ★ *"There is a feeling, that humanistic feeling, I think John Glenn got it when he went around the Earth, there's an experience like—tah dah!— and you know where he was. I was in the cellar of the Apollo."*

Frank Schiffman making an award presentation to Butterbeans and Susie on WMCA's "Harlem Amateur Hour" in the early 1950s as Ethel Waters and Sugar Chile Robinson look on. ★ *The show brought the Apollo's Amateur Night into homes all over the country through a syndicated network of twenty-one stations.*

their radios had to stay in suspense all night long, for the radio show signed off before the results were determined. The next morning the Apollo and the radio stations were inundated with phone calls inquiring about the outcome.

Amateur Night at the Apollo became a phenomenal success with the public as well as with show-business neophytes. The Wednesday night shows always attracted celebrities, and the amateur shows were the first for which the Apollo instituted reserved seating. "The amateurs would come in and register months in advance," said Bobby Schiffman. "There was always a three- or four-month waiting list to get on the show. Every Monday evening prospective amateurs would come in and register. When their turn came up, we'd send them a postcard and tell them—next week, be at the Apollo at seven o'clock. We would put them on in an order, and we always had six or seven left over that we would ask to come back the following week. You had to do that because you were on live radio and you couldn't take a chance of running out of amateurs."

Not every contestant was a budding Ella Fitzgerald or Wilson Pickett, but the audience knew that justice would be done, and calling in their own executioner became part of the Wednesday-night ritual. During the week, Norman Miller was the stagehand in charge of sound, and he was also well known as a gruff backstage enforcer who kept wayward performers in line and the riffraff away from the stage door. However, on Wednesday nights he metamorphosed into Porto Rico, the crazed, wildly dressed nemesis of every terrified amateur and the savior of the disquieted Apollo crowd. Legend has it that at one early Amateur Night show, Miller, whose soundman's sensitive ears could no longer take the abuse of a struggling crooner's singing attempt, ran onstage, fired a cap pistol, and chased the wretched amateur off. The audience loved it, and a new Apollo tradition was born.

Miller lived for Wednesday nights, and although he never got paid for his extra duty, supplied all his own costumes. He soon filled a whole room with his hula skirts, skeleton costumes, and funny hats. "When the audience reveals its displeasure in whistles and catcalls, Porto Rico turns on a shrieking siren backstage, and rushes out to shoot the offender down with blank cartridges," reported a New York paper in the late thirties. "Then he struts around the stage a couple of times, firing off his pop gun and waving reassuringly at the audience. After two or three minutes of this, he retires to the wings, belly shaking, to wait impatiently for the next offenders. His costume for the performance is a memorable spectacle. It includes the turban of a Turkish pasha, a brassiere of funnels painted yellow and a pair of delicate pink tights."

In the fifties Bob Collins took over as Porto Rico, and later on Porto Rico was replaced by the character of Junkie Jones, who shot down the miserable into the 1970s. Another Amateur Night fixture was David "Pop" Johnson, who claimed in 1947 that he hadn't missed an Amateur Night in fourteen years. Pop reserved the same right-hand stageside box every Wednesday night. When an amateur displeased him, he took out a white handkerchief and draped it over his head. "Blow your whistle, Pop!" the audience would yell. And when he blew his whistle and began rocking back and forth in his seat, Porto Rico would make an appearance and put an end to the performance.

Pop Johnson's heir was Sandman Sims, the dancer, who was hired by the Apollo to sit in the box as a goad, dressed in a huge sombrero ringed by brightly flashing Christmas-tree lights. Sandman would cue Porto Rico by flashing the lights on his hat and coat and wailing on a dilapidated trombone. He would also break up a failing routine by calling in his sidekick Geech, an old rubber-legged comedian who could crack up the audience by merely walking down the aisle squawking for his girlfriend Hester.

Sandman claims his outfit served a practical as well as comical purpose. "You had to have a disguise," he said. "Many a night I had someone who wanted to know who was that guy that booed them off. They'd wait to go get him. They'd walk right by me after I changed clothes and say, 'Is that guy coming out?' I'd say, 'Yeah, he'll be out in a few minutes.' It was a long time before they knew who I was up there."

If the great lure of Amateur Night was the thrilling prospect of helping to discover a bright new talent, a major part of its attraction was the slightly perverse pleasure we all take in watching some poor soul fail miserably. On such occasions, one man's pathos could provide hysterical fodder for the Harlem grapevine for weeks. Bobby Schiffman remembered a particularly outrageous scene: "Jackie Wilson was probably the most exciting and talented performer to come out of the era of the late fifties and early sixties. As a result, the amateur show always had somebody who was copying him. The amateur show was live on WMCA, and there was a young fellow on the show who was doing one of Jackie's tunes. Jackie was in the audience, too. Well, in this tune Jackie always did this thing where he would come to center stage, do a spin, drop to his knees, the lights would change, a flash of powder would go off, and it was orgasm time for the girls in the first four rows. Jackie was a super

110

Norman Miller (alias Porto Rico) with singer Thelma Carpenter outside the Apollo in the 1950s. ★ *He was normally the stagehand in charge of sound. However, on Wednesday nights he metamorphosed into Porto Rico.*

Sandman Sims, sans sombrero and Christmas-tree lights, in a recent shot. ★ *"Many a night I had someone who wanted to know who was that guy that booed them off. They'd wait to go get him."*

athlete, and when he did this spin and dropped to his knees, he broke the fall before he hit the floor, and he wore kneepads. This kid had Jackie's voice down to a tee. But he didn't know from kneepads, and he wasn't the athlete that Jackie Wilson was. So the kid got to the point where he does this spin and he falls to his knees, and he hits the floor with a crash. All of sudden all you could hear over the radio was this guy screaming, 'Oh, shit!' The audience went absolutely bananas.''

If the crop of hopefuls for the Wednesday-night show looked too good, the crew at the Apollo took steps to make sure there would be at least a couple of surefire bombs. ''We had to plant some blow-offs,'' said Sandman Sims. ''If the whole show is too good, ain't nobody in there going to get blown off. We'd get us a guy and say, 'Come here, man, you got to sing tonight.' He don't know he's going to get blown off. But he knows, 'If you win, man, we gonna give you twenty-five dollars. This is your chance, man. You go out there.' He'd go out and be trying to sing and be off key, and the minute he was off key everybody would look up at the balcony at me, and sometimes I would try to hide.''

If all this sounds vaguely familiar, it may be because of a television personality named Chuck Barris whose "Gong Show"—remarkably similar in concept to Amateur Night at the Apollo—was a television phenomenon that swept the country in the late seventies. ''That was supposed to be the amateur show at the Apollo,'' Sandman said. ''But he didn't do it like it's supposed to be done.'' Ruth Brown, a onetime Amateur Night winner, agrees: '' 'The Gong Show' was a steal from the Amateur Night—a direct steal.''

• • • • •

One of the more dramatic Apollo Amateur Night stories stars Pearl Bailey. On her first trip to New York, in 1934, she was induced to put her talents to the test at the Harlem Opera House's amateur contest. But she arrived there too late and so went instead to appear at Amateur Night at the Apollo. ''They had Erskine Hawkins' orchestra as the headliner of the show,'' she wrote in *The Raw Pearl*. ''They were called the Bama State Collegians, and 'Tuxedo Junction' was their big song. . . . When the hand was held over the heads, I won . . . for 'In My Solitude,' arrangement homemade. Maybe my nice appearance helped, too. I'm grateful I didn't go down the street to the Opera House. I doubt I would have made it there, for that night a young girl walked on stage, opened her mouth, and the audience that had started to snicker ended up cheering. The girl sang 'Judy.' Her name was Ella Fitzgerald. She won, and that voice will go down in history."

It is impossible to say which of the Amateur Night triumphs was the most significant, but a leading contender surely is Sarah Vaughan's Apollo Amateur Night victory in October 1942. With that appearance, a new star for a new era was born. She was only sixteen years old, a singer in the choir at the Mount Zion Baptist Church in Newark, New Jersey. Her long, elegant gown could not quite make the skinny, buck-toothed youngster glamorous. The Cootie Williams band was playing, with Eddie "Cleanhead" Vinson as the vocalist. "I remember her standing behind us, trembling, scared to come on," he said. "I told her, 'Go on out there, everything's gonna be all right. Go on and do your best, don't be afraid.' She did 'Body and Soul,' I'll never forget that. She sat on the piano and sang. And she broke the house up."

Billy Eckstine happened to be in the theatre that evening to cash his paycheck from the Earl Hines band, and he decided to stay and watch the amateur show. "It was like a Grade B movie," the fabulous Mr. B recalled. "I rushed backstage and told her she must try out for the Earl Hines band." The Divine Sarah won Hines over, too, and went on to become the most important female jazz vocalist of all time.

Many of the big winners of Amateur Night contests at the Apollo built their careers on the kind of material used in their Amateur Night appearances. Others changed. Ruth Brown, whose "Mama He Treats Your Daughter Mean" and "5-10-15 Hours" were among the long string of rhythm-and-blues hits she produced throughout the fifties, first appeared on Amateur Night at the Apollo in the mid-forties and scored with a bland pop standard. "I was scared to death," she recalled. "I came all the way from Virginia to sing this one song. . . . Doc Wheeler, the m.c., asked, 'What are you going to sing?' I said, 'It Could Happen to You.' He kind of laughed and said, 'Who'd you learn that from?' Because it wasn't your average run-of-the-mill blues. I said, 'I heard Bing Crosby sing it.' The audience laughed.

"I sang about four bars and the audience said, 'Oh!' They started to applaud, and then they got quiet and you could hear a pin fall. When I got through I got scared 'cause it was still quiet for a minute. Then all of a sudden they screamed and they whistled and they were on their feet. I ran off the stage. Doc Wheeler called me back. All the fellas in Tiny Grimes's band applauded. Doc Wheeler said, 'You know we're gonna do something we've never done. We want this little lady to come back and

Sarah Vaughan with musicians in the Apollo alley (126th Street) in the late 1940s. ★ Eddie "Cleanhead" Vinson: *"She broke the house up."*

Ruth Brown in the mid-1950s. ★ *"The m.c. asked, 'What are you going to sing?' I said, 'It Could Happen to You.' He kind of laughed and said, 'Who'd you learn that from?' Because it wasn't your average run-of-the-mill blues. I said, 'I heard Bing Crosby sing it.'"*

LEFT: James Brown in 1956. ★
Sandman Sims: *"James Brown came to
New York and he didn't have no shoes,
nothing to dance in, nothing to sing in.
I gave him a pair of white sneakers.
Some other guy gave him a pair of pants.
Another guy gave him a shirt to come
in there and do the amateur show
that night. He won, and he ain't never
looked back since."*
BELOW: Frankie Lymon at the drums
gets an assist from deejay Tommy
Smalls, about 1957. ★ *He was
discovered at the Apollo when he
appeared on Amateur Night as the
drummer for the Esquires.*

sing another chorus of that song.' I sang it two times and I won first prize."

The fifties were an especially productive period for Amateur Night at the Apollo. The impact of the rhythm-and-blues explosion created a seemingly endless new supply of talent. The booming independent record business, largely centered in New York, soon discovered Wednesday night at the Apollo could be its single best source of fresh discoveries. Every Wednesday night the theatre was crowded with record-company scouts, who wouldn't dare miss an amateur show lest the latest street-corner singing sensations slip away.

Some fifties winners had long successful careers. For others, time at the top was brief. For example, the Crows were basically a one-hit phenomenon—"Gee"—but what a hit it was. They were discovered by talent agent Cliff Martinez at the Apollo amateur show and brought to the top independent producer at the time, George Goldner. "Gee" was their second release for Goldner, and it was one of the best and most important r-and-b records ever made.

To commemorate its success, Goldner named his new label Gee. He released one of the most popular tunes of the era, "Why Do Fools Fall in Love?" on this label. It was recorded by Frankie Lymon and the Teenagers. Earlier Goldner had discovered Frankie at the Apollo when he appeared on Amateur Night as the drummer for the Esquires. Another r-and-b great, Clyde McPhatter, began singing with the Mount Lebanon Singers on Harlem tenement stoops. He first attracted attention when, against the wishes of his religious parents, he entered and won an Apollo amateur show. He went on to become a star with Billy Ward and the Dominoes, with the Drifters, and as a single. A scout from MGM Records discovered the Harps, who became Harlem favorites for MGM as the Harptones.

Among the most spectacular successes was James Brown, the greatest black star of the sixties. He made an Amateur Night appearance at the Apollo in the mid-fifties. Sandman Sims remembered it: "James Brown came to New York and he didn't have no shoes, nothing to dance in, nothing to sing in. I gave him a pair of white sneakers. Some other guy gave him a pair of pants. Another guy gave him a shirt to come in there and do the amateur show that night. He won, and he ain't never looked back since." Leonard Reed was the theatre's manager at the time. "He came there and begged me to put him on the amateur hour," said Reed. "I said, 'No, we're filled up.' He just kept saying, 'I'm better than anybody on the show. I'm better than Little Willie John.' I said, 'Okay, we'll see.' That made me mad. I remember he had this straw suitcase and he was singing something about crying. He got down on the floor and he performed. He ripped that show apart."

The tremendous productivity of the amateur shows continued into the sixties and seventies. As Bobby Schiffman examined a photo montage of a June 1965 Apollo bill, he marveled that every one of the performers that week had come from Amateur Night: "This show includes Joe Tex, The Ronettes, Gladys Knight and the Pips, King Curtis, Inez and Charlie Foxx, and Billy Stewart. Gladys Knight was very good, and she won the amateur show a couple of times. We put her on one of our professional shows. King Curtis was also off the amateur show. He came and played saxophone and won. Inez Foxx was a beautiful local girl. She and her brother came up and sang and won a couple of times in a row, so we gave them a week. Ronnie [later Ronnie Spector] of the Ronettes—her uncle owned a greasy spoon next to the theatre, and she was in and out of the theatre all the time because her uncle owned this place; he was the one who asked me to put her on the show. Billy Stewart, he was very heavy and died very young. But he came on and he was wonderful. He had a unique singing voice and style. All of these people came off the amateur show and all of them became headliners."

The extremely popular gospel shows also produced new talent at their Amateur Nights. Dionne Warwick had grown up in the world of gospel music. Her mother was a member of the Drinkard Sisters. Dionne often accompanied her mother to nearby engagements, and on one of these visits to the Apollo she made her stage debut. "Every Wednesday night was Amateur Night, and it was no different when they had gospel shows there," she said. "But it was for gospel singers. Our group decided to go up there and get the prize, and also an appearance at the Apollo on the next gospel show. And we did. We went up and sang and won first prize. But we never went back to sing again." At the time, in the late fifties, Dionne was more interested in preparing for a different type of amateur contest—the Van Cliburn competition for new classical pianists. Of course, she made her name as a pop singer and song stylist, thanks to the talent, drive, and ambition that was provided its first outlet at Amateur Night at the Apollo.

· · · · ·

Amateur Night and every night, the Apollo audience was the power that made or broke careers. But it was much more than that. It was the heart and soul of the black community, the embodiment of the spirit of

Bobby Schiffman marveled that every one of the performers on this June 1965 Apollo bill had come from amateur hour.

Harlem—the force that truly made the Apollo great. As appreciators, the audience enforced a standard of excellence to which all performers, amateur and professional, aspired. Those performers who failed to give the Apollo crowd their all, or attempted to elevate themselves at the audience's expense, always regretted it.

For example, recalled Bobby Schiffman, "Nina Simone was, for a while, a very hot commodity who had a super big record called 'Porgy.' We secured her at the Apollo, and she came with a very highfalutin attitude toward her people. She wasn't ready to get down with the people, and when you were at the Apollo you had better get down with the people. Well, she was there on a Wednesday night. Amateur Night. The theatre is jammed with people who had come to see her. About the fifth number in the show, she still hadn't done 'Porgy.' The people in the back started to yell for her to please sing 'Porgy.' She got up from the piano and said, 'I knew that this was Amateur Night. The interesting thing is the amateurs are not backstage. You're the amateurs. I'll sing 'Porgy' when and if I get ready to sing 'Porgy.' The audience got up and walked out en masse. The next time she came to the theatre on the first show on Friday, three women got up from the back of the audience, walked down the aisle, threw a handful of pennies on the stage, and walked out. They hated her."

The Apollo's mainly black audience—so vulnerable in the white world beyond the theatre's doors—sat at the center of the greatest city in the world, in the middle of the most important black community in the country, right on Harlem's main street, in the top black theatre of all time. They were invincible here. But as Harold Cromer said, "They didn't come out to boo you. It was just, 'Hey, Jim, I paid my thirty-five cents!' " Their intention was not to be malicious, but to demand and reward greatness. Wise entertainers realized this, and learned from it. "The Apollo was really the basis for my becoming the kind of performer I am today," said Ruth Brown, "because it taught me stage presence. It taught me how to have rapport with my audience. It taught me humility. It taught me not to be so grand, not to get so carried away that you feel these people are idiots that are coming out here to watch you—because that is not the case. It taught me that my audience was always first and foremost."

Playing in front of the Apollo audience was like schussing downhill for the World Cup, racing at Le Mans, or stepping into the ring at a championship fight—it was an exhilarating but nerve-racking experience. As Sammy Davis, Jr., put it: "In the Apollo at the opening show—

119

when the band started playing 'I May Be Wrong (But I Think You're Wonderful)' and the house lights would come up on the curtain—you'd start to get the itchy feeling and nervousness. Because it seemed like a dual thing. It wasn't just being accepted as a performer. It was being accepted by your own people."

The relationship between performer and the Apollo audience has been compared to that of preacher and congregation, and often that was an apt analogy. But it could also, at a moment's notice, dissolve into a match between Christian and lions. "When performers hit the Apollo stage, no matter how celebrated they were, no matter how successful they were, they were nervous," said Bobby Schiffman. "When Ella Fitzgerald was ready to go at the Apollo she was nervous as hell. Every performer was, but it keyed them up. It spurred them on to do the best they possibly could, thirty-one times a week. They put out every fiber of their energy, emotion, and ability to please that audience. I don't care if there were twenty people in there. They did their best at the Apollo because they knew that if they sang it wrong or didn't give their all, the audience would jump right on them."

The Schiffmans may have been particularly prophetic weathermen, but it was mainly because they had daily access to one of the finest barometers around—the Apollo audience. While the Schiffmans ran the theatre, even they would acknowledge that the audience was the real boss. Johnny Otis described an incident involving a song-and-dance man who bombed when he unsuccessfully tried a comic monologue. "Oh, man, they cut loose on him," said Otis. "He struggled through his act, and he actually was bad. He came backstage, and as he walked through, he said, 'Screw those m.f.'s. I wouldn't work here if they paid me a million dollars.' In other words, he quit. Frank Schiffman was standing there, and he said, 'You see, Mr. Otis, I hired him in good faith, but the people overruled me and they fired him.' "

The audience at the Apollo inspired both fierce competition and a wonderful spirit of cooperation among performers. As the crowd demanded more and more, each performer tried to outdo the other for its approval, and spurred his colleagues on to greater and greater heights. But it was a generally friendly competition generated by the excitement of being at the world's greatest theatre, and most seasoned performers were eager and willing to help newcomers. "There was a running joke at the Apollo," said Dionne Warwick. "When a guy walks onstage he's supposed to own it. I don't care if it's five minutes or fifty minutes. Go out there. That's your stage. And if somebody's coming onstage after

Nina Simone in the early 1960s. ★ Bobby Schiffman: *"The audience got up and walked out en masse. The next time she came to the theatre on the first show on Friday, three women got up from the back of the audience, walked down the aisle, threw a handful of pennies on the stage, and walked out."*

A 1947 Apollo crowd. ★ *The audience was the heart and soul of the black community, the embodiment of the spirit of Harlem—the force that truly made the Apollo great.*

you, you're supposed to give it to the point that they can't follow you. That's consummate performance. You passed that person going onstage, and you have to take a hose—cool that stage off. Too hot to trot out there; and that was the thing: 'Don't think you're going on tonight.' You know?"

"We were proud when we came onstage," said Gladys Knight. "To whoever was coming after us, we'd say, 'Kill! Go out there and wipe 'em out.' That's the way it was in those days. Or we could say to each other, 'Hey, maybe if you do this like this, it might go over better.' Everybody's so into himself nowadays—or herself—you talk about going up and telling somebody some advice about what they're doing and you're liable to get hit in the mouth. You can always learn, you know, and the Apollo was just that kind of venue. It was a school, that's what it was, maybe more than a theatre it was a school."

"It was a competitive place to play," said Little Anthony. "If an act would come off, and they got a standing ovation, they'd walk offstage like this [he struts around, cocky]. They'd say, 'You better call the fire department. I feel sorry for you coming behind me.' The first act would set the pace for the rest of the show. That's why opening acts were so darned good: they knew they had to come out smoking. If the audience liked the opening act, before the end of the week, that act was not the opening. You knew you were making it if you moved out of the opening in the same week you started. I remember Schiffman sending down a notice: 'The Imperials can't be third, move them down to fifth.' We were killing the act that was coming down, and they couldn't handle it.

"There was a competitive high as performers, but they were very liberal and nice after the performance. For instance, maybe one of the Dells would say, 'Hey, man, don't be looking straight out like that. You see them girls over there at the top, now you got to play to them.' Or a group like the Flamingoes, they used to show us footwork and dancing things. We just literally learned as we went, from the Apollo. It was the most disciplined place in the world. I learned comedy timing, rhythm, relaxation, and articulation from the Apollo. They were the toughest audience in the world. You'd better do good, or they'd throw a bottle. There were days I didn't do well and I cried. I didn't want people to see me." The Apollo stimulated a performer to do his or her best. Dionne Warwick commented, "I think the greatest performances of anybody have been at the Apollo Theatre."

To be a part of the Apollo audience was to be a part of the show. This implicit link with the performers onstage created a charge like that between the two poles of a battery, and it electrified the atmosphere at the Apollo. As Phyl Garland wrote in *The Sound of Soul*: "Some anthropologists have linked this sort of interaction with the African past when art was regarded as an inseparable part of life that was not to be purchased for a two dollar ticket. If there is some truth to this, nowhere in modern-day America is it more apparent than at the Apollo."

All of the jazz musicians, blues singers, soul stars, street dancers, and *lebenspilder* comedians at the Apollo addressed the black experience. It was the source of their inspiration; and their interpretation raised the common black experience to the level of art while their personal and professional stature elevated and confirmed the hopes and desires of everyone in the audience.

"Black music is a demonstration of emotion," said Bobby Schiffman. "Black audiences have a Sarah Vaughan. When she sings a love ballad you can feel the passion, the pain, the joy, because the emotion comes out in the voice. Sarah Vaughan is feeling it from her life experience, and the audience recognizes that. Also to black audiences the accomplishment of black performers who got out of the ghetto is something to be admired. So that what the audience is saying when they are screaming and yelling about how much they love what the artist has done is, 'Yeah, I like what you have done, and I admire the fact that you have gotten out and I could get out the same way. And I love it that the opportunity is presented, and I am applauding not only your achievement as far as the song you just sang, but your achievement in doing all the other social things that stardom spells out.' "

The everyday Apollo customer was black, but the racial makeup of the Apollo audience changed through the years. Just as the Harlem riot of 1935 signaled the end of the white nighttime encampment uptown, so subsequent riots in 1943 and the 1960s further stemmed the flow of white tourism to Harlem and the Apollo. In the thirties and early forties, the audience at the Apollo was often 40 percent white during the week, and up to 75 percent white at the Amateur Night and Saturday midnight shows. By the mid-sixties Frank Schiffman estimated that only 15 percent of the weekday and 25 percent of the weekend audience was white. Audiences for the last regular shows at the theatre were virtually all-black. One welcome exception to this trend was the busloads of European tourists who descended upon the Apollo in the summertime. The ebb in the tide of white visitors to Harlem hurt the theatre financially, but as Harlem grew increasingly isolated from the rest of the city, the Apollo grew more important to the local community.

A night out at the Apollo was something special, but for the people in the audience, like the performers onstage, the Apollo was home. Mothers often brought their babies because it was cheaper than paying a sitter, and they were an accepted part of the scene. Also, since the Apollo management was well known to many, on their way out people would stop in the office to congratulate the Schiffmans on a fine show or to give them a piece of their mind. Unlike any other cultural institution, the Apollo was an oasis of comfort, security, and relaxation for its community. It arose within an atmosphere of grave racial injustice, and the great tradition of the Apollo audience is founded in the daily struggle of being black in America. Society forced blacks into a straitjacketed existence where there was no room to move, no margin for error, no freedom. One suspect glance, one false move, one harsh word, one shout, one laugh, one tear—any of these could bring white notice, white alarm, white wrath down upon them. So out in the world they stayed cool, they played dumb, they held it all in. But not at home. At home it could all come out—the laughter, the sorrow, the violence, the joy, the eloquence. At home in the Apollo, all the pent-up emotions and reactions of the day were released in a free and uninhibited display that proclaimed their worth and dignity and freedom.

When the movie ended and the master of ceremonies announced, "Ladies and gentlemen, it's showtime at the Apollo!" a roar of glee would erupt from the kids in the first few rows and way up in the second balcony, moving like a wave between the nearest and farthest extremes of the theatre. Soon the whole audience was enveloped, screaming and cheering. A performer hitting the stage was greeted by this frenzied scene, which was amplified by the sheer physical closeness of the audience. The popular performers always emptied the first few rows of the orchestra as the kids rushed the stage, which stood no higher than chest-level to them. Even the first balcony, which hung so low that it blocked the sight lines of some of the rear orchestra seats, seemed to loom unnaturally close to the stage. The stageside boxes, usually filled with celebrities, framed the stage. There were guards on hand to keep the action manageable. But it became mandatory for performers to grasp as many wildly waving hands as possible, and many, finding the opportunity for open communion with their fans irresistible, waded into the crowd.

By tradition and design, the atmosphere at the Apollo encouraged audience involvement. "It really was kind of special," said Sammy Davis, Jr. "There was a marvelous rapport. The audience talked back to the performer. The performer talked back to the audience. It wasn't heckling so much as we know it now. But the guy in the audience would say, 'You ain't doin' shit.' And the performer would say, 'Yes, I am!' right back to him.''

Sometimes the rejoinders took the form of slick putdowns that upstaged the act onstage. ''There were guys in the audience that were funnier than you,'' said Scoey Mitchlll. ''If you got up there and you were dying, they'd start throwing lines at you from the audience. And I mean, not just 'get off the stage.' They'd do funny lines. Once I started to sing a song and I was just joking around. A fellow walked up to me and he had a pencil and paper. He walked up to the edge of the stage and he put it on the stage, and I said, 'Hey, so you want my autograph?' He said, 'No, just write the line, don't sing it.' '' But the pros took it good-naturedly, because entertainment was the main objective. ''Your ears will pick up comments that people are making,'' said Screamin' Jay Hawkins, rhythm and blues' precursor to rock's Alice Cooper. '' 'Look at that damn fool.' They're dyin' laughing, but they're enjoying themselves. That's the ultimate goal. I made them forget their welfare checks that didn't come or the job they don't have.''

Indeed, providing enjoyment and a release was the ultimate goal of the Apollo, and the audience was willing to accept and encourage quality entertainment of any type free from analytical or emotional constraints. ''That's one thing about the Apollo,'' said Scoey Mitchlll. ''If you were doing something good—I mean you could be an opera singer and come in the Apollo, and though they may not really understand the fact that you're singing in Italian, if you were singing good, they'd let you know it.''

This unique compassion and genuine feeling kept top performers coming back to the Apollo even as more lucrative places had opened up to them. ''I played the Apollo long after I needed to, basically because there was no audience like the Apollo's,'' said Nancy Wilson. ''I went back and stood out there one night. I finished the show and took my bow. When I stood up, people were rushing the stage. It was the warmest and most beautiful feeling I've ever had. There is just no way to describe the warmth and how they embraced you at the Apollo if they loved you. They just don't make them like that anymore.'' Perhaps Billie Holiday expressed it best when she wrote in her autobiography: ''There's nothing like an audience at the Apollo. They didn't ask me what my style was, who I was, where I'd come from, who influenced me, or anything. They just broke the house up.''

It was sometimes a challenge to keep the masses of people who

A proud father shows his sons some of the Apollo greats in one of the photo murals in the lobby in 1954. The stairs to the second balcony are on the right, the ones to the first balcony are beyond that, and the main entrance to the theatre is at the rear. ★ *For the people in the audience, like the performers onstage, the Apollo was home.*

RIGHT: A comic works the crowd in 1937. ★ *The first balcony, which hung so low that it blocked the sight lines of some of the rear orchestra seats, seemed to loom unnaturally close to the stage. The stageside boxes framed the stage.*

flowed into the Apollo every week from literally breaking up the theatre. The Apollo sold at least 800,000 to 1 million tickets annually. A so-so week might draw 16,000 customers. An especially hot attraction could triple that number. In more genteel days, before the rock-and-roll revolution upset things, the Apollo handled the crowds with thirteen young male and female ushers, but by the mid-sixties two dozen husky men were employed to keep things under control.

Standing in line was a part of the Apollo scene for most shows. Because of the theatre's general-admission–stay-all-day policy, the theatre did not clear after each show, and there were usually people waiting to take seats as they became available. When superstars such as Lionel Hampton or James Brown appeared, eager fans would wait outside, in any weather, for hours. Ushers would queue them up in two lines, one going west down 125th Street, around the corner, and up Eighth Avenue to the Braddock Hotel, the other stretching east and around the corner on Seventh Avenue to the old Alhambra Theatre.

While official policy allowed patrons to stay as long as they liked, the management sometimes used subliminal methods to ease people out. "We used to have a film called *The River*," said Doll Thomas. "It was a documentary of all the main rivers in the country. Come in there and look at twenty minutes of all that water falling, and they're going to want to get up and go to the bathroom. The minute they got up, we put someone in their seat."

When acts like James Brown began packing them in as never before, and demanding a percentage of the house receipts, the Schiffmans began clearing the Apollo after each show to allow for maximum turnover. But the audience did not adjust easily to this. "The moment the last act was over they'd turn the lights up," said Harold Cromer. "The ushers would run up and down the aisles getting everybody out. The offstage announcer would ask everybody to please clear the theatre. But the disgruntled characters would say, 'Hey, man, I paid my money. I can stay in this motherfucker all day.' There would be a lot of arguments, fights. But they'd send them out the side door onto 126th Street. They'd have a fight, but they'd get them out."

The most vociferous and vocal segment of the audience was the kids. Their uninhibited joy and freely expressed displeasure were catalysts for the rest of the audience. As rhythm and blues, and then soul music, became the dominant entertainment forms at the Apollo, the kids increasingly dominated the audience. Young people were always the first on line. As soon as the doors opened, some would try to sneak past the

The line for James Brown's 1965 show, stretching east along 125th Street, around the corner, and up Seventh Avenue.

Kids in the front rows digging a 1970 Stevie Wonder show. ★
Leslie Uggams: *"Those first three rows, everyone wanted to be there, because when the artist came down and put their hand out you could say, 'Oh, I touched him, wow!'"*

ticket booth. Leslie Uggams, who grew up near the Apollo, described the scene: "We were on line at nine in the morning on Saturday waiting for the theatre to open at noon, in order to be in the front seats. And, let me tell you, you could not go to the bathroom because somebody would jump in your seat and you'd have a fistfight if you tried to get them out. So you had to make sure you went to the bathroom, you had your popcorn, and everything. Those first three rows, everyone wanted to be there, because when the artist came down and put their hand out you could say, 'Oh, I touched him, wow!' "

The kids hung on every word, and always kept performers on their toes. "On weekends," said Harold Cromer, "the first show, the kids were there, and they were very astute. So the second show, we found that if you repeated the routine, it was no good. They were right with you. So we used to switch up on them. They'd screech, 'You didn't say that the last time!' "

From the earliest days, going to the Apollo was a ritual for the youth of Harlem. "If you lived in Harlem during the 1930s, you had to make it to the Apollo each and every Friday to catch the new show," recalled playwright Loften Mitchell. "Truant officers would have had a picnic if they had invaded the place. There was a definite pattern. You left your schoolbooks under the bed, then strolled around the block until it was show time. Then, you paid for a second balcony ticket and made it up those long steps. You 'fell' into the balcony, looked for someone you knew on the other side, and you always found someone there waiting to be recognized. You called out: 'Hey, daddy-o! How's every little thing?' The fellow on the other side greeted you, gratefully, and answered: 'Jumping.' Then, fortified and recognized, you sat down, generally among friends who had suddenly appeared. You reached over and found some excuse for speaking to a fine brown 'chick' who sat in front of you. Before the Apollo theme song was through, you were 'spieling' and singing, too, 'I Think You're Wonderful.' "

The second balcony was notorious. Performers called it the Buzzard's Roost, because if you died onstage they'd pick your bones clean. "That second balcony, man, they'd throw a chair," said Sandman Sims. "Or some singer would go off key and get hit with a beer bottle or something, and everybody'd have to leave. It was arson, man! Happened all the time." These were the cheap seats, populated by kids and those least able to afford an Apollo show. It was so steep that people had to hold onto the brown iron railings for safety. Those in the front row had to lean forward to peer over the rail, and to those in the rear, the stage appeared a spot in the distance. The second balcony also is famous for its leapers. Many have told stories of people overcome with emotion and euphoria jumping from the second balcony. The gospel shows were often the scene of what might be called leaps of faith, but it always seemed, as one report put it, "The Lord was watching over, and no one got hurt." It has also been said that one rendition of Count Basie's "One O'Clock Jump" inspired a fan to take the tune literally at the appointed hour. But the most famous incident involved a reefer-smoking hipster who got carried away during a rousing rendition of "Flyin' Home" by the Lionel Hampton band. He stood on the rail, shouted "I'm flyin', I'm flyin'!" and tested his wings into the orchestra section below. Again, miraculously, no one was hurt. It is said this incident inspired Jerry Valentine to compose the hit tune "Second Balcony Jump" for Earl Hines.

The most outrageous element in the Apollo audience was the transvestites who became an Apollo Amateur Night fixture in the fifties and sixties. As Bobby Schiffman recalled: "There was a group of transvestites who used to buy the C Box, which was right over the stage on the right-hand side, every Wednesday night. They had those tickets permanently reserved. They used to carry on. They came in dressed in outrageous clothes and gowns. It became an attraction. People used to come to see what they were wearing and what they were doing up there."

Ruth Brown, who was famous for her fine costumes of fluffy crinolines and petticoats as well as beautifully sculpted gowns, was often a target of their bitchiness. "For years it was that way," she said. "They had this box and they would stand and tell you, 'You don't look half as good as I do, darling.' So you had better be dressed or when you came on they'd tell you from the box, 'That's some bad crap you're wearing!' They'd challenge you."

Yet, like all the other memorable characters in the Apollo, they helped make the theatre's shows something special. "Our gay friends would fill that box," remembered Gladys Knight. "On Wednesday night when we came onstage we felt their presence. They'd say, 'There's our girl!' or, 'Look at those Pips!' And they would ooh and aah about our costumes. And I was proud, because they were proud of us."

THE FORTIES

· · · · · · · · · · ·

They called him "Bean." In 1940, Coleman Hawkins was the hottest sax man in the world. On the strength of his phenomenal solo on "Body and Soul" he had been touring the country with his own sixteen-piece band. Hawkins was onto something new. He expanded the presumed capabilities of his instrument. His inventiveness ripped apart the growingly complacent world of swing and foreshadowed a major shake-up of the big-band scene. Musicians everywhere wore out copies of his record trying to figure out what Hawkins had done.

One very early Friday morning in late June, after completing his week at the Apollo with Ralph Cooper and Pigmeat Markham, Hawkins celebrated by calling a few friends up onstage for a jam on Fats Waller's "Honeysuckle Rose." These Friday morning get-togethers had become quite popular at the Apollo, and helped create the atmosphere of artistic freedom that led to the famous Harlem jam sessions that produced the new sound of bebop. Even to the Apollo crowd used to the best, this particular gathering was awesome. Hawkins kicked off the Waller tune. Tommy Dorsey peered through his wire-rimmed spectacles down the slide of his trombone to his guitarist, Carmen Mastren, while fellow trombonist Jack Jenney looked on. Harry James and Bunny Berigan blew their trumpets side by side. Reedman Joe Marsala was there and so was Count Basie, comping away at one of his idol's finest compositions. And behind it all, bassist John Kirby, fresh from his sextet's triumph at the formerly all-white Waldorf-Astoria, provided a steady beat along with fiery drummer Gene Krupa.

What a marvelous release it must have been for these men—because, while swing music was at its peak of popularity, it was becoming increasingly smarmy and commercialized. There was little room for improvisation or creativity in swing's stylized arrangements, and although the top bands competed furiously for the services of the great instrumental soloists, there was often little for these artists to do.

Big bands continued to be the major attraction at the Apollo until the postwar years. However, wartime conditions and changing tastes made it increasingly difficult for them to go on. Paradoxically, as some of the top black bands began to break into formerly all-white territory, Schiffman relied on newer black bands, those of Erskine Hawkins, Buddy Johnson, Cootie Williams, and Lucky Millinder. Yet no band could survive merely on occasional gigs at the Apollo, and world events were affecting the employment picture for the bands around the country.

Because of gas rationing and other restrictions, travel became problematic. Many white bands turned to the rails, but black bands were further hampered by Jim Crow restrictions on trains below the Mason-Dixon Line. Until the NAACP prevailed upon the Office of Defense Transportation to ease its ban on charter bus travel for black bands, many outfits were faced with extinction. But only five buses were made available. Gas shortages also made it more difficult for fans to get out and see the bands. Two other wartime curbs, a 20 percent amusement tax and the midnight "brownout" curfew, severely hurt business. The bands might have turned more to recordings to supplement their reduced performing income, but in 1942 the American Federation of Musicians called a recording ban that dragged on for two years. War service claimed many leaders and sidemen, and the remaining musicians often demanded inflated salaries.

Within a few weeks of December 1946, eight top swing bands succumbed: Benny Goodman's, Woody Herman's, Harry James's, Tommy Dorsey's, Les Brown's, Jack Teagarden's, Benny Carter's, and Ina Ray Hutton's. "It was too expensive," explained Eddie "Cleanhead" Vinson, who led his own band in the mid-forties after quitting as Cootie Williams's vocalist. "The big names lasted longer than anybody. But the Erskine Hawkinses and Buddy Johnsons—everybody was breaking

ABOVE: The Coleman Hawkins Orchestra at the Apollo, 1940.
★ *Coleman Hawkins was the hottest sax man in the world.*
BELOW: 1947 Apollo handbill for Johnny Otis and his
soon-to-be-disbanded big jazz band. ★ *"There were no
more jobs. We had to struggle too hard."*

down. During the year of 'forty-seven it started petering out with the big bands. And you had television, and people weren't going to shows that much. That kills a big band. There wasn't no places for you to play."

Johnny Otis, whose own big jazz band came in on the tail of the era, agrees. "There were no more jobs. We had to struggle too hard. I remember, Billy Eckstine and I met in Washington, D.C., and he had a big band and I had a big band, and he said, 'You know, I'm breaking mine down. I'm sorry.' When I got home [to Los Angeles] I was forced to reduce the size of mine out of sheer economic necessity. I couldn't function with fifteen or sixteen." But, in the end, Otis added, "Our art and our entertainment is a reflection of our way of life. . . . It was a change of life-style."

. . . . .

The 1940s was a transitional period for the Apollo and for American society in general. Americans lived through the end of the Great Depression, four years of world war, and the dawn of the atomic age. Although less earth-shaking, the changes at the Apollo were dramatic in their impact on its constituents. In the early forties, Harlem was still a popular hangout for whites. Malcolm X, then an itinerant dishwasher and hustler known as Detroit Red, described the scene in his autobiography: "Especially after the nightclubs downtown closed, the taxis and black limousines would be driving uptown, bringing those white people who never could get enough of Negro *soul*. . . . Inside every after-hours spot, the smoke would hurt your eyes. Four white people to every Negro would be in there drinking whiskey from coffee cups and eating fried chicken. The generally flushed-faced white men and their makeup-masked, glittery-eyed women would be pounding each other's backs and uproariously laughing and applauding the music. A lot of whites, drunk, would go staggering up to Negroes, the waiters, the owners, or Negroes at tables, wringing their hands, even trying to hug them, 'You're just as good as I am—I want you to know that.' "

The war years brought expectations in the black community that perhaps white people meant what they said. Black participation in World War II was thorough—nearly one million served. As in the First World War, when its nation called, the black community responded. The Apollo supported the men and women in uniform. Thirty-five tickets were set aside each day for the soldiers at the Harlem Defense Recreation Center. Also, headliners on each week's bill—Billie Holiday, Ella Fitzgerald, Bill Robinson, Lucky Millinder, Cab Calloway, Earl Hines, Willie Bryant, the

Ink Spots, and Lena Horne—entertained and socialized with the service-men, making Tuesdays at the U.S.O. Center "Apollo Night."

On the home front, thousands of blacks found lucrative jobs in the defense industry, and for the first time their economic situation improved measurably. But frustration soon replaced optimism, and by the mid-forties many blacks were mired in disappointment. When blacks fought in the war it was generally in segregated units, and when some branches of the service finally were integrated, blacks usually served in menial positions. Stories of black servicemen being beaten and killed by white "crackers" near Southern military bases turned up all too frequently in the Harlem newspapers. And the euphoria of finding high-paying war-time jobs soured as blacks realized that decent salaries did not mean they would be welcome in decent neighborhoods. Harlemites were further upset when Mayor Fiorello La Guardia temporarily closed the Sa-voy Ballroom, he said, to prevent incidents arising out of interracial mingling.

In Harlem, events came to a head on the night of Sunday, August 1, 1943, in the worst riot ever experienced in that community. The trouble began when a white policeman answered a call for help at the Braddock Hotel, a favorite neighborhood hangout for Apollo entertainers at 126th Street near Eighth Avenue. He attempted to arrest a woman causing a disturbance. When a black soldier intervened and allegedly assaulted the police officer, the policeman fired, wounding the soldier in the shoulder. He arrested the soldier, and as he marched him to nearby Sydenham Hospital, a crowd gathered.

Waiting outside the hospital for word of the soldier's condition, the crowd grew restless. Somehow a false rumor spread that the soldier had died. The crowd turned into a rampaging mob. Hundreds of white-owned businesses on and around 125th Street were gutted. But the Apollo remained undamaged. Some reports said a cordon of Harlemites formed spontaneously to protect the theatre. Mayor La Guardia was ignored and jeered as he rode through the streets in a sound truck urging calm. The riot raged until dawn. When it was all over, hundreds had been arrested, hundreds more wounded, and at least six people were dead. Adam Clayton Powell, Sr., called it "the hottest hell ever created in Harlem."

Although the Apollo was spared any physical damage, the 1943 riot hurt the theatre at the box office by scaring away some of its white clientele. "After the riot things got very tight in Harlem," wrote Malcolm X. "It was terrible for the night-life people, and for those hustlers whose main income had been the white man's money. The 1935 riot had left only a relative trickle of the money which had poured into Harlem during the 1920s. And now this new riot ended even that trickle."

While the Apollo was hurt, it was far from crippled. The Wednesday night and Saturday midnight shows, especially, continued to be so popular that in 1945 the Apollo instituted reserved seating for these shows. The Apollo was such a great deal that it was almost impossible for it to be badly hurt. The top price for a ticket in 1947 was one dollar after 5:00 P.M., and it was the only theatre in New York to change its ticket prices four times daily, starting at fifty cents before noon.

The events of the forties made the Apollo more important than ever to the community and to black entertainers. To a demoralized and dejected people, the Apollo was one of the few sources of hope and pride. For the audience it was an escape, but also an assurance of their own worth, of their culture's uniqueness and importance, and a portent of a better life far beyond the troubles of the ghetto. For entertainers, the Apollo was a refuge: as whites took over the swing scene, as blacks were forced to accept second-class status in the growing recording industry and many were left unprepared to cope with changing styles in show business and culture, the Apollo remained home. There they felt the love and understanding of a family. In the forties the Apollo became more than just another theatre. It was a boisterous, bouncing, bobbing cork in a sea of troubles.

. . . . .

Rich as it had always been in talent, the Apollo also continued to lead the way in innovation. The critical musical development in the forties was bebop. Frank Schiffman became a booster of the new sound, though bebop didn't please everyone in Harlem. The *New York Age*, which at first had condemned swing, now complained that bebop was killing swing. "Large expensive bands were no longer in vogue," the *Age* stated in 1949, "swing, which had its heyday after the demise of jazz, suddenly had to step aside for a 'bastard-type' craze known as bebop which needed only a small combo to bring out its—well, virtues. Where Cab Calloway and his hi-de-ho formally [*sic*] held the spotlight, was now a young man with a horn, Dizzy Gillespie, by name, who took a new riff, an off-beat with an accented fifth, and built himself a cult of beret-topped, chin-whiskered followers with flashy clothes and big, flowing bow ties."

Bebop began to emerge as more frustrated musicians and young rebels got together to jam and experiment with new sounds and means of expression. But the burgeoning jam-session scene had the local musicians' union worried. Schiffman and others were reaping a financial benefit from all this unexpected free talent. The union people feared a trend toward free jams instead of paid gigs. The Friday-morning Apollo sessions and many others ended soon after the union began handing out fines of $100 to $500 to musicians for playing without a contract.

The scene then went underground to the smaller clubs of Harlem, most notably Minton's Playhouse and Monroe's Uptown House. Even at these clubs, musicians risked an encounter with the union's so-called walking delegates. But the sense of frustration with the big bands and the youthful exuberance of the daring new players was too great to be put off by such threats.

Minton's, in particular, became the hip spot to jam, thanks to the innovations of the club's new manager, ex-bandleader Teddy Hill, who took over in January 1940. On Monday nights, traditionally musicians' night off, Hill instituted a "down home" dinner for everyone in the band at the Apollo that week. After a rough weekend at the Apollo, these events often became riotous affairs, and were very popular throughout the early forties. Another reason for Minton's popularity with musicians was the fact that the owner, Henry Minton, was one of the first black delegates to the union, so the musicians could jam with virtual impunity. But the greatest attraction was Minton's little house band—a group designed to encourage jamming. The pianist was Thelonious Monk, then barely out of his teens; on drums, the innovative Kenny "Klook" Clarke; Nick Finton on bass; on trumpet there was Joe Guy and, occasionally, Dizzy Gillespie; and the most famous and important member at the time was the great improviser, guitarist Charlie Christian.

A new style of music was being invented, partly through experimentation, partly by accident. The more the Minton's musicians and others—such as Charlie "Yardbird" Parker, Ken Kersey, Little Benny Harris, and Idrees Sulieman—played together, the less inhibited and more in touch with each other they became. All were big-band alumni grown impatient with clipped solos reliant upon the harmonic structure of swing arrangements. They refused, to the consternation of many, to be beholden to an incessant dance beat, and their solos became much more complex and melodically innovative. As in the twenties, improvisation was the key. Instead of remaining within the confines of an established melody, the pianist and rhythm section would "feed" the soloist groups of chords meant to intimate the melody while freeing the soloist to improvise upon an array of harmonic structures. To many it sounded like

RIGHT: Dizzy Gillespie, 1946. ★
*The New York Age: He "took a
new riff, an off-beat with an
accented fifth, and built himself a
cult of beret-topped, chin-whiskered
followers with flashy clothes and
big, flowing bow ties."*
BELOW: The Earl Hines band
(Hines is at the piano) with
vocalist Billy Eckstine, 1941.

nonsense, and it was often deridingly called "Chinese music," but the music became known, onomatopoeically, as bebop. It was music for a new age—aggressive, cynical, troubling, modern.

Certainly, in the early forties, while the new music percolated in the small clubs, few outside the small circle of fans at Minton's and Monroe's knew what was happening. But the Apollo led the way in exposing bebop to a larger audience. By the late forties, bebop had far more than a cult following. It was Frank Schiffman who first booked the experimental bop band of Earl Hines early in 1943—with Dizzy Gillespie, Charlie Parker, and Little Benny Harris. And from 1944 until 1947, the greatest bebop band ever, Billy Eckstine's, helped make its mark at the Apollo. This vitally important unit featured, at one time or another, such giants of modern jazz as Dizzy, Fats Navarro, Miles Davis, Kenny Dorham, Gene Ammons, Dexter Gordon, Lucky Thompson, Charlie Parker, Leo Parker, John Malachi, Art Blakey, Tommy Potter, and Sarah Vaughan, and arrangements by Budd Johnson, Tadd Dameron, and Jerry Valentine. While the new music was not as accessible as swing—you couldn't readily dance to it, and sometimes couldn't even hum it—the Apollo audience soon welcomed it.

Dizzy Gillespie and Charlie Parker were bebop's most brilliant stars and Apollo appearances by them were major events for jazz fans. The life of John Birks "Dizzy" Gillespie often revolved around the Apollo Theatre. As a penniless unemployed musician, he used to hang around backstage, keeping his ears open for job opportunities and his eyes open for opportunities to hustle a dollar or two. Here he met his wife, Lorraine Willis, an Apollo chorus girl. She would stake him to a meal or lend him money until he found a job, and he has said that one of his motivations in getting serious about the band business was to earn enough money to allow Lorraine to quit the Apollo. He sat in as third trumpet when the Savoy Sultans supplemented their band for Apollo engagements. And when Woody Herman needed a hand at the theatre, Dizzy was there. He broke into bands as a full-time member with Teddy Hill at the Apollo, playing in a style that owed much to his idol, Roy Eldridge. While at the Apollo with Hill, Cab Calloway asked Dizzy to join his band. It was his big break, but, in an incident that helped him earn his name, when Calloway accused Gillespie of shooting spitballs at him, an argument developed and Dizzy stabbed Cab.

Later, at the Apollo, Les Hite hired Dizzy for his band but, because of the Calloway tussle, Hite kept his distance from Dizzy. Despite his demeanor, Dizzy was always a serious musician, and he had been perfecting his new style backed by Kenny Clarke's bop-style bass-drum accents and "chink-a-ching" drumming. Hite's drummer, Oscar Bradley, employed a more old-fashioned style, playing "paradiddles and flams and double flams" behind Dizzy's solos. Gillespie asked Bradley to play in the style he was comfortable with, and the drummer agreed. When the band began playing, Dizzy stood up for his solo, but Bradley let loose with the obnoxious "ratamacues." Gillespie sat right back down without completing his solo. Hite gave him the evil eye but, out of fear, said nothing. After the show, rather than fire Dizzy, Hite fired the entire band, then hired back everyone he wanted—everyone but Diz.

Like Clark Terry, whose true talents were first discovered by Louis Armstrong while Terry was playing with George Hudson at the Apollo, it was at the theatre that Lionel Hampton first heard Dizzy and realized that he was onto something new. "I went down to the Apollo Theatre. . . . That's where I first heard him," said Hampton in Dizzy's marvelously titled memoir, *To Be or Not to Bop*. "I was sitting behind the stage, man, and I heard this guy playing all this trumpet, you understand. I said, 'I wanna hear him at this recording session.' I had a contract at this time. . . . He came out with a new style, a bebop style. He came out with a different style than we'd ever heard before." Hampton asked him to play on his 1939 recording session of "Hot Mallets" and the resulting records, some feel, were the first to feature the infant sounds of bebop.

Dizzy was a leader in more ways than one. His goatee, beret, and jive patter set the style for a generation that culminated with the Beats of the 1950s. As a bandleader he was relaxed, yet always in control. The Apollo audiences loved his band's high-spirited playing and Dizzy's ad-libbed introductions, and Dizzy usually tried to keep things light. "Once, when we were working at the Apollo," said trombonist Ted Kelly, in Dizzy's memoir, "after one of the shows, Diz said, 'Hey fellas, why you guys so stiff, man? This is a show. Don't be sitting up there so stiff, and playing to relax people.'" The following show one of his sidemen, dressed as a cop, chased another band member across the front of the stage with a billy club. Dizzy looked askance, but said nothing. The next show another musician pushed a wheelbarrow containing a colleague around the stage. This proved too much for Dizzy, who felt he had been upstaged. He realized he was licked. "'All right, fellas,'" Kelly reported him saying. "'That's enough of the comedy. Let's go back to like you were before. Tighten up, turn it loose, you know.'"

As Dizzy Gillespie was the light side of the bebop revolution Charlie "Bird" Parker was the dark side. His is one of the most tragic stories in

A bloated and weary-looking Charlie Parker in 1953, two years before his death at the age of thirty-four. ★ Jackie McLean: *"When Bird was at the Apollo, we would go early in the morning, and stay and watch the show all day long."*

the cultural history of America, although the Apollo supported him even in his darkest hour. Soon after leaving school in Kansas City at the age of fifteen, Charlie was immersed in hard drugs, alcohol, and dissoluteness. He suffered devastating abuse from other musicians when he began sitting in at the myriad of cutting sessions on bandstands all over Boss Pendergast's town. But his immature style began to develop, and by the time he came to New York with the Jay McShann band in 1941, he was attracting attention from the cognoscenti.

Charlie Parker was a genius. Whenever his alto sax wasn't in hock, he developed new musical ideas and modes of thought that continue to influence improvisational musicians today. But he lived day to day, hustle to hustle, bed to bed, fix to fix. Those who recognized his greatness loved him and forgave him his excesses, but his antics often got him into nonmusical jams.

One of Bird's favorite hangouts was the Braddock Hotel bar next to the Apollo. There he could socialize with musicians before or after shows at the theatre and take advantage of its policy of two drinks for the price of one. Charlie couldn't even afford the price of the initial drink—he was so destitute that on one night he appeared at the bar dressed in a stolen overcoat that concealed the fact that he had hocked his only suit. However, Bird appreciated the twofer policy because he could amble up and down the bar grabbing the extra drinks that went overlooked.

His friends didn't mind the gambit, but once he was caught in the act by a group of local hard guys. They told Charlie he'd better come up with a round of drinks for them or they'd teach him a lesson out on 126th Street. Bird tried to sweet-talk them, to no avail. Suddenly, he remembered that his old pals in the McShann band were playing next door at the Apollo. He told the toughs to hold on for ten minutes and he'd get them their drinks. He ran to the stage door and sent a note inside. Luckily, the band was between shows, and his old friend Gene Ramey lent him two dollars. He dashed back to the Braddock, and successfully settled the affair, once again managing to stave off disaster.

Although his way of life helped create the Charlie Parker legend, it was his music that made him a hero. One fan followed him wherever he went, recording everything Bird played on a surreptitious old-fashioned wire recorder. Some argued that the flock of bird-name groups in the early 1950s—the Orioles, Cardinals, Robins, et al.—represented an "underground handshake" with Bird.

His Apollo engagements were eagerly awaited by the jazz cognoscenti in Harlem. "I went to see Bird with his five pieces around 1948,"

Jackie McLean told A. B. Spellman in *Four Lives in the Bebop Business*. (McLean, an important altoist, so revered Bird that he not only copied his playing style, but later, like many other impressionable young players, emulated Parker's heroin habit.) "When Bird was at the Apollo, we would go early in the morning, and stay and watch the show all day long. We would watch him from the first show until after three o'clock, when it was time to go home from school. We used to go home and put our books up, and then tell our parents that we were going to the Apollo, and they'd let us go and we'd split and go and watch Bird again until nine, when it was time to go home at night. We'd run out and get some hot dogs at intermission, and that would be all we had to eat all day long."

In 1951, at the recommendation of the narcotics squad, Parker's cabaret card was revoked. The card was issued by the New York State Liquor Authority, and was required of any performer working in establishments that served alcohol. The revocation effectively curtailed Charlie's successful career in the jazz clubs of Fifty-second Street, and it left the Apollo as the only New York venue open to him. Although he played the Apollo whenever he could, the restrictions took their toll on Bird emotionally, physically, and musically. His agent finally got his card reinstated in 1953. But Charlie had burned himself out. His revue, "Charlie Parker and Strings," was a flop at the Apollo and elsewhere. He seemed to have lost heart. At every performance, an overweight Bird led his band, supplemented with a section of classical violinists, through a turgid set of uninspired arrangements of "April in Paris," "I Didn't Know What Time It Was," "Just Friends," and "Summertime."

On March 12, 1955, Charlie Parker began coughing up blood, collapsed, and died in the apartment of the Baroness de Koenigswarter, a friend and patron to many New York jazz musicians. No one knew Bird's age at the time, but the attending doctor estimated him to be between fifty and sixty, based on his physical condition. Charlie Parker was thirty-four years old.

· · · · ·

Paralleling the growth of interest in bebop among the avant-garde, was the increasing demand from the mainstream audience for ballads—love songs sung in the intimate tones of Billy Eckstine, Sarah Vaughan, Nat King Cole, and other singers, black and white, who established themselves in the forties. The trend was a wartime phenomenon, inspired by the separations forced by the war and the sentimentality it spawned. But the trend continued strongly even afterwards and helped turn the infant jukebox business into a booming industry, while also setting off a boom for records by popular singers. Virtually every public gathering place had a jukebox, fed by the coins of eager customers and the records of popular singers.

During the 1930s only twenty-six records each sold a million copies or more. Between 1940 and 1945 the figure rose to sixty-eight, and between 1945 and 1950 there were eighty-two. At first, the record companies complained that 75 percent of their output was going to jukeboxes, but as home record players became increasingly popular consumers began buying discs themselves. By the time *Billboard* instituted its "Honor Roll of Hits" (the so-called pop chart) in 1945, Americans got into the habit of buying whatever the top records were that week. Almost all the pop hits were by whites—Frank Sinatra, Perry Como, and Peggy Lee. Black stars, except for occasional crossovers such as Nat Cole and Billy Eckstine, were relegated to the "Harlem Hit Parade" race charts. But, all over America, the new stars were the singers who could produce hit records.

The first of the new generation of black star vocalists to emerge was Billie Holiday. Her career as a solo artist began in 1938 with an historic two-year stand at Barney Josephson's Café Society in Greenwich Village—the first integrated American nightclub outside of Harlem. This engagement led to her first successful recording in 1939, and she became one of the most critically acclaimed vocalists of the forties. Billie was a great blues singer, but she also epitomized the attractiveness of the pop singer in wartime America. "If you find a tune and it's got something to do with you, you don't have to evolve anything," she said. "You feel it, and when you sing it other people can feel something, too. Give me a song I can feel and it's never work. There are a few songs I feel so much I can't stand to sing them, but that's something else again."

One of those songs was "Strange Fruit," the 1939 recording that made her career. Lewis Allen wrote this gripping song—strange fruit referred to lynched black bodies dangling from the limbs of trees—especially for Billie. Despite the song's success and obvious affinity for the Apollo audience, Frank Schiffman was against her singing it in his theatre. He didn't protest directly to Billie, but rather "by complaining to me," said John Hammond, her mentor and producer. "He said, 'I don't know what she thinks she's doing.' As a showman that was not Schiffman's idea of what would entertain his audience."

Yet the song went over at the Apollo as it did nowhere else. "At the Apollo the song took on profound intimations," Jack Schiffman wrote.

As Billie finished, "a moment of oppressively heavy silence followed, and then a kind of rustling sound I had never heard before. It was the sound of almost two thousand people sighing."

"Billie ruled the roost at the Apollo," said John Hammond. "They loved her, but at the same time she got too far out for the Apollo audience. Now, Pearl Bailey was the Apollo ideal of a singer." Pearly Mae could sing and dance and crack jokes, and became, in the late forties and early fifties, one of the theatre's biggest draws. Her 1953 show with Duke Ellington grossed $40,000 and set an Apollo attendance record. She first appeared with Noble Sissle in the thirties, not as a singer, but as a specialty dancer. Then Pearl built her reputation as a singer with the bands of Edgar Hayes, Cootie Williams, Cab Calloway, and the Sunset Royal Band. She appeared frequently at the Apollo even while her career expanded into nightclubs, Broadway, film, and television. But she always remained loyal to the Apollo. In the early seventies she once called Bobby Schiffman and said, "Hey, Bobby, when can I come home?"

Another great singer who called the Apollo home was Nat "King" Cole. "The biggest thing that happened with me," said Andy Kirk, "was when Nat King Cole and his trio appeared with me at the Apollo." In the fall of 1945, Cole's act was such a smash that Schiffman had to hold him over for a second week—a most unusual occurrence. The trio's recordings of hits such as "Straighten Up and Fly Right" and "Nature Boy" sold in the millions, and by the time Cole went solo in the late forties, his was the top black act in show business.

The Ink Spots were a vocal group who, unlike their colleagues the Mills Brothers, remained favorites in the black community even after they achieved great success among white listeners. The Ink Spots were perennial Apollo darlings from the time their leader, Bill Kenny, was discovered at an early Apollo Amateur Night show. Their first million-selling disc came in 1944 with "Into Each Life Some Rain Must Fall," performed with Ella Fitzgerald, but they scored their first hit in 1939 with "If I Didn't Care" (today's generation is perhaps more familiar with this song through Redd Foxx's loving mimicry of Bill Kenny's passionate crooning on the "Sanford and Son" television show). Kenny was revered at the Apollo and whenever he sang in his winsome high-pitched tenor, the theatre would fall silent, save for the scattered sighs and muffled wimpering of his female fans, overcome by the Kenny charm.

Billy Eckstine's solo career got off to a rocky start on Fifty-second Street. After his 1944 debut at the Yacht club, *Metronome*'s Barry

ABOVE: Billie Holiday at her
loveliest, with photographer
Gordon Anderson in the late
1940s. ★ John Hammond:
*"Billie ruled the roost at the
Apollo."*
RIGHT: Pearl Bailey, late 1940s
or early 1950s. ★ John
Hammond: *"Pearl Bailey was
the Apollo ideal of a singer."*

Nat King Cole and the Trio. ★ *In the fall of 1945, Cole's act was such a smash that Schiffman had to hold him over for a second week—a most unusual occurrence.*

The Ink Spots at the Apollo in the early 1940s. Bill Kenny is at the mike. ★ *The Ink Spots were perennial Apollo darlings from the time their leader, Bill Kenny, was discovered at an early Apollo Amateur Night show.*

Ulanov wrote that "X-Tine," as he was then billed, had a "shattering tremolo and a pompousness in phrasing not unlike that of an operetta performance." But Eckstine's seat-rumbling vibrato and lachrymose facial contortions really got to the youngsters uptown. He was awarded a plaque as Outstanding Male Vocalist of 1945 on the stage of the Apollo, based on the tremendous success of "Cottage for Sale" and "Prisoner of Love." He continued with his important big band until 1947, when he again went solo with "Everything I Have Is Yours."

In the late forties he really took off, and the kids at the Apollo began to call him "The Fabulous Mr. B" or just plain "B," while whites were apt to dub him the "Sepia Sinatra." From 1949 into the early fifties he was the hottest thing at the Apollo, fueled by hits like "Fool That I Am," "My Destiny," and "I Apologize." Like Sinatra at the Paramount, Eckstine had a fanatical following of squealing adolescents at the Apollo. Black teenaged boys wore "Mr. B Shirts," and girls reverentially kept his picture on their mirrors. To quiet the throngs at the Apollo, he'd smile, fix his eyes on the audience, and murmur "steady now." Even after Eckstine broke into the white big time of the Copa and the Waldorf, he continued to play the Apollo. At his annual show reopening the theatre after its summer renovations, which became a Harlem tradition, he greeted his audience with a heartfelt little speech. "Thank you so much. It's so good to be home again."

Eckstine once said, "Diz and Bird were the biggest and most important contributors to modern jazz. And in the vocal field [it] would be Sarah Vaughan." "Sassy," as she was known among musicians, made her debut with the Hines band at the Apollo on April 23, 1943. She also played piano and organ, and along with Eckstine, augmented the Hines band to create some of the most beautiful big-band sounds ever heard at the Apollo, or anywhere else. Musicians loved to play for the "Divine Sarah" because she had perfect pitch and used her voice as an instrument, bending and coloring notes like a true improviser. Charlie Parker drew inspiration from her when she was with the Hines band, and later when she left to help Eckstine form his own band. Dizzy Gillespie, who was in the Eckstine band along with Parker and Vaughan, arranged for her first solo record session on New Year's Eve, 1944.

Her perfect pitch was something of a problem at the Apollo, and she continually complained that the theatre's piano was out of tune. Even when Frank Schiffman began having it tuned before every performance, she would sometimes take tools in hand and fine-tune it herself. An established pop star by the late forties, she continued to produce hit records into the late fifties with tunes that included "Broken-Hearted Melody," and is still one of the greatest jazz vocalists.

Dinah Washington was another great vocalist. She combined jazz stylings with the blues to produce one of the gutsiest sounds in music. Like Sarah Vaughan, she had roots in gospel music, having begun as a singer with church choirs in Chicago. Her big break came in 1943 when she was discovered by Lionel Hampton. "My manager, Joe Glaser, happened to be in Chicago," said Hampton. "A friend of his named Joe Sherman had a nightclub in the Loop. They had a young lady working in the ladies' powder room and every time the band was to come out to play, why, she would pop her head out the door and sing with the band, 'cause the ladies' powder room and the bandstand were right next to each other. I was at the Regal Theatre in Chicago, and so I heard this girl sing and she sounded good. She came out and sang with me on one of the shows. I liked her singing very well. So I said to her, 'What's your name?' She said, 'Ruth Jones.' I said, 'I don't like that name, can I call you something else?' She said, 'I don't care what you call me as long as you give me the job.' So out of the clear blue sky I said, 'From now on your name will be Dinah Washington.' "

Dinah was one of the greatest characters in American popular culture. She had a great deal of success with pop records, among them "Unforgettable" and "What a Difference a Day Makes." But she was known as "Queen of the Blues" in her heyday.

Like an earlier blues queen, Bessie Smith, Dinah had quite a temper. Ruth Brown remembered one show where Dinah was to be lowered onstage inside a huge globe of the earth. "It was supposed to come down and open and she would step out," said Brown. "But when it came down, it hit a little harder than it was supposed to and the door jammed, and she couldn't get out. Boy, was she cursing."

In the early fifties, Bobby Schiffman was having the star's dressing room completely rebuilt for an upcoming appearance by Eartha Kitt. "On Friday morning Dinah came in and saw that she wasn't queen bee in that dressing room," said Bobby. "She came up to the office and cussed me out. She had a mouth like a sailor. Her favorite expression was j.a.m.f.— jive-ass motherfucker. She cussed me out something awful." Yet her bark was worse than her bite, Schiffman recalled. "She was always reaching out and trying to help people, and she would help performers and put them on her show. She was the most gracious lady. I remember there was an act by the name of Cook and Brown. One of them had a very sick mother, and they put her in Harlem Hospital. They had a very

Dinah Washington at her first Apollo appearance in 1945. ★ Lionel Hampton: *"She said, 'I don't care what you call me as long as you give me the job.' So out of the clear blue sky I said, 'From now on your name will be Dinah Washington.'"*

modest income, no medical insurance, and she was a ward patient. Dinah went to see her, and when she saw she was in a ward, she had her transferred to a private hospital downtown and picked up the entire bill."

When Dinah Washington sang, she drew upon a thirty-year-old legacy of the blues that she interpreted and updated for a modern audience. The blues was a staple of every singer's repertoire at the Apollo, but in the late forties a new breed of blues shouters gained prominence. In contrast to Billy Eckstine or Nat King Cole, they relied upon sheer vocal power to put a song over, and their style was too rough to appeal to a white audience, so their records never appeared on the pop charts. But in their vocal stylings the roots of yet another revolutionary popular music form—rhythm and blues—can be found. Wynonie Harris was a top shouter who first gained recognition as a vocalist for Lucky Millinder. Backed by the wailing sax of Illinois Jacquet, he first reached the Harlem Hit Parade on his own with "Playful Baby" and he later made successful cover versions of "Drinkin' Wine, Spo-Dee-O-Dee" and "Good Rockin' Tonight." To cure a hoarse voice before an Apollo show, Harris was fond of downing a couple of heated shots of whiskey. His hard-living and hard-drinking ways caught up with him, and he faded after 1951.

Another leading blues-based singer was Eddie "Cleanhead" Vinson. Unlike Harris, Vinson persevered to play in clubs around the country in the 1980s. He was the vocalist with the Cootie Williams band, and also led his own big band in the mid-forties. As a single, he played the downtown clubs as well as the Apollo. But he was always conscious of who he was playing for. "You'd pick different numbers for downtown than you would uptown," he said. "Uptown, I'd do 'Cherry Red.' I did a lot of ballads downtown, but I wouldn't dare sing a ballad uptown."

．．．．．

While vocalists overshadowed most of the bands in the forties, two bands, one big and one little, not only survived, but became the hottest black attractions of their time. Lionel Hampton and Louis Jordan were not just fine musicians but true showmen who would do almost anything to pump energy and excitement into their shows.

Hampton gained instant fame in 1936 when Benny Goodman heard him in Los Angeles and tapped him to play vibes in Goodman's important integrated group. He played and toured with Goodman for four years and also made recordings on his own, such as the "Hot Mallets" set with young Dizzy Gillespie. Hamp had a great ear for talent and the sixteen-piece band he brought into the Apollo in December 1940, to the delight of the Apollo crowd, featured soloists Dexter Gordon and Illinois Jacquet on saxes and Joe Newman on trumpet. With such an outstanding lineup, Hampton began letting his men work out on longer and wilder solos that often whipped audiences into a frenzy.

"Flyin' Home," a number he wrote and originally recorded with Goodman, became his showstopper after his big band hit with it in 1942. "I would come up with things like this at the Apollo," said Hampton. "I used to have this part in 'Flyin' Home' where the lights would go out and you'd see airplanes projected on the scrim behind the bandstand. You'd hear the motors humming and that's when the saxophone player, Illinois Jacquet, and [later] Arnett Cobb, started playin' their famous solo. The band would be shouting down, and we used to have a lot of acrobatic stuff with the horns; the trumpets would be going up like this, and the trombones would be going around and the saxophones would be going up this way. Everybody'd be rockin'. We were the originators of that.

"In the last part of 'Flyin' Home' there was a section that went rapapapapapop pow! Everybody used to wait for that. I would jump on my drum, and in the meantime the Apollo's electrician, Bob Hall, would push a button and a smudgepot would come up like the stage was blowing up. One time we did that and everyone ran out of the theatre. Another time when I jumped on the drum, everybody in the balcony jumped up with me and cracked the balcony. Everybody heard the balcony crack and they again started running out of the theatre."

Hampton had a penchant for clearing the Apollo, even if it meant leading the audience out with his own band. Sammy Davis, Jr., who worked for Hampton when young Sammy was still a member of the Will Mastin Trio, explains: " 'Flyin' Home' would go on for twenty minutes. He killed two drummers. . . . I don't mean that. He'd go parading out in the audience and go right out the theatre on to 125th Street, to entertain the people waiting on line. You'd look up and hear him, and then suddenly he'd disappear, and the only person left onstage would be the drummer and the bass player. You know regular drumsticks are normal size. Military drumsticks are big—parade sticks. But that wasn't loud enough. He had to turn the sticks around to the other end to keep that beat going. It was a fantastic thing to see Hamp perform, and nobody could say to Hamp, 'I don't feel like doing this show.' Because Hamp would be out there working just as hard. He'd come off wringing wet."

Hampton's wife, Gladys, handled his business affairs. "Her deals in business I never knew," said Hampton. "And I didn't want to know,

ABOVE: Wynonie "Mr. Blues" Harris, late 1940s. ★ *To cure a hoarse voice before an Apollo show, Harris was fond of downing a couple of heated shots of whiskey.* LEFT: Eddie "Cleanhead" Vinson, late 1940s. ★ *"Uptown, I'd do 'Cherry Red.' I did a lot of ballads downtown, but I wouldn't dare sing a ballad uptown."*

Lionel Hampton in the 1940s. ★ *"I would jump on my drum, and in the meantime the Apollo's electrician, Bob Hall, would push a button and a smudgepot would come up like the stage was blowing up. One time we did that and everybody ran out of the theatre."*

because I trusted her so much. I idolized her. I looked up to her. She was something special, different. I couldn't question her about anything. She always told me, 'If I were to leave you, look here and you look there and everything will be like a book.' That's the way it was. She passed away. So I bless her." One of Gladys's deals was to convince Frank Schiffman that Hampton should get a percentage of the receipts. Thereafter, his band began doing more shows per day than anyone else—at least seven, and Hampton claims nine or ten. "We just blew up the community with happiness and joy and excitement," he said. "Fourth of July every day."

Hampton gradually moved away from jazz into more and more jumping numbers that presaged the oncoming of rhythm and blues. "All that rock-and-roll stuff the guys're doing now, it all started with us," said Hampton. "All that dancing and things onstage started with us. It was all my ideas. I had a dance group with me called the Hamptones. Now you see all that stuff that James Brown's doing and all these groups do. The Hamptones were the greatest. Nobody did choreography before they did."

Louis Jordan made an even greater impact on rhythm and blues and rock and roll, influencing everyone from Bill Haley and Chuck Berry to English rocker Joe Jackson. Jordan began his career playing alto sax for Chick Webb in 1936. In 1938, he began an extended engagement at Harlem's Elks' Rendezvous with his Tympany Five. Then he grew tired of jazz, saying that jazzmen "play mostly for themselves." He said, "I want to play for the people." That's what he did. Blending well-played hot jazz, a jumping rhythm, a genius for showmanship, and humorous down-home lyrics unlike any heard before, Louis Jordan became a smash. Starting with his first hit, "What's the Use of Gettin' Sober (When You're Gonna Get Drunk Again)," in 1942, he was regularly on the "Harlem Hit Parade" until the early fifties. In 1946 alone he scored eleven hits.

Jordan modeled himself after Cab Calloway and, like Calloway, Jordan clowned in films and in white establishments as well as black ones. Also like Calloway, Jordan served as an interpreter of black street lingo to the white world. In tunes like "Knock Me a Kiss" and "Reet, Petite and Gone," he not only hipped whites, but provided black young-sters with a lexicon they could identify with. In songs like "Gonna Move to the Outskirts of Town," "Is You Is or Is You Ain't My Baby," "Choo, Choo Ch'Boogie," and "Jack, You're Dead," Jordan created a new way of looking at popular music. It was based on an existential outlook on life portrayed through humorous, often ironic lyrics and propelled by a steady shuffle beat. It was action-oriented, and at least subtly antiestablishment. That may be why it appealed to the pent-up youths of the forties and early fifties, and why Louis Jordan's music is still fascinating to today's nihilistic rockers.

Jordan's relationship with the Apollo audience was blissful. In 1948, he became one of the few artists held over at the theatre for a second week. As late as 1960, he could still pack them in, and that year he ran a mock "Louis Jordan for President" campaign from the theatre.

His relationship with the Schiffmans, however, was another matter. Although he said Frank Schiffman was a "great man" and "one of the best managers of theatres I have ever worked for," he did not get along well with the Apollo's management. Jack Schiffman claims he once walked out without explanation, and never finished the week. "Every time I used to go to the Apollo, I'd get hoarse," he told writer Arnold Shaw. "Why? Because it was a filthy theatre. And [Frank Schiffman would] say, 'I'm gonna close it up for two or three months during the summer and clean it up.' He'd close it up and set mothballs around, and then open it up next year. The same dirt was there from year to year. To tell you how I know—I used to put a mark in it. And I'd come back to play there again, and my mark would be there. Great theatre! Did a whole lot for Negroes, made a lot of Negro stars. If he'd cared, he would have fixed it up and made it a first-class theatre. . . . If you care about a thing that you made millions out of, you would have it fixed up. . . . And still it's number one of the Negro theatres."

·····

Although Frank Schiffman was scorned by some of his performers, he was generally well respected in Harlem as a community-minded individual, if only because in the thirties and forties he was the only entrepreneur on white-owned 125th Street to employ blacks at all levels of responsibility. But there was so much resentment of the other 125th Street merchants that a boycott was organized in 1947 by the Reverend Adam Clayton Powell, Jr., and the *Amsterdam News*. In January 1948, a report reached Mayor William O'Dwyer's desk on the "125th Street Controversy" in which the Harlem-based Consumers' Protective Committee summarized its charges against the merchants:

1. They sell inferior merchandise.
2. They charge exorbitant prices.
3. They use a two or three price system.

4. They practice double dealing.
5. They fail to absorb through the process of employment skilled Negro professionals of the community.
6. In most instances they refuse to label price and quality of merchandise.
7. They refuse to advertise their products in local newspapers for comparative value.
8. There is a general lack of cooperation on the part of local merchants to community institutions.
9. They have no interest in the improvement and appearance of the community.
10. Through some process of collusion it is impossible for Negro businesses to be established on the street.

The tone of the "Mayor's Committee on Unity" report was skeptical, and belied a lack of understanding or compassion. It stated: "The inference that these patterns are due to the fact that the merchants are white is unfortunate, for there is no assurance that were the merchants themselves Negro, there would be a difference of behavior." The boycott ended when some concessions were made, but the problem was far from settled.

By the late forties, there were rumblings of discontent in the entertainment world, too. While white entertainers worried about being blacklisted, black entertainers worried about being listed at all. In August 1949, the *New York Age* began a series of articles by Bill Chase titled: "What's Wrong with Our Show Business? (The Rough Deal Given Negro Performers)." Chase wrote: "It is safe to say that the Negro, as far as show business is concerned, is just about at rock bottom, and slowly, but surely, starving to death—in the profession. . . . They've been pretty well put through the old squeeze in a monopolistic vise operated by a well organized mob who've gotten rich in the field and who have it so well sown [sic] up that nobody's going to muscle in their 'Take.' " The culprits were identified as insensitive and dishonest managers, agents, producers, club owners, bookers, lawyers, record company executives, and theatre operators. One question raised was, "Why Harlem, with its more than 400,000 entertainment-and-theatre-conscious population, is denied the right to have more than one theatre, keeping hundreds of talented actors and entertainers out of work?

"Except for a lucky few who have hit the jack pot via their popularity on jukeboxes," Chase wrote, "the average performer today

LEFT: Louis Jordan, 1944. ★ *"I want to play for the people."* BELOW: The Will Mastin Trio with Mastin, Sammy Davis, Jr., and Sammy Davis, Sr., late 1940s. ★ *"I lived fifteen blocks from [the Apollo]. So we'd walk home at night. To live at 140th Street and Eighth Avenue and to walk to the Apollo, that's big time."*

has had to put his favorite profession down for more lucrative employment. . . . Gone with the wind, too, is the big money which so many of our stars could demand and usually get. . . . Outside of Lena Horne, Billie Holiday, the Ink Spots, Billy Eckstine, Pearl Bailey, Louis Jordan and few more, I think you would find a sharp drop in the dollar department."

. . . . .

One who would soon be added to that list is Sammy Davis, Jr. Sammy grew up in a family of vaudevillians who constantly toured the country as part of the act of his adopted uncle, Will Mastin. At first, Sammy was strictly a dancer, and Bill Robinson was so impressed that he volunteered to tutor the boy. Mastin made the act a trio during the depression, with Sammy Sr. and Sammy Jr. When he first appeared at the Apollo in 1947 with the Will Mastin Trio, Davis split $650 for the week. Nine years later, as the most successful black entertainer of his time, he earned over $21,000 for a week at the theatre as a single. Sammy, the hoofer, was a success, but not an immediate smash, at the Apollo, despite the fact that he was an excellent dancer, and in Bojangles's opinion "a perfectionist."

"My mother had worked the Apollo Theatre as a chorus girl," said Davis. "So everybody knew my mother. When I came in, though I was part of the Will Mastin Trio, I was really Baby Sanchez's son: be nice to him. Also, the funny part of it was, the first time I ever worked the Apollo I worked with a white band, Louis Prima's. Half the people who came to the theatre thought that Louis was black anyway. Mixed. So he was a big favorite. We walked in and we wrapped the show up, and Louis was so pleased with it. He said, 'I wish I worked places where you could go, I'd take you with us.' It was like I was on Cloud Nine. I lived fifteen blocks from there. So we'd walk home at night. To live at 140th Street and Eighth Avenue and to walk to the Apollo, that's big time. We went on and we did well. There was no rush—like everybody rushing backstage saying you're great—like the stories you hear. It was just like we were accepted, and that already was talk enough. The stagehands told us, 'Yeah, you'll be back.' "

The next time the Trio came back to the Apollo, Sammy added impressions to his act. He had wanted to try the impressions at his debut, but Frank Schiffman forced him to cut them because the show ran too long. After a false start, the new material helped catapult the act to stardom. "The second time we came back with Louis Jordan, and they had heard about the colored kid that does impressions," said Davis.

160

" 'He's great.' So this time there was no objection to it at all. When I went in the second time, the audience scared me so bad, because I was doing the impressions, I lost my voice. First show, I went [he opens his mouth] and nothing came out. Will and my father went, 'Hit it!' and went right back into the dance thing, and I couldn't talk. I came off the stage and a couple of the guys in Louis's band and my dad said, 'You're just scared. They just scared you.' Next show my voice came back. That's how bad that audience was noted to be at the Apollo. Scared the voice out of me . . ."

"Sammy was always regarded as an outrageous talent," said Bobby Schiffman. "I remember sitting in Sammy Davis's dressing room when he was getting $1,500 for the week for the Trio. He called the William Morris agency office while I sat there and said, 'Listen, I want you to know that there were lines down the street, around the corner, and back into the block for the Will Mastin Trio.' And he said, 'I want you to know that we're no $1,500 a week act anymore. All you got to do is come up to the Apollo and look at the lines of people waiting to hear us, and you'll see that we're headliners.' "

Indeed, they became headliners at the Apollo, and Sammy appeared in Las Vegas, on Broadway, in films and on television; and, of course, he also became a singing star. Despite the negative image and charges of pandering to whites that began to plague Davis in the sixties, the generation that had frequented the Apollo in the forties and early fifties continued to consider him one of the greatest and most versatile performers of his time. Besides his talent, Harlem bathed in the reflected glory of his success and fame in the white world.

Sometimes he impressed his hometown with his new friends. "One night when Marilyn Monroe was in town she came to the Apollo with some friends of ours," Davis said. "She wore a black fur coat and was sitting in the box. I said, 'Ladies and gentlemen, there's a friend of mine up there, and I would like for you to meet her. It's her first time at the Apollo. Make her feel at home. Ladies and gentlemen, Marilyn Monroe.' You heard gasps, and I said, 'Will you put the spotlight over her.' She stood up and shook her hair and it fell down, and she was in this gown. Well, that was the end of the show. I thought both balconies were going to come right down on the people. You have never heard such a scream.

"After the show she came backstage, and I said to one of the stagehands, 'Would you take Miss Monroe across the stage?' I was talking to my friends, and I was lagging back like this, and the stagehand says [with deepest respect and graciousness], 'Right this way, Miss

Monroe.' So he gets to the steps that go up to the dressing room, and the other stagehands are standing on the steps checking her out. Not doing anything rude. The stagehand walks up [with consummate politeness], 'Right this way, Miss Monroe.' Up the steps is where the dressing room is. So the stagehand says, to the other guys on the steps, 'Motherfuckers, don't you know this is Marilyn Monroe! Get the fuck out of the way!' It never occurred to him—it was the language of the theatre. But it was so cute, and she just laughed. Everybody laughed."

Thanks to his great versatility, Sammy Davis, Jr., avoided the pitfalls that met other dancers of his time. "By the mid-forties," wrote Marshall and Jean Stearns, "and the emergence of jazz with more complex rhythms, the few dancers who survived were forced into a subordinate role. No longer the innovators who led drummers toward more flowing rhythms, they dwindled to dependent followers, who, to get along, adopted jazz fashions and often found it expedient or exciting to emulate the activities of such pioneers as Charlie Parker and others, who seemed bent on self-destruction. . . . By the forties their eccentricities, anticipating the excesses of jazzmen, became more tragic than comic. The process was hastened by the fact that they were trying to make a living in a dying art."

Teddy Hale was one of the more tragic cases. By 1936, ten-year-old "Little Hale" already had five years' professional experience behind him, and in another five years he had become a popular dance attraction in black theatres. Downtown at the Paramount in the mid-forties he developed a routine to "Begin the Beguine" that became his trademark. He was one of the cleanest and clearest tappers ever, but his life was usually fogged by his addiction to heroin. He was in his early thirties when he died.

Deborah Chessler, songwriter and manager of the landmark rhythm-and-blues group the Orioles, was in Frank Schiffman's office at the Apollo when the call came from Hale's manager, Nat Nazarro, that the dancer was dead: "Nobody wanted to believe it. Nat had called Frank earlier in the week and told him Teddy was due to come into the Apollo. See, they didn't know if he was going to make it because he had been arrested for something, being held on drugs, and then Nat got him out in time for the show. So this happened all in one week. It was a real shock because this was a young kid with nothing but talent. Teddy Hale was a little guy who for sheer dancing ability was matched by no one. You know one time you see something you can never forget—that was Teddy Hale."

"If Teddy Hale's ankles were boneless," Jack Schiffman wrote, "Babe [Laurence's] were made of bananas." Babe or Baby Laurence was a contemporary and friend of Teddy Hale's and, like Hale, a junkie. He also did time in jail, where, the Harlem rumor mill said, he was busy working out new steps while he awaited release. When he got out, the Apollo immediately booked him, and tried to keep him straight by rationing his draws to a few dollars at a time. But he disappeared before the week was over. In fact, he frequently missed engagements; but the Apollo was always happy to have him for however long he stayed.

Dancers were in awe of Hale and Laurence. "Sammy Davis came to the Apollo, and he was doing everything. He was a one-man show," said Sandman Sims. "Baby Laurence, myself, Teddy Hale, and a guy called Groundhog [a legendary shadowy figure among hoofers] decided to go up there. So Baby Laurence and Groundhog went on one side of the stage, and me and Teddy Hale went on the other side. We stood in the wings and looked at him. He knew Baby Laurence, but he didn't know the rest of us. So we said, 'If you dance one step, we're all coming out to dance.' He found out who we all really were and he didn't dance. He wouldn't do a step. After the show was over, everybody was asking, 'Why didn't you dance?' He said, 'Man, are you kidding?' He wouldn't dance a lick in front of us. We laughed. So the next show he danced for us, and then he called us up onstage."

Bunny Briggs, one of the great dancers of what the Stearnses dubbed "the Dying Breed," was among those who avoided the fate of Hale and Laurence. Briggs was blessed with a peaceful countenance that helped make his one of the few happy stories of the era. As a child in the early thirties, Briggs sang and danced with the society band of stride pianist Luckey Roberts. He played in the homes and on the private yachts of the Wanamakers and Astors and learned impeccable manners. His mother was the guiding force in his life, and her watchful eye kept him out of trouble.

He learned much of his art from Baby Laurence, with whom he worked at the Ubangi Club in front of Erskine Hawkins's band, and he thrilled Apollo audiences with his own version of a famous dance routine known as Paddle and Roll. Keeping one leg ramrod straight, he would "roll" the other foot, producing machine-gun taps with the toe and heel. At the appropriate points, he would "paddle" the foot to produce accents to the beat. The talented and reliable Briggs worked steadily through the sixties, often with Duke Ellington, and he has remained active.

. . . . .

Photographer Gordon Anderson with dancers Bunny Briggs
and Peg Leg Bates, backstage at the Apollo, early
1950s. ★ *Briggs was blessed with a peaceful countenance
that helped make his one of the few happy stories of the era.*

Apus and Estrellita at the
Apollo, late 1940s. ★
*"Every time we hit the
stage, you could hear,
'Ooh, ah, look at Apus!'"*

It was a pivotal and meaningful era for black comedy. The controversy over the use of blackface makeup had raged since the mid-thirties, yet the issue was not resolved until the late forties. Vere E. Johns wrote in the *New York Age* in 1934: "As long as paper and ink are made I'll be saying, 'To hell with blackface comedy.' First because it is filthy; second because it is ignorant; third, because it is unnecessary, and fourth because the white man uses it to belittle us." In a rebuttal, William E. Clark maintained that blackface was a tradition that was honored. Johns replied that it was also traditional "for the Negro to be the servant of the white man." Clark shot back, "It is also traditional that the Negro is of a patient and genial disposition, that he is a good singer and that he possesses a good sense of humor. Should these also be abolished simply because they are liked by white people? . . . Now, I maintain that there is such a thing as racial comedy, despite Mr. Johns's assertion to the contrary. And if there is, why should not the Negro comedian wear the badge of his race?" Getting in the last word, Johns responded, "Mr. Clark is afraid that if we don't black up, the white man might claim us if we were any good. That argument should apply to everybody. I shall send a ton of burnt cork to . . . Bill Robinson . . . Paul Robeson . . . and Buck and Bubbles. We are in grave danger of having the white people claim them. And beginning next week we'll print the *Age* in black paper with red ink."

The main resistance to change came from the old-time comedians themselves. "They were all doing blackface," said comedian Timmie Rogers. "And when I came along in 1944, I says to John Mason, Crackshot Hunter, and Pigmeat Markham, 'It's time to get the black off your face. You don't need it.' They gave me hell. 'Who in hell do you think you are? You just started your comedy act last year. We were doin' this for forty years, son. We know comedy. You have to learn comedy.' I said, 'I've learned one thing; that you don't need blackin' your face.' I only had one valid point that stuck in the guys' minds. That was, 'Suppose you were on radio? Would you wear black on your face?' Stopped them cold. Because that was it. But it was tradition. A mask to hide behind. About two years later they all took the black off their faces and they were just as funny without blackface, because the makeup, the clothes don't make you. What you say makes you."

Black comedians were still not ready to come onstage in everyday dress. Into the fifties, crazy clothes in wild colors were standard gear for black comics. Apus Brooks, of Apus and Estrellita, was typical. His wife,

Estrellita, described him: "Every time we hit the stage, you could hear, 'Ooh, ah, look at Apus!' You could hear it: 'Man, where'd you find those pants? Gee, I like your hat.' Shoes were this long. That's what comics were really wearing at that time. As the years went along we dressed up in tuxedos. Beautiful dress suit, sport clothes, and everything. But in those days it was comedy clothes, all very bright colors. Pants were maybe Kelly green, and the coat was probably red. Or striped pants, probably yellow." Still, an important break with the past had been made that paved the way for more changes to come. But the Apollo was about to enter a dynamic new phase. The whole entertainment scene was about to change, and with it the Apollo's treasured vaudeville variety format— and for the entertainers dependent upon this format, there would be nothing funny in that at all.

5

THE FIFTIES

· · · · · · · · · · ·

The kids in the audience buzzed. Something was up. It wasn't just the normally boisterous front two or three rows; the murmuring enveloped a good portion of the orchestra section. "Dig this, man," one boy said as he nudged his friend. "This is gonna be good," said another. The Schiffmans were puzzled. Noro Morales, the headliner, was a solid performer, but they had never expected him to elicit such extraordinary anticipation. As it turned out, the crowd was waiting not for the headliner but for the "Extra Added Attraction"—a new, up-and-coming group called the Orioles. It was the second day of their engagement, August 13, 1949.*

"On the first day, Friday, there was nobody in the theatre," said Bobby Schiffman, "except for a nucleus of people we used to have who came to the first show every Friday. They would review the show for the street. They would go out of the theatre and say, 'Oh, man, it's outrageous.' Or 'Oh, shit, it stinks.' Depending upon what they said, we did business or didn't do business, unless you had a superstar. [This time] they went out and spread the word, and Saturday you couldn't get near

*There is considerable confusion over the date and circumstances of the Orioles' debut at the Apollo, and 1947 and 1948 have been cited elsewhere. However, based on a week-by-week examination of the Apollo's ads in the *New York Age*, I believe the Orioles' triumph could only have been in 1949.

the theatre. It was as if you had done a full-page ad in the *Daily News* and been on every radio station every thirty seconds. The people just came, and the Orioles were responsible for the whole damn thing."

So successful was this show that for the first time in the history of the Apollo, Frank Schiffman canceled his scheduled show to bring the Orioles back a week later. "The lines were unbelievable," said Deborah Chessler, the group's manager. "They hired extra police. Most of the time the first ten rows would end up partially on the stage. The police would run down there and pull them off. One time somebody stole [lead singer] Sonny Til's ring right off his finger. It was hard to keep the audience away from them. They clawed at them and got their ties, shirts—tore them off. They were dancing in the aisles. It was like what you have today. It was unreal."

No greater tale has been recounted in the Apollo mythology than the epic of the Orioles' conquest of the Apollo Theatre. Few remember the Orioles today, but they were one of the seminal rhythm-and-blues groups, and the first r-and-b attraction to create a sensation at the Apollo. Their success presaged a change in the way the Apollo presented its shows, and signaled the downfall of the Apollo's variety acts.

The story begins in 1948. All over the country Americans laughed and wept as they watched Irene Dunne in *I Remember Mama* or cheered Duke Wayne and Monty Clift in *Red River*. The sweet sounds of Perry Como, Bing Crosby, Doris Day, Billy Eckstine, and Peggy Lee soothed war-frazzled American nerves. It was a relatively complacent time, but it was also the beginning of a period of apprehension. We had entered the nuclear age, and we did not know what lay ahead—only that it would be something different.

No one could have imagined that a disparate linking of people would help to rock America to its foundations: the lovely and unusual harmonization of a quintet of black youngsters calling themselves the Vibranaires began to attract a bit of attention, first on street corners, then in the local taverns. At the same time a young Jewish girl, Deborah Chessler, who still lived with her mother, also began to attract attention as a songwriter with a tune called "It's Too Soon to Know," which was covered by a number of artists, including Dinah Washington and the Ravens. A mutual friend played her a demo record of the group, and she agreed to manage them.

According to the Apollo mythology, as told by the Schiffmans and recounted in several books, this disparate group—Chessler and the boys—piled into a dilapidated 1934 Ford, and spent their last quarter getting from Baltimore to New York. One Thursday, their car came to a sputtering halt on 125th Street, right in front of the Apollo. Without an appointment, the bedraggled bunch managed to get in to see Frank Schiffman. Finally, convinced that they were talented and broke, Schiffman took pity on them and, with a touch of showman's instinct, agreed to book them for seventy-five dollars a week on the show starting the next day. They had a new sound, look, and feel that knocked the Apollo audience out. The crowd went wild, Frank Schiffman had been proved a genius, the old Apollo variety format went out the window in favor of all-rhythm-and-blues revues, a new era had begun. . . .

A nice romantic tale, but not so. According to Deborah Chessler, "I told my mother, 'The only way I'm going to do this group any good is to go to New York with that demo record and see what I can do.' " Chessler went to some of the music publishers she knew, and they suggested she try to get the group on the Arthur Godfrey radio show. The Vibranaires were at first unsuccessful on that show, although they later returned triumphant. Booking agents wouldn't touch the group until Jerry Blaine, of Jubilee Records, signed them. They changed their name to the Orioles, after the Baltimore baseball team, recorded Chessler's prophetically titled "It's Too Soon to Know," and signed with Billy Shaw, who then worked for the Gale Agency.

"I told him, 'We want the Apollo,' " said Chessler. But they were booked into the Baby Grand bar on 125th Street. "While we were there we kept saying, 'We want to play the Apollo.' It was even harder to take, because here we were playing right up there so close to the Apollo," she said. Finally, five or six weeks after the record was out, Shaw got them the Apollo. "We were so happy," Chessler said, "we didn't even ask about the money."

The Orioles knocked out the Apollo crowd with a new look and a new sound that was early rhythm and blues. They owed much to the Ink Spots, whom the Orioles loved, and Sonny Til had the same devastating effect on women as Bill Kenny did. But their sound had more bounce and emotion, and their choreography was slick and sexy. The Orioles were the first vocal group to draw upon the blues, as Dinah Washington had, and create pop music. "The Orioles, in my opinion, probably started the whole rhythm-and-blues scene in black music," said Bobby Schiffman. "They were the innovators in rhythm and blues because they were the first ones who didn't try to represent melody as written. They were the ones who fucked over melody and did it their own way." As Deborah Chessler said, "The harmony was not perfect harmony, but it was wonderful harmony. Anybody listening could remember the melody, and went away singing Orioles songs."

. . . . .

This new sound of rhythm and blues was an entirely black phenomenon. After World War II, and the promise of the war years, the disappointments and discrimination became more unbearable for blacks. Instead of integration and equality, blacks faced continued ghettoization and lack of opportunity. Turned in upon themselves, unable to reach beyond the limits of the ghetto, black people channeled their creativity into creating a music for themselves.

Rhythm and blues has become the term used to describe the sounds of such different performers as Lionel Hampton, Dinah Washington, Clyde McPhatter, and James Brown. The term became popular after *Billboard* magazine stopped calling black hits "race records" and started its "rhythm and blues" chart in 1949. As Arnold Shaw wrote in *Honkers and Shouters*: "R & B was liberated music, which in its pristine form represented a break with white mainstream pop. Developing from black sources, it embodied the fervor of gospel music, the throbbing vigor of boogie woogie, the jump beat of swing, and the gutsiness and sexuality of life in the black ghetto."

Ruth Brown described the position of the r-and-b singers this way: "We were working under all kinds of adverse situations . . . consequently, there was a lot of hurt that went along with it. What really sustained us was the music. All of the things that went wrong during the travels, or the harassment, you took that out onstage. You got up and started to sing, and I think that's where the feeling for the lyric comes from. It was a total experience. The rhythm covered up for the blues. That's my estimation of what rhythm and blues was. The rhythm, the beat, covered up the blues, but the blues were inside."

Swing was, at first, maligned, and bebop misunderstood, but rhythm and blues met with open derision and outright hatred from various segments of society. Middle-class blacks were ashamed of its vulgarity and embarrassed by its primitiveness. Many whites thought it musically atrocious, evil, possibly satanic, and when white youngsters like Elvis Presley adopted and adapted the sound to create rock and roll, they began treating it like a disease to be eradicated. Black-music purists saw rhythm and blues as a derivative corruption of the blues. The jazz world felt it was a trifling entertainment, lacking imagination. But, the masses

170

of ghettoized blacks felt its vitality, shook under its power, and were liberated by the emotional expressiveness of rhythm and blues.

Some who helped create the new music, like Los Angeles bandleader Johnny Otis, were resented by their old colleagues. "I had begun to see through the years," said Otis, "when my big band did a blues—for instance, with all those men in the band we could play the most powerful swing-bop-jazz thing—the people would like it, but when the piano player would play 'After Hours,' what we used to call the Negro national anthem, the house would come apart." Otis realized that he did not need a full-scale big band: "I said to myself, 'With a boogie-woogie piano player, a guitar player, a couple of horns, and a drummer, it probably would please these people more than a big full-blown jazz band.' It was true. I saw rhythm and blues coming. But I was like a traitor to some of the brothers when I made that move. I felt uneasy around some of the jazz establishment; like I was breaking a sacred trust of some kind. Well, I was never a great jazz man, and I knew it from the beginning. So I didn't betray a sacred trust."

As early as 1948, Otis began calling his act the Johnny Otis Rhythm and Blues Caravan. In 1950, Otis hit with a tune called "Double Crossing Blues," thanks to the vocal efforts of his thirteen-year-old discovery, "Little Esther" Phillips, and the Caravan came to the Apollo. Johnny Otis is a most unusual man. He is white, genetically—Veliotes was the surname of his Greek immigrant parents. But in every other way he is black. He grew up in a largely black neighborhood in Berkeley, California, and has written, "I did not become black because I was attracted to Negro music. . . . I became what I am because as a child, I reacted to the way of life, the special vitality, the atmosphere of the black community. I cannot think of myself as white."

Today Otis's music is ill-remembered, and Californians are as likely to know him as the famed disc jockey, or as Reverend Otis, the leader of his own church in Watts, or as a politico, the right-hand man of Congressman Mervyn Dymally, whom Otis met at his Apollo debut:

"I was backstage in the alley," recalled Otis, "and there was all these Harlem kids standing around. They wanted to bullshit, and they wanted autographs. I see this one little dude standing over on the periphery, a pleasant little guy, looking a lot younger than even the others." It was Mervyn Dymally, fresh from his native Trinidad. "So I just walked over," said Otis. "That's how we became friends. He later moved to California and we kind of raised our kids together."

Johnny Otis also owes another of his careers to the Apollo. In a

The Orioles in the alley behind the Apollo, with a girlfriend, about 1950. Sonny Til is second from the right. ★ Bobby Schiffman: *"It was as if you had done a full-page ad in the* Daily News *and been on every radio station every thirty seconds. The people just came, and the Orioles were responsible for the whole damn thing."*

Big Joe Turner recording in the early 1950s. ★ *When the six-foot-two, 250-pounder let loose his bellowing voice, people listened.*

discussion backstage at the Apollo on the difficulties of maintaining hit records, Frank Schiffman told Otis, "What you ought to do while you're still a young man is get yourself a disc-jockey show." Otis picks up the story: "I said, 'A disc-jockey show?' He said, 'Yes. Establish yourself as a disc jockey, then you don't have to have a hit record. They have hit records every day that somebody else sweats for.' " When Otis got home to L.A. he gave it a shot. "I said, 'The Old Man's smart.' I called KFOX and I said, 'My name is Johnny Otis, I'd like to get a disc-jockey show.' So there's a big pause on the other end and he said, 'Johnny Otis, the Duke Ellington of Watts?' I got the job."

The Orioles, like Otis, despite their important place in the history of rhythm and blues, have been neglected by music fans today. In addition to initiating the rhythm-and-blues hysteria at the Apollo, the Orioles were primarily responsible for hatching the flock of bird-name groups that took flight in the fifties, such as the Penguins, Flamingoes, Robins, Larks, Falcons, and Cardinals. They were productive hitmakers in the black community, and whenever they appeared at the Apollo, they were besieged by songpluggers. "These songpluggers worked for music publishing firms," said Deborah Chessler. "They would get new material, and they'd try to get an act to record it. They were always backstage at the Apollo. Somebody would come up and say, 'Here's a new tune, or here's one we found that just suits you.' Every songwriter was trying to get up to the Apollo with a demo record, or just a lead sheet and say, 'Would you please record it?' Well, you had to go over it. Maybe it was a hit. Not only for us, but for all the acts."

The Orioles' last major hit, and the greatest of their career, was a remake of a country-and-western tearjerker called "Cryin' in the Chapel." It was recorded in New York while the Orioles were at the Apollo, and it was introduced at the theatre. The Orioles' version was the final link between rhythm and blues and its fabulously successful offspring, rock and roll. In the fall of 1953, "Cryin' in the Chapel" became the first r-and-b song to hit the pop charts. "While we were at the Apollo," Chessler remembered, "the record company called. I knew we had a recording session coming up, and we didn't have any material for it. They told me they had a couple of good songs they were sending out, and there was one we should look into right away. It had just come out by Darrell Glenn. So we called a rehearsal for that night. In between shows at the Apollo we listened to records in the dressing room. They had 'Cryin' in the Chapel,' ran it down a few times, and learned it that night. We had a lead sheet. They played it again and picked up the harmonies.

They did it the next night in the theatre. The following morning we were down at the recording studio. That hit overnight."

Another seminal rhythm-and-blues performer to whom time has not been kind is "Big" Joe Turner. He began as a singing bartender in Kansas City during that town's wild years in the thirties. When the six-foot-two, 250-pounder let loose his bellowing voice, people listened. He first gained wide attention during the late thirties when he performed at the Apollo and Carnegie Hall as part of John Hammond's "From Spirituals to Swing" concerts with boogie-woogie pianists Pete Johnson, Albert Ammons, and Meade Lux Lewis. However, Turner soon fell on hard times. He picked up gigs where he could, and sang a mixture of pop standards like "Pennies from Heaven" and beloved Kansas City blues such as "Roll 'Em Pete." Some of the work was degrading. "The Apollo Theatre people, the manager and them, didn't know me," said Big Joe. "So they had me, instead of doing one spot, they had me workin' all through the show. I was pushing a cart, hollerin', 'Popcorn man! Here comes the popcorn man!' I didn't know what was happening. I thought that went along with the deal. I was on every shift."

In 1951, with the rhythm-and-blues revolution gaining momentum, Joe was rediscovered at the Apollo by Ahmet Ertegun, who with Herb Abramson had started Atlantic records four years earlier to record the black music they loved. In the early forties, the teenaged Ertegun, son of a Turkish diplomat, held a series of parties in Washington featuring top black musicians like Sidney Bechet, Vic Dickenson, and Joe Turner, who had been hired in New York by Herb Abramson, a top record collector. "Quite a bit after that," recalled Ertegun, "after we started Atlantic records, we thought Joe Turner was one of the great blues singers of all time. But, we didn't know where Joe Turner was. We heard he was out in California, or in Texas or Chicago, and we didn't have enough money to really go traveling around the country in those days. Then I read somewhere that Jimmie Rushing had quit the Basie band, and that Joe Turner had taken his place.

"The following week I saw that Count Basie was playing at the Apollo Theatre. I went down to the first show, and he'd just joined the band. Joe Turner sings strictly traditional eight- or twelve-bar blues. But [Basie] had refined those arrangements as the years went by, and the arrangements for the stage had become much more sophisticated. They probably hadn't had many rehearsals, if any. So Joe Turner was announced, and he came onstage and started to sing 'Sent for You Yesterday' or whatever. As he was singing there'd be like—instead of the usual two-bar fill at the end of the twelve-bar frames, they'd extend them. Joe came back right on the beat where he was supposed to, but the arrangement went another way. So halfway into the song they were completely off, which sent the crowd into hysterical laughter.

"I felt very bad for Joe Turner. I went backstage during the break, but he'd already left. I walked down 126th Street to the corner and I saw him in Braddock's bar where he was having a drink. I walked in and he looked kind of dejected. I said, 'Man, forget about all this shit. I know I can make hit records with you. We're going to do a whole new thing.' That sort of cheered him up. I wrote, with his help, a song called 'Chains of Love,' and Jesse Stone wrote a beautiful arrangement. That became a big hit. After that Jesse Stone worked very closely with him and we made 'Shake, Rattle and Roll.' " Turner achieved a string of hits in the early and mid-fifties, when he was in his early forties, but he couldn't keep up with the youngsters for long, and his hit-making years ended, although he continued to work steadily. Enjoying little material benefit from his musical contributions, and hobbled by debilitating illnesses, Joe Turner carries on. In his seventies, moving with painful slowness on crutches, Big Joe Turner still belts out the blues he loves.

· · · · ·

Every revolution has its key turning points. And yet, while the Orioles' triumph at the Apollo Theatre was a major step toward the demise of the theatre's traditional policy of presenting variety entertainment, the variety shows did not disappear overnight. From their initial success through the mid-fifties, the Apollo played the Orioles on variety bills with a wide-ranging and seemingly mismatched array of performers, such as Buddy Rich, Sy Oliver, Charlie Parker, Johnny Hodges, Little Leslie Uggams, and Bunny Briggs. As Deborah Chessler said, "It wasn't really smart booking, but it worked. That's the thing."

In fact, while it may have worked artistically, it wasn't really working commercially. The Apollo was going through hard times. Frank Schiffman seemed to have broken stride temporarily with the black community that had in the past led him to the new sounds and styles. He played the early purveyors of rhythm and blues—Ruth Brown, Big Joe Turner, Little Esther, Johnny Otis, and others—but they, like the Orioles, were programmed into the old-style variety shows.

Bobby Schiffman, however, realized that not only had a new sound arrived, but with it a whole new way of listening to music. "With the cooperation of a disc jockey on WWRL named Dr. Jive—his real name was Tommy Smalls—we thought out that people weren't coming to see the tap dancer and the [other ancillary] acts," said Bobby Schiffman. "They were coming to see the vocal act that had the hit record that was being played on the radio. So together we spawned the idea of eliminating the other acts and putting in acts that had hit records. That became known as the r-and-b revue." By the mid-fifties these revues, featuring as many as a dozen singing acts on one bill, became the dominant form of entertainment at the theatre. "The Apollo was the pioneer in that type of presentation," noted Bobby, "and the guys that followed us into the white marketplace, like Alan Freed with his Rock and Roll Revue, took his idea right from the Apollo Theatre." Actually, if Freed were still alive, he might debate this, since his first rock-and-roll show was scheduled for March 1952 in Cleveland.

When Frank Schiffman saw his first r-and-b revue, he "couldn't believe it," according to Leonard Reed, then the Apollo's manager. "We had done shows with variety entertainment, and when you come up with a format of all these singing acts in a row you say, 'What the hell is this?' But it was packing the house. I got sick of this because I had nothing to do. All I had to do was go downstairs, see the band rehearse, and say, 'You go first, you go second, you third, you fourth.' One day I asked, 'Mr. Schiffman, when are we gonna go back to a good show?' He said, 'Hold it. What do you call a good show? One that doesn't do us any business? I want to show you something.'" He took Reed outside, stood under the marquee, and pointed to the long lines. "He said, 'When the line gets right here, that's when we'll change. I don't like it either, Leonard, but you must learn that money coming through that gate is our business.'"

"The rhythm-and-blues revues turned the theatre around financially," said Bobby Schiffman. "Because the people of the community loved and bought it, and continued to buy it. You could go in the Apollo and see seven or eight acts with hot records all on one show. It was much more expensive to produce than the variety shows, but the proceeds were much greater. An empty seat doesn't mean anything. During that era the theatre was operating at capacity more than anytime else. There were situations where we were doing as many as seven shows a day. That's unheard of."

Unhappily, for many of the variety acts—the dancers, comedians, and old-style songsters—it was the beginning of the end, and many of the old-timers resented the Apollo's new approach. Speaking today, they do not bother to distinguish between rhythm and blues, soul, and rock

176

and roll; to them the new sounds that proved their swan song were all just rock.

"In the fifties when the rock came in," said Harold Cromer, "the regular variety acts were on the wane. They wanted one group after the other, and the kids were not interested in what you'd call experienced talent. They just wanted to listen to the music and holler and scream. The Apollo became a different place. The generation changed. The kids coming up knew nothing about the other guys who began the theatre."

Cromer's partner, Jimmy Cross, recalled, "You ask them about Pearl Bailey, and they'd say, 'Oh, the lady that sells chickens.' That's all."

"Not that the rock stuff's not good," said Harold. "I'm not saying it's not good. What I'm saying is they became just record hits. They'd perform their record, and after that there was no performance involved. A lot of them developed talent, but there was no real *theatrical* talent involved." Still, like it or not, rhythm and blues was here to stay, and nothing would ever be the same again at the Apollo.

As rhythm and blues began to take over the Apollo and the glory days of the great dancers and the *lebenspilder* comedians came to an end, Harlem was also changing, and not for the better. "If black Harlem was once a heaven," wrote Jervis Anderson in *This Was Harlem*, "or was seen to be by the migrants and the commentators of the nineteen twenties, it had ceased to be that by the beginning of the nineteen fifties. When the early optimism had been exhausted, there remained, among the majority of the population, almost all the racial and social hardships that many had hoped would be nonexistent in the finest urban community that blacks had ever occupied in the United States."

Whites had generally abandoned the area—both the private citizens who used to flock to Harlem for their entertainment, and the public servants who were supposed to represent it—and so, too, had the black middle class and the black intellectuals and artists who had helped make Harlem such a vital and stimulating community. As the clubs, theatres, and ballrooms that once defined Harlem faltered or closed, the Apollo Theatre became the last bastion of black expression, entertainment, and fun left uptown, and that meant it was more important than ever to the community.

Like Harlem, the Apollo changed but also remained the same. Although r and b was now dominant, the Schiffmans did not abandon their older clientele. They continued to present regular variety shows, at least occasionally, throughout the rhythm-and-blues era, and into the sixties and seventies. They also tested other attractions in the fifties, including Mambo Shows featuring all Latin artists and made several unsuccessful experiments in presenting revivals of Broadway dramatic hits such as *Rain, Detective Story,* and *Anna Lucasta.* Also, new variety artists emerged, and older acts updated their material to fit into the rhythm-and-blues shows.

. . . . .

In comedy, the old-style performers had to move over for the new breed who knew better how to deal with the frustrations and increasing anger of the black community in the fifties. The Apollo began featuring a new style of comedy, one that was topical as well as satirical. The emphasis was still on entertainment, of course, but the new comedians no longer relied on the comic aspects of blackness. It was becoming harder and harder for black people to find humor in the "pictures of life" scenes portrayed by the *lebenspilder* comedians. In the fifties, comedians at the Apollo satirized the absurdity of black people's social position in a segregated society and, even more important, they strove to portray blacks as people, just like other people: sophisticated and backward, handsome and ugly, intelligent and stupid, brave and cowardly.

One of the earliest purveyors of topical comedy was Nipsey Russell. He is remembered in Harlem for his unprecedented twenty-year stand at the Baby Grand bar, just down the street from the Apollo. He became a popular attraction at the Apollo as a comedian and master of ceremonies, and it was at the theatre that he was given his nickname, "Harlem's Son of Fun." Born in Alabama, he consciously eliminated any trace of dialect from his speech and act and, rather than play the buffoon, faced his audience straight on and delivered his monologues, poems, and stories with dignity.

One of his best-known bits, as related in *The Redd Foxx Encyclopedia of Black Humor,* involves a black man fleeing the racial turmoil of the South. Sitting in the bus station, he notices a machine that tells one's fortune and weight. He tries it out, and receives a card that reads: "You weigh 150 pounds, you are a Negro, and you are on your way to Chicago." Amazed, he tries it again. Again he receives the same message. Now he is perplexed, and he attempts to outsmart the machine. Spotting an old Indian, he borrows his blanket and feather. He wraps himself in the blanket, sticks the feather in his hair, and sneaks up on the machine. When he deposits another coin, out comes a card reading: "You still weigh 150 pounds, you are still a nigger, and by fucking around you've missed your bus to Chicago."

178

Latin stars at the Apollo in the 1950s. Front row (left to right): Miguelito Valdez, Gilberto Valdez, Tito Puente. Back row (left to right): Mambo Ace Joe Centeno, Joe Loco, Mercedita Valdes, Lucy Faberi, Mongo Santamaria, Mambo Ace Anibal Vasquez, Bobby Quintero.

Timmie Rogers in a recent shot. ★ *He led the final attack on blackface comedy in the late 1940s, and was the first black comedian to wear a tuxedo in his act—a revolutionary move at the time.*

Nipsey was also a regular in the Apollo audience. He usually came to the first show on Friday, and he always sat in the front row. "Nipsey loved to see comics die," said Scoey Mitchlll, who played the Apollo frequently as a comedian and m.c. "He came into the Apollo one day when I was working, and I told some joke. Nipsey laughed and jumped right up in front of the audience and says, 'Boy, I'm going to use that joke. I'm telling you right now, I'm going to steal that.' And I said, 'Hey, it's cool. But just be careful where you use it because the guy I stole it from might not be as understanding as I am.' "

Another comedian who helped modernize black comedy was Timmie Rogers. He led the final attack on blackface comedy in the late forties, and was the first black comedian to wear a tuxedo in his act—a revolutionary move at the time. "My first attempt to go onstage in Hollywood, I got fired for wearing a tuxedo," said Rogers. "I got fired by a white man because I dressed my act like a white man. When I came into the Apollo with these different clothes on, and doing comedy, I was a welcome sight."

Timmie's great trademark gag line—a broad-grinned "Oh, yeah!"—was arrived at by accident at the Apollo. As he tells it, "Frank Schiffman wanted me to come in and read the coming announcements before the show started. I didn't want to come on early because I'm scheduled to come on next to closing, before the headliner, Nat Cole. But Frank was an ex-schoolteacher, and he had a way of doing things. He said, 'Oh, Timmie, please. Oh, come on, Timmie. Don't be difficult.' So I came in and I caught myself lousing it up. I would say, 'Ladies and gentlemen, good morning and welcome to the Apollo Theatre. Next week coming up will be the great Duke Ellington and his great band. Oh, yeah! And Miss Ella Fitzgerald. Oh, yeah! And Bunny Briggs. Oh, yeah!' When I walked onstage that morning, the whole second balcony, what we called 'the jury,' hollered back at me, 'Oh, yeah!' If I'd have known it would be that big, and my identification for life, I never would have hesitated. I owe all my thanks to Frank Schiffman. I found myself a gem."

In April 1957, Timmie Rogers became the first comedian to headline at the Apollo. His was an innovative show called "No Time for Squares," inspired by Timmie's feeling that: "I didn't believe in a show of just acts, acts, acts. I had to have a little something to hold it together—a small thread. My late partner, Al Fields, and I wrote 'No Time for Squares' and Frank Schiffman caught it at the Club Elegante in Brooklyn. He said, 'You're going in, Timmie. I'm bringing the show to the Apollo and you're going to headline the show.' Coming into the

Apollo we had to have something that was hip. I was so tired of hearing 'Cotton Club Revue.'

"Opening the show we would sing, with the curtains closed, 'Is it true what they say about Dixie?' My head went through the curtain and I said, 'Oh, yeah!' Then we would go into our opening number, 'No Time for Squares': 'Come one, come all. It's time for having a ball. Each one does what he dares, 'cause it's no time for squares. Get hip, be wise, break society's ties. But being a drag ain't nowheres, 'cause it's no time for squares.' "

The show featured a variety of entertainers like pianist Buck Washington, singer Jackie Starr, and the Three Chocolateers, who created pandemonium by running through the audience bobbing their heads, craning their necks, and singing the "Pecking" song. They rehearsed in Rogers's living room, and this gave Timmie an idea. "We were sitting around one day. While we were sitting on the couch, I look around and think, 'That's the idea.' I said, 'Al, we got our set. We're moving the apartment into the Apollo,' " and he did that. As each performer did his bit, the others sat onstage, on the sofa or by the piano, smoking or biding their time until their turn came. "It was different," said Rogers. "It was very casual and very unique, and Harlem just went wild about the idea."

Stump and Stumpy (Jimmy Cross and Harold Cromer) began their careers in the thirties, but they became a very popular comedy act in the fifties. They were masters of the straight comedy bit, but they also mixed in elements of topicality. "One time we had a tax audit," Harold Cromer remembered. "They had an injunction on us at the Apollo. They had a lien, and were going to take our entire salary. So we had to go downtown, and by the time we got out we were late for the first show. We got to the theatre after a cab ride through Central Park, dressed in street clothes. The band is playing the last number, and the curtain is closing. We run through the theatre and holler, 'Don't close the curtain!' The audience is screaming and hollering, and we walked right through the audience up on the stage and did the whole act. We explained what had happened. We did a talk bit then. We were open—if something came out in the newspaper, we would throw that in. It was ad-libbed. Johnny Carson's doing it now. Timing. We were doing it then."

Nostalgia carries with it some resentment. "People copied from us," Cromer recalled. "Martin and Lewis stole from me and Jimmy."

"Wherever we were, they came," said Jimmy Cross. "Or their manager."

"Jerry Lewis would do Jimmy," said Harold, "and Dean Martin

LEFT: Stump and Stumpy, about 1950. Jimmy Cross (Stump) is on the left, Harold Cromer on the right. ★ *"Martin and Lewis stole from me and Jimmy. . . . If you've seen Martin and Lewis in the old days, you've seen me and Jimmy."*
BELOW: Handbill for the 1953 Joe Louis show with Leonard Reed at the Apollo. ★ *"He said, 'What corner do you think is luckiest for you?' I said, 'Any corner in San Francisco, because I'm a long-distance fighter.'"*

would watch me, because I was the straight man. See, we played two different kinds of colored people. We're not black, we're colored, Stump and I. Jimmy played like he was a simple type, and I was the intelligent one. He was screwing up, but I really became the butt end of the whole thing. I'd say, 'Wait a minute, Jimmy, you don't even know what you're talking about. You know linole-uh, how do you say that word?' "

"I don't know. These words are hard for me to say," said Jimmy, playing along. "Like the stuff on the floor, linolemumum."

"No, no, Jimmy, you mean linoleum."

"Linolemumum."

"No, no, look: L . . ."

"L . . ."

"I . . ."

"I . . ."

"N . . ."

"N . . ."

"O . . ."

"O . . ."

"Leum . . ."

"Linolemumum."

"Now that would work," said Harold. "We did a lot of that, and then Martin and Lewis got the idea, too. When we worked the Cotton Club in Hollywood, Martin would come by every night. We'd have a couple of drinks afterward, and he'd find out how do you get this feeling, this rapport with one another. Jimmy and I hang out together, and they found out that was the key, as long as they were constantly with one another, all they had to do was play off of what happened. They invited us for dinner and said we'll give you $2,000 and some of our old radio scripts. I said, 'We don't need your old radio scripts. We don't need your $2,000. You're making more money than you ever did doing Stump and I.' That was the way they were trying to buy us off. It's true. If you've seen Martin and Lewis in the old days, you've seen me and Jimmy."

Probably the greatest comedy sensation at the Apollo in the fifties was far better known for his expertise in the ring than on the stage. But Harlem's heavyweight idol, Joe Louis, proved himself a superior showman—when he had an excellent foil like his buddy Leonard Reed to play against. Their first show in April 1953 was so successful that the Apollo brought them back for a return engagement three weeks later. Reed met Louis in 1935 in a Detroit nightclub, and they became great friends and occasional business partners.

"He had retired successfully in 1947," Reed recalled, "and he said to me, 'I want to go in show business.' So I wrote material for him to do an act, and we broke it in in Europe. Johnny Weissmuller was there, and they had a big health and holiday show. Joe and I went over there for eighteen weeks. When we came back we took it on tour and then we played the Apollo in 1953.

"In this act Joe and I fought. I'd throw a punch, and he'd throw a punch. I was younger then, I was agile. He'd knock me out. I'd do flips and end up in a headstand." Reed, looking like nothing but skin and bones, dressed in oversized baggy shorts and wore a boxer's protective headgear. "We had a mock fight: the Bearcat, that's what my name was, and the Brown Bomber. Joe said, 'Come on, let's say suppose you were fighting me.' I said, 'Suppose I ain't fighting you.' He said, 'Oh, we'd just pretend.' I said, 'Shit, I can't be that deceitful.' He said, 'Just look out.' I said, 'Okay. Is this the championship fight?' He said, 'You're right, it is.' I said, 'The Bearcat against the Brown Bomber. Where're we fighting?' He said, 'Madison Square Garden, New York. What corner do you think is luckiest for you?' I said, 'Any corner in San Francisco, because I'm a long-distance fighter.' He'd knock me down two or three times and the last time he knocked me down, I just fell flat out. He said, 'Come on, get up.' I said, 'Shit, you didn't get up when Marciano knocked you down!' The people would just scream."

Bobby Schiffman remembered a time when Joe didn't pull his punch, and Leonard, as well as the audience, got knocked out. The Apollo, like all vaudeville theatres, had a tradition known as burying the show, in which the cast added a little something extra, or unusual, or zany to the final show of the week.

"On the closing night of the show," said Bobby, "it had circulated that Louis was going to drop Reed in his tracks that night. Everybody in the theatre knew it, including Reed, but Reed never said a word. This comedy dance bit, which usually lasted two minutes, stretched to eighteen minutes because Leonard was afraid to get too close to him. Louis wasn't a great monologuist, and all the talk emanated from Reed and his fear that Louis was going to pop him. But the bit couldn't end until he got close enough for this to happen, and Leonard is trying to figure out how the hell to end this bit. Finally, he got too close and Louis [really] hit him. Instead of doing the flip and ending up on his head, he just sank right to the ground. It was like he was cold cocked."

. . . . .

Along with a heavyweight like Joe Louis, the Apollo, continuing its efforts to try anything to grab the Apollo crowd, also eagerly presented a remarkable new crop of bantamweights. In the early fifties a number of talented child entertainers arrived, to the delight of the Apollo audience. Some, like Sugar Chile Robinson or Toni Harper, produced hit records, but once the novelty of their precociousness wore off, they faded from the scene. Others, Little Leslie Uggams and Little Esther Phillips, for example, were natural talents and continued as successful performers as they grew.

The Apollo audience had always been receptive to child performers, but they made no allowance for age. They demanded the same level of quality from them as from their elders. Bobby Short, a child prodigy who played the Apollo in the late thirties, wrote in his autobiography: "People said I was too downtown for [the Apollo audience]. They didn't care about my size or age, people were interested only in my ability, and this was being measured in terms of my familiarity with the hit songs of the day in Harlem. . . . I recall singing 'Love Is the Thing, So They Say,' an Ella Fitzgerald hit, and the audience totally forgetting that the provocateur up on the stage was a child—just leaned back and clapped as though I was a thirty- or forty-year-old blues singer. They didn't care who was doing it as long as it was being done."

Backstage at the Apollo was no day-care center, and the stagehands were hardly a mother's ideal baby-sitters, but it was all the child stars had. Leslie Uggams, who sometimes worked with Dinah Washington, recalled: "Dinah was very, very special. Dinah could cuss better than anybody I ever heard in my life, but she had a heart of gold. When it got real heavy, and she'd get to cussing, she'd say, 'Okay, Juanita,' which was my mother's name, 'take baby into the dressing room. I got some strong cuss words I gotta use here.' My mother would take me in and close the door, but Dinah's voice carried everywhere, it wasn't like you couldn't hear it."

Little Esther Phillips sang the blues like a worldly adult, but she was only thirteen when she came into the Apollo in 1950. "My most vivid thought about the Apollo is Porto Rico," she said. "The first time I met him he called me a bitch and talked about my mother, and I just broke down in tears. I can't speak for any other child stars, but he was very, very hard on me. I don't feel he really meant me harm, but that was the only way he could express his compassion or feeling. He didn't want me loitering around. Like between shows I would get kind of fidgety

Little Esther Phillips outside the Apollo, about 1950. ★ *"Between shows I would get kind of fidgety because I had nobody to play with. So I'd go down and play with the lights and mess up the movie. Well, I was kind of a little brat, I guess, but I was bored."*

Leslie Uggams, age nine, at the Apollo in 1952. ★ Deborah Chessler: *"That voice just filled the theatre. She knew just what to do with her hands, and how to stand and bow and talk. She was more professional than a lot of people were at thirty."*

because I had nobody to play with. So I'd go down and play with the lights and mess up the movie. Well, I was kind of a little brat, I guess, but I was bored. I guess Porto Rico was really trying to protect me, even though he hurt my feelings. But really, I liked him, and I still love him. I really do."

Leslie Uggams got her start when, at age seven, she appeared on the Apollo's Amateur Night radio program and caught the attention of Jack and Bobby Schiffman. They arranged for bandleader Lucky Millinder to create an act for her, and her first professional engagement was at the Apollo with Louis Armstrong. "I did 'When You Smile'—that was my opening number—and 'Pennies from Heaven.' I did impressions—Johnny Ray, Kaye Starr, and Ted Lewis. I was telling this on the 'John Davidson Show' and John said, 'Those were all white people. At the Apollo you did that?' I said, 'Well, we weren't prejudiced.' I tapped also, and did 'Exactly Like You,' and I had my own special spot, and later Louis brought me out and we did a duet. I also worked with Ella Fitzgerald and Dinah and I'd do the same thing. In New York I could work the midnight show, but when I went on tour and worked, like, the Howard Theatre in Washington, I could not. But in New York everything went as far as the show was concerned."

Leslie still has a framed copy of Frank Schiffman's rating card for her on a wall in her Beverly Hills home. "Here's my rating, 7/11/52: I got $250, plus $100 for special services. I don't know what that means—thank God I was only nine years old. It says, 'A very cute nine-year-old youngster whose voice is not very good, but she is a bundle of personality.' In 'fifty-four: 'Very cute, sweet, went over nicely.' Then in 'fifty-eight, I got $500. It says, 'Good singer, worth using, slightly overpaid.' I love that." Deborah Chessler remembers Leslie when she played with the Orioles: "She was fantastic, absolutely tore up the house. That voice just filled the theatre. She knew just what to do with her hands, and how to stand and bow and talk. She was eight years old and more professional than a lot of people were at thirty."

Sugar Chile Robinson was a pint-sized piano player and singer who was a frequent headliner at the Apollo in the early fifties. Sitting at a white grand piano dressed in shorts and saddle shoes, Sugar Chile delighted audiences with his hit rendition of "Caledonia." But his career ended in controversy. "The stories you used to hear about Sugar Chile," said Leslie Uggams. "He was the size of Gary Coleman, and the rumor around was that he was a midget. But he was a dynamite performer. Now you know Spayne [the stagehand] and that crew were wonderful, but, boy, if you gave them any static, sometimes somebody would slip up to your dressing room that shouldn't be there, and I think they got you back in that way. It seems one day at the Apollo a fan got upstairs without them knowing and opened Sugar Chile's door and he was sitting there in his shorts smoking a cigar. Of course that hit the black newspapers, and they weren't too thrilled about that. He was supposed to be a kid, and I think he just got some grown-up habits that came a little too early. I think, though, they were passing him off as twelve when he was really sixteen or seventeen."

. . . . .

While the latest black musical form, rhythm and blues, remained confined to the black ghettos of America, a few black artists aimed their performances at a wider audience, and were able to succeed in the white world.

Josephine Baker—the "Dark Star"—had created a sensation in Paris with the Folies-Bergère in "La Revue Nègre" in 1925, and twelve years later she became a French citizen. "She was a star in Europe, and not very significant in this country, in our opinion," said Bobby Schiffman. "But for years we had heard the name and we were dying to play her because she was such a grand, elegant lady. We finally played her the week before Christmas, 1951. It was the only time she was available, and that is traditionally the worst week in show business, especially in relatively poor communities, because people are saving for other things. The engagement went five days before Christmas, Christmas day, and two days thereafter. Well, the first days before Christmas you could have shot a deer in the theatre—nobody there. But she was up there breaking her ass to do the show, and she was outrageous. Christmas day you couldn't get in the theatre. Jammed to the walls; the two days after, too."

When she played the Apollo at forty-five she was no longer a youngster, yet she was still breathtakingly beautiful, and she sang and danced like a young woman. Josephine played the grand lady to the hilt. She was attended by two French maids, and her entourage and her quarter-million-dollar wardrobe took up three dressing rooms. "She had some costumes that were so outlandish that she couldn't walk in them," said Bobby. "We had to plant her." Her segment of the show lasted an hour, and she made seven or eight costume changes. "She had a private dressing room built right off the stage," recalled Doll Thomas. "After each number, the minute she came off, one maid would help her off with one costume, and the other would have the next costume ready. Once or twice when she wanted to catch her breath, she had a clever white comic, Pat Henning, with her to fill in. But she'd step out of that costume into this one, and she would do that in eight bars and on the same rhythm."

Bobby Schiffman can best tell the story of another great lady's triumphant arrival and debut at the Apollo Theatre, because he is the one who made it happen: "As a young man I went to my father and said, 'I'm going to go after the superstars of black music.' And he said, 'Yeah, sure.' I wrote a letter to Eartha Kitt—a lady who I had the greatest respect and admiration for. I thought she was a brilliant performer, and there was an aura about her that stimulated my juices to want to get her in the Apollo because I knew she would do super business in there.

"I had been trying to get Eartha Kitt to come into the Apollo through her agency, William Morris. I was a youngster just out of college. Every time I would call—I had no credibility with the agency, they didn't even know who I was—the answers were always no. No, she doesn't want to play it. No, she doesn't have the time. No, she won't do it. No, she's not a black act. Ten thousand other reasons they were giving me, and I knew they were just to get Bobby Schiffman off the phone. They were talking to me because of my father, for whom they had a great deal of respect, but I was just a brash, bold young punk. When I found I couldn't get to her through them, I wrote her a letter, and for some reason she said okay.

"I went to visit her in her apartment on Fifth Avenue. She invited me for lunch and we sat and talked. At the end of that conversation, while I was sitting there, she called the William Morris office and said, 'Listen, I want to play the Apollo. I want to play it whenever Bobby Schiffman wants me to play it, and if there's anything else in the way of a proposed date that makes sense to Bobby Schiffman, I want to cancel the other thing.'

"When Eartha came to the Apollo, it was right after she married Bill McDonald, who was a white man. There was a great deal of resentment in some of the nationalistic black intellectuals about Eartha marrying a white man. Here was one of the great sex symbols of American music who was going out of her race to marry a white man, and a great deal of thunder came down about it. She got all kinds of hate mail, and all kinds of threats, and when she came to the Apollo she was scared out of her wits. She thought she was going to be put down.

"When Eartha walked on that stage at twelve-thirty on a Friday afternoon, the theatre was jammed to the walls. When she walked on the stage, and before she uttered a single word, the people in the audience

189

Josephine Baker at the Apollo, in the 1950s. ★ Bobby
Schiffman: *"She had some costumes that were so outlandish
that she couldn't walk in them. We had to plant her."*

Eartha Kitt at the Apollo, in the 1950s. ★ Bobby Schiffman: *"She got all kinds of hate mail, and all kinds of threats, and when she came to the Apollo she was scared out of her wits."*

stood up and applauded for ten minutes. What they were saying to her was, 'We hear all this bullshit about the hate letters, and we know you don't have to come to the Apollo, and we know the only reason that you came to the Apollo was because you wanted to come. And we thank you for coming.' That girl stood on that stage and cried. I mean the tears just streamed down her face. She was absolutely speechless. Absolutely paralyzed to move, and for ten minutes that tumultuous reception went on. At the end of it she did a show—she will never do a better show than that one. She killed the people and they loved her to death."

Yet as times changed, and perhaps Eartha's attitude also, she received a markedly different reception. "The Black Panthers hated me because I supported Martin Luther King," she told *Village Voice* columnist Arthur Bell. "They threw stones at me when I appeared at the Apollo." Bell wrote, "Politeness forbade my mentioning that I had seen her at the Apollo, too, in the early '60s, and the verbal stones were thrown because she came on stage in ermines and pearls and sang Jewish and Turkish songs. She used the Apollo to break in her hoity-toity Persian Room act."

Another black star whose plaintive melodies appealed to whites as well as to the softer side of the r-and-b audience—Johnny Mathis—had a rocky relationship with the Apollo. His entry into the theatre was unusual even by Apollo standards. "Some guy was peddling Johnny Mathis at one of the record companies," related Bobby Schiffman. "He said, 'Bobby, come in here. I want you to hear something.' So I went in and listened to 'It's Not for Me to Say' and said, 'Wow! Who the hell is that?' He said, 'It's a kid named Johnny Mathis that we're going to release.' I said, 'Outrageous! When are you going to release him?' He said, 'I guess it will come out in a couple of weeks.' I ran back to the theatre and said to my father, 'There's a young kid by the name of Johnny Mathis. You got to find him and book him for three months from now.' My father said, 'Well, who is he?' I said, 'Dad, please trust me. He's a young black singer that's coming out. I heard the release date. It's going to be a smash!' So my father found him and booked him for $350 for thirty-one shows. When Mathis came in, 'It's Not for Me to Say' was the number-one record in the world. We had him for $350."

But trouble lay ahead. Harold Cromer was the master of ceremonies for Mathis's debut show. "Johnny came by early Friday to rehearse," said Cromer. "He did a regular nightclub act, which was unusual then. The music was great. But Johnny was frightened like mad. He was really out of his bird because he had never performed before black people, and

Johnny Mathis at his Apollo debut in 1957. ★ Harold
Cromer: *"Johnny was frightened like mad. He was really out of
his bird because he had never performed before black people, and
he'd always heard about the Apollo audience."*

he'd always heard about the Apollo audience. So I said, 'Believe me, you'll do okay.' Mathis said, 'But I'm nervous. And I don't know. They may not like me.' I said, 'I'm emceeing the show. I'll make sure you go over.' They had Johnny way up on the top floor, where I was. In the dressing rooms at the Apollo Theatre, when the show closes, they hang all the chairs on hooks on the wall. So he walked into the room and all the chairs were on the wall, and, man, was he nervous. All he had was one suit. He refused to take the chairs down, and he took the suit bag and hung it on top of one of the chairs, took his suit out, and changed.

"Now, with five minutes to go he's nervous, and the perspiration is coming off his head." Cromer and Reuben Phillips, the house bandleader, had come into the wings after each act finished to reassure Mathis, then Cromer brought him on with a big buildup. "He's nervous and shaking, and he sings his opening song, and he's hot. Second song, even bigger. Third song, he is really smooth. Then he did 'That Old Black Magic' and the people really loved him. Then he did his hit recording. But he only did three shows."

The Schiffmans were delighted with Mathis's performance and realized that, to be fair, he was worth far more than they were paying him. "I started to rub Mathis down with kid gloves," said Bobby Schiffman. "At the end of the week Mathis would have gotten a $2,000 bonus from us. On Saturday I got a call in the office. Mathis wants to see me. So I go backstage and he says, 'I can't go on.' I said, 'You what?' He said, 'I have laryngitis. I can't sing.' I said, 'I can't hear you, John.' He says, loud, *'I got laryngitis!'* I said, 'Come on.' The long and short of it is, he walked out on that Saturday. He insists that he had laryngitis. I think he's full of shit."

· · · · ·

Like many other attractions from the variety-show days, most of the big bands had broken up. But the Apollo still needed a band to play for the old-style acts that remained and to back up the new rhythm-and-blues performers who needed musical accompaniment. So Frank Schiffman searched for a house band that would play the Apollo every week. In the late forties and early fifties he employed Lucius "Lucky" Millinder and his band on a semiregular basis. Millinder was a colorful and popular figure in Harlem, and although he played no instrument and couldn't read a note of music, he was an excellent and well-disciplined bandleader. Later, as Lucky got more and more involved in the music publishing end of the business, he dissolved his band. In 1953, Schiffman turned to Reuben Phillips, a saxophonist who had played with a number of bands, including those of Andy Kirk, Count Basie, and Louis Jordan, and asked him to assemble the finest New York musicians he could find to form a permanent Apollo house band. That Phillips did, and his band played for all the acts at the Apollo nearly every week until well into the 1960s.

"He played for all of the singing groups," said Harold Cromer. "When rhythm-and-blues first started, they had a minimal amount of instrumentation with them; mostly it was vocals. The record companies would supply the musical background for them, and they would have charts of their arrangements for the band. They would bring the staples with them—a bass player, maybe, or a guitar player. They would augment the house band and Reuben Phillips would become the conductor for it."

As the house band replaced the cavalcade of big bands that had been a part of every Apollo show in the thirties and forties, so the disc jockeys supplanted the producers as show packagers at the Apollo. The rise of the disc jockey may be one of the few instances in the history of industry where men replaced machines. At first jukeboxes were the means the recording industry used to merchandise and publicize its product. In fact, the demand for records to fill jukeboxes during the war years was so great that the major record companies had trouble meeting it, especially in the neglected area of "race" records. Into the gap stepped a growing number of small independent labels such as Exclusive, Beacon, Apollo (no relation to the theatre), and National. As more and more music was produced for the jukes, radio stations became increasingly interested in playing the new tunes on the air.

But record companies initially resisted the playing of their discs on the air. It was thought that airplay would dissipate the retail sales potential. Some companies even banned radio play of their records outright. Gradually, the situation began to change. "By the end of World War II," wrote Arnold Shaw, "the collapse of the big bands and the growth of small stations enhanced the possibility that deejay turntables might serve as a medium of exposure and promotion. The advent of television cast the die. The decline of network radio shows and the introduction of the transistor gave new importance to the 'indie' station and the 'Knights of the Turntable' who became the medium through which the small record company could economically reach the public." A synergistic effect developed among the record companies that multiplied

Disc Jockeys & Apollo Theatre Masters OF Ceremonies

Rocky G

George Hudson

Symphony Sid

Jack Walker

Jocko Hinderson

Mort Fega

Herman Amis

Frankie Crocker

Hal Jackson

Doc Wheeler

Fred Barr

Eddie O'Jay

Tommy Smalls

A page from a 1965 Apollo souvenir program. ★ Ruth Brown: *"At the time the disc jockeys started headlining the shows, all of a sudden you didn't see the performers' names on the marquee—you would see Dr. Jive's."*

in number throughout the r-and-b era, the artists who were suddenly in great demand, and the disc jockeys who purveyed the sound to eager youngsters around the country.

Thus the disc jockeys became the organizers and hosts of the Apollo's new rhythm-and-blues revues. The shows capitalized on the popularity of the deejays, and they, not the performers, were usually the headliners. These shows often featured as many as a dozen different acts performing their hit tunes and were tremendously popular. However, while the audience got its money's worth, performers were often exploited in various ways. "At the time the disc jockeys started headlining the shows," said Ruth Brown, "all of a sudden you didn't see the performers' names on the marquee—you would see Dr. Jive's. The artists started to be diminished because all of a sudden the disc jockey was in control. If he played your records, okay, if he didn't, you're dead. And you got your records played according to your familiarity with him. There was payola and everything else. The disc jockey was almost in control of who got to work the theatres because he was bringing the shows in."

The disc jockeys wielded a great deal of power, at least until the federal payola investigation of 1959–1960. "The deejays would sit with me and plan who to buy," said Bobby Schiffman. "They were trying to take advantage of the fact that they played the records on the air to get the acts to work for a lower price, because they always had a percentage agreement [with the theatre]. So they would try to get the acts to work for less. The FCC took away that power by not letting the deejays pick the songs that they could play. It's now in the hands of a program director, and the object is to keep it from being payola. That was a form of payola. You would get the acts to play for little or nothing because you were playing their record on the air."

The first Apollo r-and-b disc jockey was Dr. Jive (Tommy Smalls), who brought his first rhythm-and-blues revue into the Apollo in 1955. But soon others such as Alan Freed (the man who coined the term *rock and roll*), Doc Wheeler, Rocky G, later on Clay Cole and Frankie Crocker, and, in the jazz arena, Symphony Sid Torin, regularly brought their shows into the Apollo. One of the most successful and popular deejays was Douglas "Jocko" Henderson whose "1280 Rocket" show on WOV was launched by space commander Jocko as his space theme blasted over the airwaves. Jocko favored argot such as "well all roother" and "great gugga mugga shooga booga." A typical Jocko rap, reported by Arnold Passman in *The Deejays*, might go: "From way up here in the stratosphere, we gotta holler mighty loud and clear 'ee-tiddy-o and a ho,' and I'm back on the scene with the record machine, saying, 'oo-pap-doo,' and how do you do!"

When commander Jocko first came into the Apollo, the Schiffmans didn't quite know what they were getting into, and neither did Jocko. "There was a record-store owner named Bobby Robinson," recalled Bobby Schiffman, "who had a little store on 125th Street. He came to me and told me I ought to play this guy Jocko. I never heard of Jocko, and Bobby had to convince us to play him. I had put a show together with a fellow who was a promoter for Fats Domino—who was already a major star. By the time we put the show together we had eight acts, and about five of them had records in the top ten. At the last minute we decided to ask Jocko. When he came into the theatre the first day, he was so scared, he didn't know what to do. He said, 'Do I have to clean my dressing room? Can I come out and sell tickets? What do you want me to do? I'll do whatever you want.' The end of the week, Jocko went out like a lion. The theatre was jammed all week, and he of course thought it was *he* who did the business."

· · · · ·

A star who continued to headline his own shows, even at the height of the disc jockeys' power, and one who may have been the greatest rhythm-and-bluesman of the era, was John Davenport—better known as Little Willie John. Johnny Otis discovered him in Detroit in 1955 when he was seventeen, and that year he had his first hit with "All Around the World," a soulful r-and-b wailer. The girls sighed when the diminutive singer shouted: "If I don't love you, baby . . . Grits ain't groceries, eggs ain't poultry and Mona Lisa was a man!" Soon afterward he achieved his greatest success with "Fever," a tune that was copied and made famous by Peggy Lee in 1958. But ballads were his specialty. "Willie John in my opinion was the best male singer I ever heard," said Bobby Schiffman. "He used to send chills up and down my spine, and I never met a singer who had that kind of emotion and feeling in his songs. Willie would appear at the theatre and do thirty-one shows, and I would stand in the wings and watch every show. He was incredible. He used to do a medley of two tunes, 'Talk to Me' and 'Let Them Talk,' and the ripples would run through the audience, because Willie was such a romantic. There was such feeling in what he did. If he were alive today, he would have sold a gang of records."

Willie John was irrepressible, and irresponsible, too. A heavy

Jocko Henderson with singer Baby Washington, backstage at the Apollo in the late 1950s or early 1960s. ★ *"From way up here in the stratosphere, we gotta holler mighty loud and clear 'ee-tiddy-o and a ho,' and I'm back on the scene with the record machine, saying, 'oo-pap-doo,' and how do you do!"*

Little Willie John, 1956. ★ *"I'm going to just spend my money up. Nobody will have anything to fight over. They enjoy it with me or they won't enjoy it at all, 'cause I'm spreading it out."*

drinker, he had a dangerous habit of carrying a gun. He was active in promoting the nascent career of his friend James Brown, who used to open for Willie John at the Apollo in the early days, and James remained true to him until the end. Danny Ray, Brown's longtime master of ceremonies, and St. Clair Pinckney, band director for Brown for more than twenty years, talked about Little Willie John: "Willie was a very active type of person," said Ray. "If he comes inside the place, you're going to know he's there. Everybody from the front desk on up would know Willie was in the house. He had that kind of charisma. Things happened at such a young age for him, and he tried to handle things, but he wasn't ready. That's why he got into difficult scrapes."

"If he wanted to do it, he did it," said Pinckney, "without even a moment's hesitation. That's the way he was. Carefree."

"He was a riot, a constant riot all day long," said Ray. "He'd always test you to see how sharp you were. We were at the Apollo. Schiffman said, 'I'm glad you all came this week, but I'm going to be twice as glad when you leave.' They were talking about having a party, getting some liquor, upstairs with the Coasters. Willie says, 'You should all get at least fifty dollars apiece.' He collected money all over the place. He had a handful of money. Then he hollers back upstairs, 'Thank you all for this collection very much. I knew I could be a preacher.' He left out the door with the money. Got in the car and pulled off. The guys were standing there with their mouths open.

"He always said, 'I'm going to just spend my money up. I can't take it with me. I'm gonna spend the hell out of it.' I think in the back of his mind he knew he wouldn't last through this whole thing. That's why he said, 'Nobody will have anything to fight over. They enjoy it with me or they won't enjoy it at all, 'cause I'm spreading it out.'"

"Willie John was a terrible money handler," said Bobby Schiffman. "He would squander his money all over the world. He was always borrowing from people, especially the people who he did business with. When a guy would borrow money and not pay it back, the agents had a way of attaching the salary when they sent us a contract. I signed a contract that was sent to me by the agency, with Willie John's signature on it, that said I was to deduct most of his money and give it to the office to whom he owed the money. Well, Willie came in on draw day and said, 'I'd like to draw $1,500.' I said, 'There's not $1,500 left.' Now I was a young kid at the time. I was directly under my father's tutelage, and damn near afraid to do anything in regard to money unless I checked it. Willie said, 'You're kidding me. Show me the document.' I got out the document and he snatched it out of my hands, crumpled it up and stuck it behind his back. Now I got scared. I thought my father would raise hell with me for losing that document, which was the only copy we had. So, I said, 'Willie, give me the paper.' He said, 'It's my money. I'm not giving you the paper.' Well, I grabbed that little son of a bitch off the ground, picked him up by the collar, swung him against the wall, and held him up there with one hand. I said, 'If you want to come down with all of your teeth, drop the paper. If you want to stay up there and come down without your teeth, hold the paper.' I had a flash of hostility in my eyes, and he knew it. He dropped it."

After 1961 his career faltered, and this, combined with his natural recklessness, led to trouble. He killed a man in a bar fight, and although he claimed self-defense, he was sent to the Washington State Penitentiary for manslaughter in 1966. James Brown and Bobby Schiffman spearheaded an unsuccessful effort to gain his release. Even in jail, Willie John remained his happy-go-lucky self. "The last time I saw him," said St. Clair Pinckney, "me and James and Ben Bart [head of Universal Attractions] went up to the penitentiary. He said, 'I don't think I'm going to get out of here.' He had been sick and was riding in a wheelchair, and he'd say, 'This wheelchair is my pleasure here.' James would get kind of upset about Willie, and Willie would say, 'Don't ever let it worry you that way. 'Cause I might not come out no way. If I get out, I get out. If I stay, I stay. Still gonna be the same man in or out of here.' " He died in prison of pneumonia in 1968, at the age of thirty.

A contemporary of Willie's, and one who had to deal with the pitfalls of stardom at an even earlier age, was Frankie Lymon. Discovered at the Apollo, Frankie and his group, the Teenagers, hit it big with their first record, "Why Do Fools Fall in Love?" a song written by the precocious thirteen-year-old. The song became a tremendous international hit. Leslie Uggams, who grew up in the same Harlem neighborhood as Frankie, remembers him and his group: "All of a sudden they became teenage idols. He couldn't handle it. Then he started with the older women, and it just got all out of proportion. Before he knew it, Frankie was heavily strung out on drugs."

Another teenaged star, who was taken under the wing of the younger Lymon, was Little Anthony. "He was younger," Little Anthony said, "but he was smarter than I was. He was a man. I was a kid. Frankie was a tragedy. He was the hottest thing in the world. He had just come in from playing England—it was the first black group to play for the Queen at the Palladium. He had this tall girl with him. She's got to be twenty-five or thirty years old. He was about fifteen or sixteen. Really, he was that kind of guy. He was way ahead of his time. That's what killed him: too much too soon.

"He was an addict since he was about fifteen. But Frankie, bless his heart, never once ever offered me heroin, not one time." Although he made periodic attempts to kick the habit, Lymon inevitably fell back into addiction. His habit began to affect his performances. One night at the Apollo, Anthony remembers: "He hadn't had any in a long time and he was trying to stay away. But he got mixed up and got some more and went on it one night. He evidently shot up and it took him to another space. It was so bad that—there is a thing where you grow to nod—well, it was that bad and he had to go on, and he walked into a wall. He walked out like this, and everybody knew it. At the time it was no news, even to the audience. I shot a sharp look at him and said, 'Oh, man!' They got him offstage and took him upstairs and Spayne or somebody said, 'He got hold of that stuff again.' That wasn't a performance, that was ridiculous. That was a tragedy." His career sputtered out. At the age of twenty-six, Frankie Lymon, penniless, was found dead of an overdose in a Harlem apartment.

Little Esther Phillips was another teenaged heroin addict, but unlike her unfortunate counterpart, Frankie Lymon, she has managed to constantly battle the habit, and maintain a successful career—reemerging in the early sixties and, again, with a version of Dinah Washington's "What a Difference a Day Makes," in the late seventies. According to Johnny Otis, he discovered her at a theatre in Watts. But she remembers the event occurring at Otis's nightclub in Watts, the Barrel House. "My sister, who's older than me, and her friend wanted some white port and lemon juice," said Esther. "They didn't have any money, and Johnny held amateur shows at the Barrel House, so they dressed me up and put lipstick on me and took me in there. I won first prize."

Otis signed up the thirteen-year-old and recorded "Double Crossing Blues" with her. It became one of the biggest rhythm-and-blues hits of 1950, and she went on the road with Otis. "We were on the road one year," said Esther. "We traveled from Los Angeles all through the South doing one-nighters. Then we ended up in New York City and the Apollo. We had a bus that said 'Little Esther and Johnny Otis' on it. As we rolled down 125th Street people just stopped and stared, because we were going into the Apollo. I remember they had lines and lines of people."

Esther became a major r-and-b star. At a time when a rhythm-and-blues record that sold 100,000 copies was a hit, her "Double Crossing

Blues" sold millions. It was hard for people to come to terms with her youth. "Little Esther's record must have sold two or three million," said Ahmet Ertegun. "I went backstage at the Apollo to see Ruth Brown, and Esther was coming up as the next show; it was Ruth's last show. Ruth said, 'Oh, I want you to meet this little child here.' She said, 'Esther.' Esther said, 'Yes, Miss Brown?' Ruth: 'Come *over* here, Esther. I want you to meet Mr. Ertegun.' I said, 'Don't talk to her like that. This girl sold more records than you and I put together!' "

"We had her dressed like a little Southern girl," said Johnny Otis. "Some people criticized us for that. Well, what's wrong with how a little Southern girl would look? That's what Esther was, a little Southern girl. So after the first couple of shows at the Apollo, Dinah Washington comes backstage. She takes Esther with her, and brings her back with her hair done, high-heel shoes on, nylon stockings, and a form-fitting dress. She looked like she was thirty. Dinah Washington said, 'That's disgraceful, having her look like she's in the cotton fields.' I couldn't tell Esther anything, because Esther was a very precocious child, like a woman at thirteen, and she liked it." Once again, the headiness of early success led to tragedy. Soon after she left Otis in 1952, Little Esther was on heroin. Although she finally kicked the habit as an adult, it continued as a temptation, but Esther Phillips has finally won her battle—one of the few of her peers in show business to do so.

· · · · ·

Although the Apollo itself was relatively drug-free, there were always dealers lurking about the stage door in the alley on 126th Street. The temptation was especially great for the new young stars of the rhythm-and-blues era who had come from the black community. "It was a kind of sad situation," said Leslie Uggams. "Everybody had their problems with their families. Come from the kind of neighborhood I came from, half the time there wasn't a father, or if there was a father, there were nine other sisters and brothers, and nobody paid any attention to you. So, with some people in the business, they finally got the attention they didn't get at home. Or a situation where you're a short guy, and the big guys always bullied you—now all of a sudden you become a big star, and people who didn't respect you, all of a sudden, 'Would you sign an autograph?' The power was like, 'Oh, hey, now I am somebody! I want to be cool. I want them to know it hasn't made my head swell. Oh, what is that you're doing? I'd like to try that.' "

Why was the black community inordinately affected by this problem? And why did it seem that it was so often the successful ones who succumbed? Johnny Otis has a theory: "In the days when [a new star] skyrocketed to success, what kind of scars did he sustain? What kind of self-pity or self-hate or anger or hostility? Let's just assume, let's grant human beings a little bit of selflessness, maybe they care about their people. Maybe they're going good, but maybe their people are not going so good, and maybe they have enough hatred and bitterness in them, as I have. I don't care how long I go on, I'm still going to be mad about those years because my people can't go with me. My children and my grandchildren—I'm constantly reminded that they're behind, and they can't go, and it's unfair, and it's wrong. You almost want to commit suicide to escape the thought.

"When I complain about what has happened to black entertainers—I'm not talking about me. God was good to me. I'm thankful. But this system had pressured so many of us marvelous people, who didn't deserve that. They deserved rewards, not punishment. That is not to say that some people aren't just fools. Everybody isn't moved into a negative life-style because they're black. That's a lot of crap. I don't mean to idealize people unnecessarily, but that has a lot to do with it. That's why there is more dope in the black community. They're sitting ducks. The other answer is that the racists are right: blacks ain't shit. So which one do you go for? I know it's the pressure that makes for more susceptibility.

"I want to go back so you can see the pattern that is cultured in racism. Who was crowned King of Jazz? Paul Whiteman. He couldn't even play. He had some good players in his band, but King of Jazz? That was an outrage, and the black brothers and sisters who created that art form in those days were lucky if they could work in a whorehouse somewhere and pick up a few dollars. Now we move up a little bit to the swing era and the King of Swing is crowned, and he is a white man named Benny Goodman, who is in fact a fine musician, and he had a fine band. But King of Swing? Not Count Basie or Duke Ellington or Jimmie Lunceford or any of an army of black men and women who created the music? Then we come up a little further to the King of Rock and Roll, and that was Elvis Presley, who was a Southern hillbilly kind of thing, and if he could dance I could make a sledgehammer, but a lot of his success was based on his dance. He was a white boy, and he looked good, and he was a sex symbol. He was King of Rock and Roll, based on a black form of music. We know this in the black community, artists are aware of it. We know there's a rip-off. As soon as a black form is created and innovated, soon as we breathe life into it, whitey grabs it and goes with it and starts taking bows as though he invented it; and that's the unkindest cut."

In the fifties the nefarious practice of white performers covering—copying note for note—black r-and-b hits became rampant as rhythm and blues caught on in the white pop market. Since arrangements are not specifically protected by the copyright laws, cover versions could not be stopped. And since the original black versions were not played on the big white radio stations, and could not compete with the heavy promotional support the white cover versions got from the major record companies, the white versions usually became the hits, and the black originals were buried in the charts.

"Unfortunately, white kids took over black man's music and made a lot more money with it than the black performers," said Bobby Schiffman. "There was a vocal group called the Chords who had a record called 'Sh-Boom,' and they were almost at 100,000 records sold. A fellow by the name of Bob Shad at Mercury records decides that the Crewcuts [a white group] should sing 'Sh-Boom.' To show you the power of the white power structure in the music business, Shad had his a-and-r [artist and repertoire] people and his public-relations people start to call disc jockeys all over the country about the recording of the Crewcuts. The Crewcuts hadn't even recorded it yet, and here was a major campaign to let everybody know that the record was coming out by them. Then he called the group into the studio and recorded 'Sh-Boom.' Well, the Crewcuts ended up selling over a million records of 'Sh-Boom' and the Chords ended up at about 120,000."

"That was one of the things that kind of hurts when I look back on it," said Ruth Brown. "A lot of the tunes I did were covered. Unfortunately, at that time music recorded by black artists was called race music and it was only played on certain stations. You couldn't cross over, and it was because of that that when I had a tune like 'Oh, What a Dream,' Patti Page covered it, or 'Mambo Baby' and 'Please Don't Leave Me,' which Georgia Gibbs covered. They went on national TV and sang my songs. I was never even invited. To this day I have never done one: Johnny Carson, Ed Sullivan, Mike Douglas, or Merv Griffin. Never. I think if there was anything that I was uneasy about, it was that, because it diminished my eligibility to expand myself. I wasn't visible."

In addition to singing and playing by white cover artists that was often reduced to pure mimicry, the lyrics were often bowdlerized to make them more palatable to presumably more sensitive white ears. Hence

Etta James's "Roll with Me, Henry" became "Dance with Me, Henry" when covered by the plundering Georgia Gibbs. Perhaps the classic example of a cleaned-up cover version of a hit r-and-b tune was Bill Haley's copy of Big Joe Turner's "Shake, Rattle and Roll." In the original, Big Joe ordered his woman out of bed and into the kitchen to "rattle them pots and pans," but in Haley's version, references to the bedroom were eliminated. "The black community always had an honest, wholesome approach to sexuality," said Johnny Otis. Referring to a verse of "Shake, Rattle and Roll," he continued, " 'You're wearin' those dresses. The sun come shinin' through. I can't believe my eyes, all that mess belongs to you.' Isn't that nice? I think it's beautiful. It's a poetic ghetto version of 'you're beautiful.' And what's wrong with describing feminine pulchritude when you're telling a woman she's beautiful?"

· · · · ·

It would be unfair and incorrect, of course, to imply that all white artists influenced by black rhythm and blues were mere thieves or that their music was inferior and derivative. As whites got into the rhythm-and-blues field and began developing their own brand of music—the sound that became rock and roll—they, too, were featured at the Apollo. Contrary to myth, there was never an attempt to exclude white performers from playing the Apollo during the rhythm-and-blues era. Any act, black or white, with a hit song that appealed to black audiences could find itself on an Apollo bill. Bobby Darin, the Four Aces, Wayne Cochran, the Skyliners, and Jerry Lee Lewis were among the white stars of the fifties who played the Apollo.

The most famous story of a white rocker at the Apollo concerns Buddy Holly, one of the era's greatest songwriters and performers. When he and his group, the Crickets, began their first national tour in 1956, many promoters assumed the group was black, and they were booked into an otherwise all-black show that toured the "Around the World" circuit. In the movie *The Buddy Holly Story* there is a scene in which the Frank Schiffman character is stunned to discover that the group is white and worries about how the Apollo audience will react. It is possible that Schiffman could have mistaken them for an earlier black group called the Crickets, but the then-manager of the Apollo, Leonard Reed, doubts it. As he said, "Frank Schiffman never booked anyone without knowing who they were." However, most of the audience may have assumed Holly was black. But Schiffman certainly knew his audience well enough to not worry about the Crickets' reception—at least not more than with any untried group.

Leslie Uggams remembers seeing Buddy Holly at the Apollo: "I knew his records. You thought, 'Hey, another brother out there doing his number.' Then this white guy comes out and everybody says, 'Oh, that's Buddy Holly!' . . . I had him pictured totally different. You know, here comes this guy with these glasses and funny-looking suit and stuff. I said, 'He's white, isn't he?' But he was terrific. There was something really sexy and wonderful about him, and that's what made it happen. It wasn't that they didn't want any white acts up there. The thing is, as long as they do a great show, that's all the audience cared about."

The Crickets got a good reception on the early leg of their tour, and the group loved playing for black audiences. But they were unprepared for the tough crowd at the Apollo. Until they learned to take out all the stops they could not capture the Apollo audience. "The first time we went on," Cricket Niki Sullivan told Holly's biographer John Goldrosen, "it was a weekday matinee. They opened the curtains and Buddy stepped toward the mike, and there was this large black woman in the front row who said, 'It'd better sound like the record!' You could have heard a pin drop. And after we got through, I don't think five people clapped. The same thing on the evening show, and the next day—nothing. The third day we did our first song and got no response again. So Buddy turned around and said, 'Let's do "Bo Diddley."' And we went into 'Bo Diddley,' cutting up and working our buns off. I was dancing around in a big circle, going through a bunch of gyrations, and Buddy was all over the stage, and Joe B. was bouncing that bass back and forth and laying it down, and I've never seen Jerry work harder on those damn drums. And when we finished that song, the people just went bananas. From then on, we were accepted at the Apollo. Funny what it takes to please some people."

· · · · ·

The song that saved Buddy Holly at the Apollo was a cover of the autobiographical hit of a man who had just broken Pearl Bailey's Apollo house record; the man who had so dazzled a newcomer named Elvis Presley at the Apollo a year before—Bo Diddley. The maverick Chicago-based guitarist developed a thundering style, heavy on the bottom, that was widely copied. Even the great bluesman, Muddy Waters, borrowed—he took Diddley's hit "I'm a Man" and made it his theme song. But

Buddy Holly and the Crickets, 1957. ★ Leslie Uggams: *"I knew his records. You thought, 'Hey, another brother out there doing his number.' Then this white guy comes out and everybody says, 'Oh, that's Buddy Holly!'"*

Bo Diddley, 1973. ★ Bobby Schiffman: *"I remember the first time we had Bo Diddley in the theatre, I thought we were gonna have an uprising. The music was so stimulating to everybody, including me, that it was whipping everybody into a frenzy."*

Diddley, like Big Joe Turner, is stoical about the people who copied him. When asked if he thought Elvis had copied his stage routine he reportedly replied, "If he copied me, I don't care—more power to him. I'm not starving."

Bo Diddley dressed in black, wore a big black Stetson hat, and played a rectangular guitar he had designed for himself. The Apollo crowd was ecstatic. "Bo Diddley played jungle music," said Bobby Schiffman. "He used to have a bridge, and he'd tune his guitar to a chord, and all he'd do was put his finger across all the strings, and that was his chord. I remember the first time we had Bo Diddley in the theatre, I thought we were gonna have an uprising. The music was so stimulating to everybody, including me, that it was whipping everybody into a frenzy. They never heard of anything like that. It was just a complete new, different style of singing. Rock and roll's main ingredient was the beat, and he was the leading exponent of that. To him melody meant nothing, lyrics meant nothing, it was the beat that was infectious. That would drive you crazy. He really set the place on fire."

One who didn't have to worry about being copied, at least not for years to come, was Screamin' Jay Hawkins—because he was years ahead of his time. He was a wild man. "I used to love the Apollo," he said. "Directly across 126th Street there was a house where they sold white lightning, moonshine. They used to make it in the toilet. Used to get it in a little half-pint milk bottle. I used to wait until the last act before I was gonna go on, then I'd shoot across the street and get me some of that white lightning. I'd time myself as I started walkin', drinkin' that stuff. By the time I got in there, near the water fountain backstage at the Apollo, the bottle was empty. I'd set it down there by the water fountain. The guy would call my name, and I'd ease out onstage. By then an explosion went off in my head. Those hot lights on me. Every time I went to the Apollo I used to love to get that white lightning."

Hawkins hit with a tune called "I Put a Spell on You," in 1956. "Alan Freed told me with a song like that you need something weird," said Hawkins. They devised a routine for Screamin' Jay, dressed in a vampire's cape and turban and carrying "Henry"—a skull mounted on a stick—to be wheeled onstage in a coffin, after he had completed a couple of straight numbers. The lights would be blacked out, then the curtain would slowly open, and as red and blue lights blinked, Hawkins emerged from the coffin singing his bloodcurdling tune. "As the curtain opened," Hawkins said, "people began to split. They went up the aisle and out into the street hollerin' and screamin'. As I began to raise the lid of the coffin, they ran over the chairs, jumpin'. They didn't even have time to go the aisle way. One woman tore out the chairs in the Apollo Theatre, and the seats in the Apollo are screwed into the concrete floor. She was bigger than Kate Smith and Mama Cass, and how she wedged herself into that chair I'll never know. She actually wrecked the whole front row. She took some of them chairs with her 'cause there was a gap for a week."

Hawkins carried the coffin wherever he went in a zebra-striped hearse. It so spooked the stagehands at the Apollo that they refused to handle it. To keep the lid from locking, Hawkins used to stick a piece of matchbook in the mechanism. On one occasion at the Apollo, Screamin' Jay asked one of the members of the Drifters to stick a matchbook in the lock on his way down to the stage. "They never did it," said Hawkins. "They waited patiently until I got in the coffin, and they came offstage, slammed the lid, and the sucker was jammed lock tight. That's when I found out you only got three and a half minutes of air in that coffin. When I realized I couldn't get out of the coffin, boy, I got so scared I was cryin', I was cussin', I was prayin'. I had on a white tuxedo, tails, gloves, hat, cane, spats, and all. I had pissed on myself. Then I started kicking and that's what saved me because I knocked it off its display stand and when it hit the floor it busted open. I walked away. The audience thought it was part of the act, and I forgot the words. I commenced to punchin' out every Drifter I ran into. I hit about three of them, and I had my sights on Ben E. King [the lead singer at the time], and he got behind Bob Hall, the electrician. 'It was all a joke,' he said. I said, 'Not when my life was involved. That's no joke.' They didn't show for the last two shows. Took seven years before we started speaking again."

The Drifters were probably the most important group of the rhythm-and-blues era, and their story is intricately entwined with the Apollo. They took their name from the fact that the members had drifted in and out of many different groups. The Drifters' story actually begins with that of another group, Billy Ward and His Dominoes. Ward was a voice teacher who organized the group in 1950 when he brought in seventeen-year-old tenor Clyde McPhatter, who had just won the Amateur Night contest at the Apollo. Both McPhatter and Ward had gospel-singing backgrounds, and when the new Dominoes debuted at the Apollo with the Orioles, the show was tinged with the jubilant fervor of gospel music.

Ahmet Ertegun, the man who signed McPhatter, allowing him to form the Drifters, recalled: "The first time I heard Clyde McPhatter I heard him singing with the Dominoes at the Apollo. I just fell off my

Screamin' Jay Hawkins, 1956. ★ *"As the curtain opened, people went up the aisle and out into the street hollerin' and screamin'. As I began to raise the lid of the coffin, they ran over the chairs, jumpin'. They didn't even have time to go the aisle way."*

Clyde McPhatter with the Drifters at the Apollo,
mid-1950s. ★   Ahmet Ertegun: *"I thought, 'Oh,
my God, that voice is so angelic. It has so much
gospel feeling in it.' "*

chair. . . . A year or so after I heard him I thought, 'Oh, my God, that voice is so angelic. It has so much gospel feeling in it.' " Ertegun went to another Dominoes club engagement, and discovered that McPhatter had been fired the week before. With some difficulty he managed to track him down by phone. "I called him up," said Ertegun. "I said, 'Can you come down?' I couldn't believe it. 'Are you free?' He said, 'Yeah, man, they fired me.' So that was the beginning of the Drifters."

In 1953, McPhatter organized the Drifters, and Jackie Wilson replaced him in the Dominoes. The Drifters immediately hit with "Money Honey," but in 1955 McPhatter went into the army. Upon his discharge he went solo, achieving great success with "Prisoner of Love" and several other songs. He continued on his own into the sixties. The Drifters carried on without him for a while, but by 1958 their record sales slowed, and the group broke up.

However, the group's manager had signed a multiyear appearance contract with the Schiffmans at the Apollo. In order to avoid default, he asked a group called the Five Crowns, headed by Ben E. King, to become the Drifters. Atlantic records assigned two songwriting teams, Jerry Leiber and Mike Stoller, and Mort Shuman and Doc Pomus, to create new songs for the group. They came up with the biggest hits of any of the Drifters' lineups. These included "There Goes My Baby," "This Magic Moment," and "Save the Last Dance for Me." The Drifters successfully met their obligations to the Apollo, and more. After Ben E. King left in 1960, the group reorganized yet again, and continued to produce hits, among them "On Broadway," "Up on the Roof," and "Under the Boardwalk" into the mid-sixties—a time when rhythm and blues had drifted into yet another form of black music, soul.

GOSPEL
AND THE BLUES

··········

Pure blues and gospel are black strains that run through all forms of black music, and American popular music in general. The heart of many swing standards is pure blues. Substitute the word "baby" for "lord" in the lyrics of practically any gospel number and it can become a soul tune. Given the roots of pure blues and gospel, it could have been expected that each would find an audience at the Apollo. However, while gospel did prove to be remarkably popular at the theatre from the mid-fifties to the early sixties, pure blues failed to attract a wide following. Neither the pure blues artists nor the gospel artists were trained show people in the traditional sense, but the basic reason for the failure of one and the success of the other is a matter of show-business style.

Outside the South, the simple, laid-back style of the pure blues artists appealed mainly to intellectuals, black and white—except in places like Chicago that had an important pure-blues heritage. They understood the contribution of pure blues to black culture, and responded enthusiastically. Some have argued that the appeal of pure blues *was* more universal within the black community, but the fact is that the basic Apollo audience responded, for the most part, by staying away from the theatre when pure blues was on the bill.

214

Gospel performers, on the other hand, aimed for excitement; their purpose was to "raise the spirit" and ultimately create a sense of euphoria and release. The gospel artists who played the Apollo were consummate performers, seasoned before throngs of ecstatic fans in churches and auditoriums all along the Gospel Highway, and many of the great gospel singers and quartet leaders boasted voices rivaled only by the greatest opera singers.

The underlying reason for the success of gospel at the Apollo may be traced to the arrival of black slaves in America. "In the early days of slavery," wrote Imamu Amiri Baraka in *Blues People*, "Christianity's sole purpose was to propose a metaphysical resolution for the slave's natural yearnings for freedom, and as such, it literally made life easier for him. . . . The relative autonomy of the developing Negro Christian religious gathering made it one of the only areas in the slave's life where he was relatively free of the white man's domination. . . . The 'praise nights,' or 'prayer meetings,' were also the only times when the Negro felt he could express himself as freely and emotionally as possible."

The "metaphysical resolution" that religion continues to provide blacks is most fervently delivered in the music of the black church. The key words in the gospel message are hope and faith. This, coupled with the anything-goes abandon of the gospel experience, pretty much sums up the essence of the Apollo experience, too.

While gospel portended a hopeful future, the blues (actually a more recent musical development than gospel) was often an unpleasant reminder of the bad old days to many blacks. "I had a blues show at the theatre," said Bobby Schiffman. "B. B. King, Bobby "Blue" Bland, T-Bone Walker, Jimmy Witherspoon, Sonny Terry and Brownie McGhee, and Odetta. The show did very poorly, so I called the cast up to my office on Tuesday and said, 'Hey, let's sit down and bullshit. I want to find out why the show didn't do well, and I want your opinions.' So we sat in my office, and I sent out for coffee and doughnuts and bourbon, and we sat for a couple of hours and talked. . . . I'll tell you why that show did poorly, as exposed by that discussion. Blues represented, at that time, misery. Misery and blues were a throwback to slavery, to a time when the black man, intellectually, was at the lowest point in his history. And black folks from the street didn't want to hear that shit. They came to the theatre to be uplifted, to see the glamour of four-hundred-dollar mohair suits. To see the glamour of the gorgeous gowns, and the hairdos, and the beautiful makeup, and the magnificent sets. The glamour of it all took them away from their own troubles. They didn't want to reminisce or reflect on the troubles that were proposed by the blues. For that reason the blues were never a significantly popular attraction at the Apollo."

. . . . .

What exactly is the blues? B. B. King tried to get to the core of the question in a special 1974 Apollo concert for seven hundred Harlem schoolchildren. "Have you ever been hungry?" he asked the kids. "Have you ever wanted something you couldn't get? Have you ever felt bad because somebody in your family was playing favorites?" Each time the kids shouted back, "Yes!" "Then you had the blues," cried King as he twanged his trusty guitar, "Lucille."

More specifically, the blues is an indigenous black-American musical form that uses basically simple musical structures to impart an often startlingly effective emotional intensity. The blues began after the Civil War in the South and Southwest, where black men, self-accompanied by guitar, harmonica, and later piano, adapted bits and pieces of hymns, work songs, and early American secular songs to produce a music that reflected their difficult lives. The blues followed black work paths from the Mississippi cotton plantations upriver to the lumber and turpentine camps of the Midwest; from the farms and ranches of Oklahoma and Texas to the California oil fields and shipyards; from rural areas to the industrial cities of the North. Although the first recorded blues was the so-called classic blues of Mamie Smith—who inaugurated a vogue for theatrical blues in the early twenties—the great country blues artists actually came along first, but weren't recorded until somewhat later. But, by the late twenties, Blind Lemon Jefferson, Charley Patton, and Son House were all recording and selling briskly. Blues records sold exclusively in black neighborhoods, and they sold in the millions. Some 5,500 blues records involving one thousand black musicians were released between 1920 and 1942.

"I can remember telling Frank Schiffman that the blues were terribly important," said John Hammond. "This was in the forties and late thirties. I was working for the American Record Company in those days, and I was telling him that we had artists like Big Bill Broonzy and Casey Bill Weldon, and all sorts of people from the South and Southwest. Schiffman couldn't have been less interested. He said, 'This is the city and that is the country.' " The Apollo rarely played pure blues artists in the thirties and forties.

One of the exceptions was George "Huddie" Ledbetter, who was better known as Leadbelly. His blues were expressed in age-old work

Leadbelly, late 1930s. ★ *When Frank Schiffman first played him at the Lafayette in 1934, Leadbelly had just been released from prison for attempted murder after having already served another term for murder.*

songs as well as in the pure blues style, but the Apollo's interest in Leadbelly derived less from his musical ability than from his notorious reputation as a hotheaded killer. In fact, when Frank Schiffman first played him at the Lafayette in 1934, Leadbelly had just been released from prison for attempted murder after having already served another term for murder. He was released by the Governor of Louisiana, who was moved by the songs Leadbelly wrote while in prison. When Leadbelly played the Lafayette, Schiffman devised a skit in which the performer, wearing prison garb, sang in a set designed as the governor's office, and the governor, moved by his performance, pardoned him thirty-one times a week. Thanks to the publicity surrounding Leadbelly's personal life, the engagement was a great success.

But two years later, when Leadbelly headlined a show at the Apollo, he was a terrible flop. Schiffman tried to build on Leadbelly's tough reputation once again, but the notoriety apparently had worn off. Also, the calendar and a hostile review did not help matters. "The week before Easter is one of the worst weeks of the whole year in the theatre," wrote the *New York Age*'s reviewer, "the other being the week preceding Christmas. The management of the Apollo, anticipating the small turnout at the box office, has placed a show on the boards that will do its share toward encouraging the folks to stay home and keep Lent." The reviewer hated Leadbelly, but praised pop singer Midge Williams. "Top billing for the show," he wrote, "goes to George Ledbetter, alias 'Lead Belly,' a singing guitarist. The advance publicity stated that this man had been in two jails on murder charges and that the wardens, on hearing him work out on his guitar and vocally, set him free. Maybe they did, but after hearing the man myself, I'm not so sure that musical excellence prompted the two governors' actions. It may have been that both they and other inmates wanted some peace during their quiet hours. No. Lead Belly isn't the man if it's music you want." Leadbelly's poor showing undoubtedly helped form Frank Schiffman's opinion that, as he told John Hammond, the "country" had no place at the Apollo.

Nevertheless, changes in the circumstances of black people were having an effect on the blues. Between the two world wars there was a great migration of blacks from the country to the cities, and the blues made the same transition. A new generation of blues artists emerged from the cities of the Midwest and West. Concurrently, technical changes were taking place in the music world. Great strides were made in the improvement of recording facilities and record pressing. Gone were the crude field recordings and inadequate studio sessions that captured the initial wave of pure blues. Up-to-date urban studios produced a slicker sound.

The greatest technical innovation was the emergence of the electric guitar. This instrument, as employed by Aaron "T-Bone" Walker and, later, Lowell Fulson, created new excitement, and a new sound that came to be known as "city blues." The lines sometimes blurred between the new electric bluesmen and their counterparts in the also new world of rhythm and blues, and some city blues was heard at the Apollo during the r-and-b years. T-Bone Walker, who originated the pyrotechnic dance-as-you-rock style of playing (he played the guitar behind his back and lying on his back before Jimi Hendrix was born), occasionally headlined a show at the Apollo. But most of the new blues artists could not compete with the rhythm-and-blues hitmakers. Even a blues master like Howlin' Wolf was relegated to the bottom of an r-and-b bill.

Johnny Otis ran into this continuing resistance to pure blues when he tried to bring to the Apollo Willie Mae "Big Mama" Thornton, one of his many discoveries, in the early fifties. She had been singing and playing harmonica with a blues band for several years in the South and Southwest when Otis found her. "When I came into the Apollo with Big Mama Thornton, we had no hit records with her," said Otis. "I just found her in Texas and she knocked me out. I took her in the Apollo and they told me, 'Well, you can use her in the South, but a big rough thing like that—great big chick—the audience is not going to dig that.' I thought, 'Bullshit. That's what they told me about rhythm and blues.' I was convinced then, and it was borne out, that the black experience, whether it be in Boston or Mississippi, still had its roots in the South. The things that were sweet to the black souls in Meridian, Mississippi, were sweet to the black souls in Buffalo, New York, with rare exceptions.

"Anyhow, before we played the Apollo, we played Buffalo. We used a great big house, used to have three thousand people in there. I told my manager, 'Watch this.' I brought her out. Whatever it was she started hollerin' and singin', those people went crazy, because it touched them. Some things black people love. The blues. Well, when we got to the Apollo, I was told, 'She can't get up there with those cowboy Texas uniforms on, those mannish things. Get her some gowns.' I said, 'Willie Mae, you wanna wear some gowns?' She said, 'I don't care. If you want me to, I will.'

"I had a woman make her some gowns that were a sheath under-

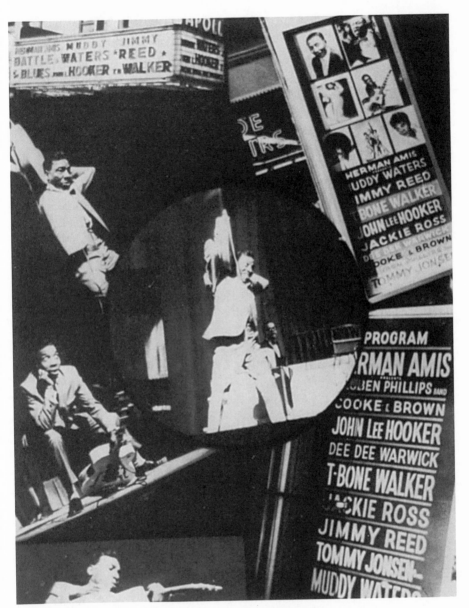

T-Bone Walker, part of a blues show in the mid-1960s. ★ *He originated the pyrotechnic dance-as-you-rock style of playing. He played the guitar behind his back and lying on his back before Jimi Hendrix was born.*

neath with a lace material over it. They were not necessarily form-fitting, but they looked form-fitting, looked nice. She came out in these things in the first show. She started singing the blues, and the people started reacting, and she kicked her legs up and she had them big ole rugged boots under her lace gown. She was really something else. They loved her at the Apollo." Whatever momentum this might have created for the blues at the Apollo dissipated when Big Mama Thornton crossed over and scored her one-and-only r-and-b hit in 1953 with "Hound Dog," the tune that Elvis Presley would co-opt three years later.

Another reason for the dearth of pure blues at the Apollo, at least until Bobby Schiffman's more tolerant regime, was Frank Schiffman's personal distaste for the life-styles of the pure-blues singers and for the subject matter of their songs. Frank Schiffman liked to think he ran a family theatre. He insisted upon at least the decorum of socially acceptable behavior backstage and onstage. He said he was physically afraid of Leadbelly. He could not have been pleased with a bluesman singing about a "black snake crawling around my room" or pleading for his woman to "draw on my cigarette, baby, until my good ashes come."

In one case he fired a well-known bluesman for his open drunkenness. "Jimmy Reed could not sing the blues unless he had a tankard of gin in him," said Bobby Schiffman. "At ten in the morning he'd be guzzling the gin. Well, at twelve-thirty opening day, Jimmy Reed was onstage drunk as a skunk. My father was straight as a dime. There was a legend with my father, if you didn't do your thing, he would pay you off for the day and let you go. Well, Jimmy Reed was stumbling on the stage, so drunk it was incredible. After the show, my father walked backstage. He was mad as a wet hen. Jimmy Reed's manager was standing outside the dressing-room door, arms akimbo. As my father walked up toward the door, he said, 'I know, Mr. Schiffman, he's packing. We're leaving.' So my dad never said a word to him about the reason. The guy knew."

Not until the sixties, when white rock musicians and college students discovered the blues and sparked a revival of pure blues, did the blues become an independent attraction at the Apollo. Bobby Schiffman tried a series of "Blues Nights" that were often critical but not financial successes. The shows featured Bobby "Blue" Bland, John Lee Hooker, Jimmy Witherspoon, Muddy Waters, and the greatest blues attraction at the Apollo—the man whom most people today identify with the blues— B. B. King.

B. B. has been called the "King of the Blues," but hard-core blues aficionados scoff at this title. They point out that he is not one of the blues originators and claim that others have been more innovative. To his credit, King has been a crusader for the blues since the late forties, when he began as host of a popular blues show on Memphis radio station WDIA. There Riley King became known as the Beale Street Blues Boy, a nickname soon shortened to B. B. For years as a performer he fought to keep pure blues alive and strove to have his sound heard before a larger audience. After he opened the ears of rock musicians, he went on to pursue an even wider audience. B. B. put together a slick show band that plays frequently in Las Vegas, where he lives. If "B," as he is affectionately known, did not come to his title of "King of the Blues" by rights, then he has certainly earned it through his ceaseless efforts on behalf of the music.

B. B. King had two potent weapons that he used to keep the Apollo audience in his grasp: his husky blues-drenched voice and Lucille, his beloved red Gibson guitar that becomes a second voice in his hands. Phyl Garland caught a 1969 B. B. King performance at the Apollo, and in *The Sound of Soul* she described the scene as King launched into "You Done Lost Your Good Thing Now":

"He begins the phrase at a high falsetto, easing down through a series of flatted blue notes into his mellow mid-range, turning his head to the side, shaking it in disbelief and grimacing at the ingratitude of this invisible woman. Squeals of delight at recognition of this common human plight issue from the audience as he repeats the statement in slightly altered form, building up to a tortured confession. Women shout out, 'No! No! Don't *do* it B. B.!' Men, seeming to identify completely with the situation, vocally nod their agreement, 'Man, do your *thing*, B. B.! All *right!*' At this, he turns to Lucille and lets her tell the story for herself as he makes the guitar speak with an almost human voice, crying, pleading, giving rise to a deliciously unbearable state of tension by repeating musically simple constructs of bent and sustained notes that are, somehow, hypnotic in their effect."

Still, B. B. has felt, "There is a fear of being identified with this music." In a dressing-room interview with a *New York Times* reporter after his 1974 children's concert at the Apollo, he said, "It's my belief that the reason they don't identify with the blues is because nobody tells them about it. The blues people have been treated like the blacks have been—unfairly, and for me it was almost like being black twice."

· · · · ·

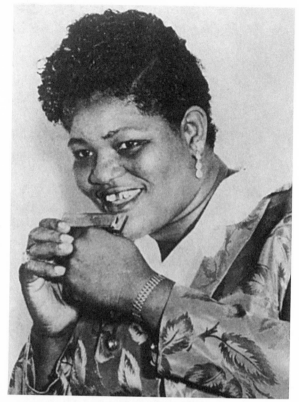

Willie Mae "Big Mama" Thornton in the early 1950s. ★ Johnny Otis: *"When we got to the Apollo, I was told, 'She can't get up there with those cowboy Texas uniforms on, those mannish things. Get her some gowns.' I said, 'Willie Mae, you wanna wear some gowns?' She said, 'I don't care. If you want me to, I will.'"*

B. B. King in a recent shot. ★ *"The blues people have been treated like the blacks have been—unfairly, and for me it was almost like being black twice."*

Committed gospel singers not only identified themselves with their music and religion, they *were* their music, for singing the gospel was doing God's work. In the beginning it was a purely religious music based on old spirituals and hymns that paid no heed to changing popular tastes or musical styles. It was a natural part of the lives of most black people and was the oldest musical form created by blacks in America.

The most popular early gospel music, at least in the relatively more staid and conservative black Baptist and Methodist churches, was the old English "Dr. Watts" hymns, written by a number of writers, but named after the most prolific hymn writer, Isaac Watts. Moving *a cappella* hymns like "Amazing Grace" and "The Day Is Past and Gone" continue as standards in any gospel repertoire. The congregations singing these hymns punctuated them with moans or humming that emphasized certain personally important phrases or passages in an inner-directed display of feeling. However, the newer Sanctified churches, including the Holiness and Pentecostal sects, sang in a much freer and even more uninhibited style. When they got the feeling they shouted it. While the Baptists and Methodists "raised the spirit" through preaching and singing, the Sanctified often created the same feeling with music alone. When Sanctified churchgoers "get happy" they scream and wail, dance and shake, speak in tongues, faint, fall to the floor in contortions, and "excite" each other to peaks of bliss and ecstasy—just like Apollo theatregoers would in the gospel shows of the fities and sixties.

Gospel entered the modern age in the thirties when even the most committed gospel believer could no longer afford to ignore the important black popular music that competed for the attention and interest of the black community. Thomas A. Dorsey, formerly a blues singer known as Georgia Tom, who was famous for his double-entendre lyrics, got religion and changed the course of gospel music. He took the majesty of the Dr. Watts hymns, coupled it with the fire of the Sanctified beat, and couched it in the feeling of the popular music of the day. He and his partner, Sallie Martin, also introduced a professional ethic into the world of gospel music. Many talented writers and soloists pumped new energy into it, and gospel moved out of the local churches, as dozens of singers and groups began to record and tour churches and religious conventions around the country.

Most of the great gospel solo performers were women. The traditional outlet for male gospel performers was the gospel quartet. These groups, which sometimes comprised more than four members even though they were always called quartets, used to be a part of the church choir. As gospel groups began to travel in the thirties, the quartets broke off on their own. The top quartets—the Dixie Hummingbirds, the Soul Stirrers, and the Golden Gate Quartet—became the most popular and exciting gospel performers.

Sometimes their message outshined the preacher's. "We started singing in churches every Sunday night before our ministers would preach," said Thurman Ruth, leader of the Selah Jubilee Singers, and the man who was responsible for bringing gospel to the Apollo. "We were broadcast on all four radio stations in Brooklyn, and when we'd sing, the church would be jammed. After we'd sing, most of the folks would get up and go out before the preaching. Then we got a lady minister and she switched it around. She'd let us sing after she'd preached, and the people would still be there."

Despite the popularity of the new gospel music, very few of its practitioners would consider bringing their music into a place like the Apollo. Even though Frank Schiffman may have tried to run a family theatre, most religious blacks considered the Apollo to be a place of sin. Clayton Riley, the writer, remembered an elderly neighbor woman preaching to him that "the Apollo is the devil's house, young man; righteous folks don't go in there and sinners can't hardly find their way out." The greatest gospel soloist of all time, Mahalia Jackson, never appeared at the theatre even though the Schiffmans and her friend, Thurman Ruth, repeatedly tried to convince her that an Apollo appearance would benefit her and her followers.

From the late thirties until the institution of the gospel shows in the mid-fifties, virtually the only gospel singer to play the Apollo was Sister Rosetta Tharpe. As a youngster, "Little Sister" learned to play the guitar and toured the country with the first wave of professional gospel performers. Although she married a preacher in 1934, and was a deeply religious person, she had a natural affinity for jazz. In 1938, still something of an oddity, she joined the Cab Calloway band at the Cotton Club, where she sang decidedly secular tunes such as "Rock Me" and "Pickin' the Cabbage."

She played the Apollo a number of times with Calloway, and then with Lucky Millinder, with whom she recorded "Trouble in Mind." By the early forties she was a popular soloist, usually performing swinging jazz numbers, but by the mid-forties she returned to a religious repertoire. Sister Rosetta remained true to her love of jazz, too. When she

The Golden Gate Quartet. ★ *The top quartets became the most popular and exciting gospel performers.*

The Selah Jubilee Singers, with Thurman Ruth, in the 1940s. ★ *"We were broadcast on all four radio stations in Brooklyn, and when we'd sing, the church would be jammed."*

thrilled the Apollo audience with inspirational songs like "Jesus Is Here Today" or "How Far from God," she was often accompanied by jazz greats like George "Pops" Foster, the bassist, or Kenny Clarke, the pioneering bebop drummer.

In the late forties, Sister Rosetta Tharpe and other gospel performers, like the Pilgrim Travelers and the Five Blind Boys, turned their gospel sound into hit records that made the rhythm-and-blues charts. By 1950 gospel had become the hottest black musical form. Yet the moral conventions of the gospel life-style prevented the sound from being heard in theatres like the Apollo.

While gospel was whipping congregations around the country into frenzies, rhythm and blues was becoming such a popular attraction that the Apollo, and then other theatres, began featuring the r-and-b revues consisting of one group after another performing their hit songs. It was inevitable that someone would think of combining the power and popularity of gospel with the successful rhythm-and-blues revue format.

That someone was Thurman Ruth. "I was a deejay on WOV in New York when I got the idea of 'Gospel Caravan,'" said Ruth. "I was with the Selah Singers, too. After we had rehearsal one day I told the fellas, 'I got an idea. I'm going to see Mr. Schiffman at the Apollo Theatre about putting gospel in like the rock-and-roll shows.' The fellas laughed at me. It had never been done. Nobody had ever gone into the Apollo Theatre with gospel. They thought I was crazy. I went to see Mr. Schiffman, and he laughed, too. He said, 'I don't think gospel will go here. They'll probably just throw eggs at you.' But he gave me a chance and told me to come back in two weeks. When I went back, he consented."

Ruth faced another, more difficult obstacle—convincing other gospel performers that playing the Apollo would be appropriate and morally correct. "Gospel at that time was considered to be sacred," he said. "Some of the groups wouldn't go in the Apollo Theatre. Even some of the preachers talked against me going into the Apollo. 'You're taking gospel into a theatre'—that was the main concern of the preachers and some of the groups. 'You're going into the Apollo, and you know it's sinning.'

"I had to tell the folks on my bill that I believed you could sing spirituals anywhere. I didn't like to change their opinion, but I believed spirituals *would* go anywhere. I once heard a minister say, and it always sticks with me, 'You want to catch a fish, you don't go to the market where the fish is already. You go to the sea; that's where you catch them.' That's the way it was with me during the theatre days. You reach all kinds of people. Those folks may never go to a church, but they were touched. God said, 'Go into the hedges and highways and compel men to come.' Folks that heard my show at the Apollo maybe left there and went to church." Or, as Bobby Schiffman put it: "The theatre's a place of sin and iniquity. But what we sold the gospel performers, and what the gospel performers sold the audience was: It makes no difference what the building is like where you worship God, and if you're here to worship God you don't have to worry that it's in a theatre that last week had shake dancers in it."

There were purely temporal temptations that finally persuaded most gospel performers to give Thurman Ruth's Apollo Gospel Caravan a try. "To get the groups," said Ruth, "I had to assure them that this would be the first time they would ever be presented in a great way. Beautiful stage, great lighting and acoustics. Above all, this was the first time they were guaranteed to have money, and knew they were going to get it regardless of whether the show was a flop or not. Usually, if you played a church or auditorium or something and the people were not there, you didn't get the money. The guy that promoted you usually didn't have money that he could pay out of his pocket. But in this case, Mr. Schiffman guaranteed the money, and he and I had a deal on the profits. I came out of the Apollo a few times with $2,000 for my part alone. The groups were paid nice money. One group in those days could make $3,000 for a week's engagement."

Thurman Ruth's Gospel Caravan made its debut at the Apollo on December 15, 1955. Ruth tried to maintain a churchlike atmosphere for the Apollo gospel shows—not pious, but joyous. All the performers on the bill stood or were seated on the stage throughout the show, helping and supporting each other just as they would in a church concert. To insure the shows had the broadest appeal to blacks of different denominational backgrounds, he featured all types of religious singing: gospel, jubilee, and spirituals. "Jubilee singing is almost what it says," Ruth explained. "Jubilation that's fast, a joyous medium. Gospel is a kind of slow thing with lots of preaching. Gospel, they almost talk it more than they sing it. Spirituals is the old traditional spirituals that started off everything. 'Swing Low, Sweet Chariot' kind of spirituals when slaves weren't allowed to even think of riding in a chariot. In the gospel world they go by the one who's able to shout the people—get folks happy. Jubilee singers, we didn't go for that much. We went for rhythm. We were entertainers. But for gospel, they feel better when they get somebody to shout or get some kind of emotion—amen or hallelujah. We had both kinds on the bill."

Most who witnessed the gospel shows at the Apollo agree that they were the most stimulating and exciting shows ever seen at the theatre. "People would get overwhelmed," recalled Dionne Warwick, whose mother was a member of the gospel-singing Drinkard Sisters. "They'd fall out of the balconies. It's true. It's not like a rock show. This goes a step further because you're emotionally involved in the spirit of God, and that makes it quite apart from anything else you've been involved in. I have seen my Aunt Rebbie literally roll in a dusty old storefront church, and not have a speck of dust on her when she got up. That is being in the spirit. I've seen her run into a wall, and not have a bruise on her. So when I say fall out of the balcony at the Apollo, it didn't bother me at all. It was just the arms of God wrapped around her. The girl was not acting. There were people who fainted. I personally cry—dance for God. There are people who wring themselves about. It's true. They had nurses to bring you around with smelling salts."

"The gospel shows were great," said Beverly Lee of the Shirelles. "You'd go there and it would be like in church, there would be such a spirit in the building. The songs they sang would reach you and touch somebody special in the audience, or a group of many people, and it just felt like the ceiling was gonna burst open. People would faint. You'd get overexcited, or we'd get happy and shout. The gospel acts would put on outstanding performances, theirs were different from ours. They just stood there and sang from the bottom of their toes or something. Seemed like it just came up, and the notes they hit were incredible. It was very, very moving."

The emotion and hysteria were real, according to Bobby Schiffman, at least mostly. "We had to have a couple of nurses in case anybody got sick," he said. "The Holy Spirit brought about tremendous mental and physical exhaustion. People would pass out in the middle of a song. Somebody would jump up and scream and take off like a shot, and the white man had never seen that before. That's commonplace in the church, but what you had to be careful of was that they didn't go into a spastic convulsion. It was not theatrics at all. It was genuine, really genuine. Now there was some theatrics, I'm sure the Holy Spirit did not arrive at 12:30, 3:30, 6:30, and 9:30 every day; yet always, in every show, the Holy Spirit would arrive. Some of the artists, I am sure,

Sister Rosetta Tharpe at the Apollo, 1941. ★ *She played the Apollo a number of times with Cab Calloway, and then with Lucky Millinder, with whom she recorded "Trouble in Mind." By the early 1940s, she was a popular soloist.*

The Staple Singers, in the 1970s. Thurman Ruth introduced them to New York at the Apollo.

although I can't document it, and don't know it to be a fact, enacted the arrival of the Holy Spirit."

"It was a reality, but it was showmanship, too," said Thurman Ruth. "The audience would know what to do and when to do it. They'd hold onto their pocketbooks. I used to tell them, 'I know this lady was real happy. She threw her pocketbook and didn't know where the money was going.' No, you didn't have any plants in the audience." With a smile, he added, "But there are certain groups that had certain folk. Maybe the Silvertone Singers carried their thing. The Soul Stirrers carried their fans."

The enthusiasm and emotion of the performers and audience were real enough to create havoc with the Apollo's show schedules. "In the theatre timing is so important," said Bobby Schiffman. "You do four, five, six shows a day, you have to stay on schedule. Well, the gospel shows had a way of throwing the schedules out of whack because when the Holy Spirit arrived, the theatre would take off into pandemonium, and time went by the wayside. It was something you could not control. One day I was sitting in the rehearsal hall and our production manager, Leonard Reed, was telling the gospel people about the importance of time in the theatre, and how it was extremely relevant that they stay on schedule. If you were allotted sixteen minutes, you should stay within it, and not thirty-six minutes. Because when the Holy Spirit came—it was takeoff time. Alex Bradford, who was one of the key gospel singers of the time, said, 'Listen, Mr. Reed, what do we do if the Holy Spirit arrives?' And Leonard said, 'Make sure He leaves by the end of the record, that's all.'"

"The groups never came off on time," said Thurman Ruth. "Most of the time the spirit would get them, and instead of singing ten minutes, they'd sing twenty-five minutes, thirty-five minutes. Some of them would stay almost an hour. But at the Apollo, I began to see that they *were* off on time. That taught them something. Get off on time, because I didn't want to go overtime. The last show, especially—you had to pay the stagehands overtime."

Excitement, not precision, was the key to the gospel shows, and the presentations were designed to thrill the audience right away and get them involved in the show. "We liked to open with a bang—give a nice fast opening," said Ruth. "I learned that from my disc-jockey days. Give a good balance; but first of all, we'd get a nice song that everyone could sing together when the curtains opened. Everybody would come on. All

231

the groups would come onstage. We had chairs out on the stage with that church atmosphere. Everybody would be singing that opening song, 'Glory Hallelujah' or 'Since I Laid My Burdens Down' or whatever. After that they introduced me as the master of ceremonies, and I'd bring the first act on. Each group used to push one another. If one group was singing, the other group was clapping or they would help you amen or something to help you out. This was cooperative. Everybody wanted to see everybody go big."

Nearly everybody who was anybody in the world of gospel music played the Apollo gospel shows at one time or another. Thurman Ruth has ranked the Swanee Quintet as "the greatest singing group that I had at the Apollo. They were terrific. I had them with another big-name group and the big name was closing. But the Swanee Quintet was so tough that I had to let them close the show. The other group was complaining all the time.

"I saw the Swan Silvertone Singers do something at the Apollo that I've never seen any other group do. The Caravans with Albertina Walker were closing the show. This was the original Swans when they were in their prime, with Reverend Claude Jeter. They had so many folks shouting and getting happy that the Caravans and Albertina Walker couldn't even go on. It was just curtain time. Just cut the last act off. They couldn't go on, the Caravans—they were out there with the Swan Silvertones and were shouting and happy themselves. Albertina Walker and the Caravans were from Chicago. They were real big. So many fine ladies came out of her group: Shirley Caesar, she made a lot of contributions, Inez Andrews was with them. Dorothy Norwood. Cassietta George. They worked so well together.

"The late Alex Bradford, I brought him in; he was on my first show. Bradford was always a winner. He was always a showman. A great singer, maybe not the best singer in the world, but he was a great singer. 'I'm Too Close to Heaven' was his big record. He went over very big at our first show. The Dixie Hummingbirds were one of my favorites. Ira Tucker was one of the greatest lead singers. They were my favorite singers. To me, they weren't real gospel, though, they weren't pure gospel. Today they are a long way from being pure gospel. They did that thing with Paul Simon, 'Love Me Like a Rock.' That group always wanted to do rock.

"Ira Tucker was with me when I first saw a group that I introduced to New York at the Apollo—the Staple Singers. When I was a deejay in

New York I wouldn't even play their songs because they sounded so countrylike, so down home. I was on vacation in Chicago, and the Dixie Hummingbirds were staying in the hotel. Ira Tucker, my good friend, said, 'Brother Ruth, let's go down and hear the Staple Singers.' I had never heard them in person, and I went down to some church with Ira Tucker and heard Mavis Staples [the youngest of the Staples girls, who sang bass]. Man, I never heard anything like that in my life. She tore the church up. I booked them right away for the Apollo and about three or four weeks later I brought them to New York. I know why the whites like them, because they were like folk singers. Some of their stuff, like 'On a Cloudy Day,' was real old-timey. Old-time folk singing. But they were different, and that's what really made them go over. Folks at the Apollo liked them. They worried me that they wanted to headline a show. So I booked them as a headline act six or eight weeks later. That's when they really got started.

"I brought Aretha Franklin to New York for the first time—she and her father, Reverend C. L. Franklin—from Detroit. He was one of our greatest Baptist preachers, one of the greatest revival ministers. He used to make a lot of records, and his records were more successful than anyone else. Folks used to get him to come to different towns to preach. Aretha was doing gospel with him, and she would come along. I was playing his record on my radio show, and I called him up and brought him to the Washington Temple Church in Brooklyn. Never played the Apollo. Aretha asked me to bring her on a gospel show, but before I got a chance to do it she left gospel and got on to other things.

"Now Clara Ward used to tour with Reverend Franklin. The folks used to come out to the Apollo to see the Ward Singers dress. They were great singers, and they'd dress fabulously, and their hairpieces were so nice. A group might outsing them, but they couldn't outdress them. They were real showmen. You knew that from the shows they went on—they went out to Vegas and places like that. They used to go back to the old landmark singing and shouting and stuff in the service of the lord. But the dressing was what really put them over. Clara was kind of ahead of her time. They had a big Rolls-Royce, or some big car. She was pretty smart. She paid some news guy to do public relations. The average gospel group at the time didn't know too much about public relations. Clara kept something about her or the Ward Singers in the papers all the time.

"Then I found an organist from Chicago who was terrific. Maceo

Woods. He used to do a thing at the Apollo with 'Amazing Grace,' and he used to take that organ and make it talk. He would talk about hearing 'Amazing Grace' when he was a youngster. He'd tell about how his mother used to take him to church, and how they would be walking—and he'd make that organ walk. Boom, boom, boom. Then he'd tell how in the morning before they went to church, his mother would be dusting around the house. He'd be playing 'Amazing Grace,' and he had a key to the organ. He hooked that key and that note would just be holding. And he'd get up and around dusting with his pretty white handkerchief like his mother used to do years ago. Then when they'd get near the church, the lightning would be flashing and the thunder roaring, and he'd make that organ sound just like that. The folks would be getting happy and falling out. The people went wild."

The success of Thurman Ruth's Gospel Caravan at the Apollo soon attracted competitors, like Doc Wheeler and Fred Barr from WWRL, who brought in their own gospel packages to the Apollo with many of the same performers. But it was usually a friendly competition. "I'd come by when they were there, and they'd come by when I had my show," said Thurman Ruth. "I'd introduce them. It was a friendly thing." However, one time things got "crossed up" and Barr and Wheeler were booked for the same time as Ruth. "I said, 'If I can't have my date I'm going to do my shows anyway.'" He opened the same day at Lawson's Auditorium just down the street from the Apollo on 125th Street near Third Avenue. "We both didn't make any money, but I didn't have the expense Schiffman had. From then on, he respected me more." Was Schiffman trying to make a better deal with the competition? "Maybe so," said Ruth.

A change was coming, though. The Soul Stirrers, another important quartet, had lost its founder and most important lead singer, R. H. Harris, by the time of the Apollo gospel shows. Harris was replaced by a young singer who would have a dramatic impact on the world of gospel and, ultimately, pop and soul music—Sam Cooke.

The gospel quartets, especially the Soul Stirrers, profoundly influenced rhythm-and-blues groups like the Dominoes and the Drifters, and later soul music in general. Harris was responsible for introducing and popularizing the falsetto voice in gospel music, an innovation that became an important element of the r-and-b and soul styles. He was a deeply religious man, committed to the fundamentals of gospel, and by 1951 he had become disillusioned with what he perceived as a trend toward showmanship in the gospel world. He was most upset with the

RIGHT: Clara Ward, in the mid-1950s. ★ Thurman Ruth: *"The folks used to come out to the Apollo to see the Ward Singers dress. A group might outsing them, but they couldn't outdress them."*
BELOW: The Soul Stirrers with Sam Cooke (bottom), in the early 1950s. ★ Thurman Ruth: *"They'd jump onstage. The women used to just go crazy when [Sam] walked out there."*

debauchery and womanizing that often accompanied the popular quartets. "That was happening with a lot of gospel folk," said Thurman Ruth. "Now, I was a pretty nice-looking guy myself. Women gonna always come after you, you know. Some guys were popular. There was always one or two in the group; what we called 'sweet men.'"

When Harris left that year, Sam Cook replaced him. He was just nineteen and had the clean-cut, but devilishly handsome look of every young black girl's dream boy next door. This, combined with his fresh tenor and part-moaned-part-yodeled vocal embellishments, packed the kids into the Apollo gospel shows. When he sang gospel favorites like "Touch the Hem of His Garment," "they'd jump onstage," said Thurman Ruth. "The women used to just go crazy when he walked out there."

In 1956, against the wishes of the other Soul Stirrers, he recorded a pop song, "Loveable." Although he used the pseudonym Dale Cook, and the song was not a hit, he was committed to pop, and his new career took off. Bobby Schiffman was instrumental in the decision of Cooke (now spelling his name with an *e*) to leave gospel: "He and I were very good friends," said Bobby. "It was easy to see the charismatic reaction he evoked from audiences at the gospel shows at the Apollo. I used to talk to him about going into pop music because the remuneration levels were much higher. When he finally decided to go, he gave me a call, and I called Larry Auerbach at the William Morris office. But they never heard of Sam Cooke. They had no eyes for gospel music, it was strictly a black thing, and they were not heavily involved in black music. But I urged Larry to sit and talk with Sam Cooke, and he eventually signed him. And Sam Cooke became one of their mainstays."

"Sam started the crossover to rock," according to Ruth, who, like others of his generation, calls rhythm and blues and soul "rock." "He just got this idea to do some rock, and he went for it and was a big hit. Made a lot of big money. Gospel people and gospel is a great thing, and I love it, but it don't pay off materially like the rock and roll. If you sell 5,000 or 10,000 gospel records that's a hit. If you sell 10,000 rock-and-roll records, that's nothing. The money, that's what changes most people. They're looking out for the money, trying to get more money."

The crossover from gospel to soul music was one of the most important developments in popular music in the sixties. Nearly all soul singers had some gospel singing in their backgrounds, and many moved, like Sam Cooke, from professional gospel to soul. The gospel element is what made soul music such a buoyant, vital sound.

The Apollo was a catalyst for this development because it was virtually the only place where gospel people and soul people met on common ground. "Anytime I'd look over the audience and see a rock-and-roll singer," said Thurman Ruth, "I'd invite him up, and they'd come up and do a number. Most of these guys had done gospel. James Brown in his heyday came up and sang 'Our Father Who Art in Heaven.' One day I introduced Brook Benton. Jackie Wilson came by one day and sang a song for me. Everybody loved gospel."

"Sam Cooke and I wrote 'I'm Alright' in the basement of the Apollo," recalled Little Anthony. "I was influenced by the gospel singers there. The Imperials needed something to make that audience come up out of their seats. The thing you do in church is reach their sensitivity mark, the emotional thing that they can relate to. I remembered a gospel thing we used to do in church, and I said, 'Wait a minute.' I told my guitar player, 'Give me that thing that we do in church, you know, that run that everybody gets up on.' We worked on it in the Apollo. I called it, from an emotional standpoint, 'I'm Alright.' It became a legend with the Imperials. I just did a gospel thing, and fell to my knees and started reaching. Then I really got into God. I went to my old gospel roots and my emotion went into the audience, and it totally blew the Apollo down. Mr. Schiffman had guards to keep the girls from jumping me. We were the first to do that sort of emotional thing. The Isley Brothers learned from us and did 'Shout' "—the record that established their reputation as gospel-in-soul wailers.

At first, "I'm Alright" was a nearly pure gospel tune with few set lyrics; then Frank Schiffman and Sam Cooke interceded. Little Anthony recalled, "We used to have big mikes, and the other artists would clap and sing in the background and make it even more exciting. The Old Man loved it. He said, 'I got you some words.' I don't know if Sam volunteered or what, but Mr. Schiffman said, 'I want you to go down and practice with Sam. He's gonna put some words to it.' So Sam took a little paper and started writing: 'When my baby holds me in her arms—I'm alright, I'm alright. When I taste her many charms—I'm alright, I'm alright.' So it went from a religious gospel thing to what you see today—realizing that you can take an emotional thing and turn it from a spiritual thing to a sensual thing. We opened up a can of worms that I regret to this day."

As with Anthony, many gospel artists or gospel-influenced performers had a difficult time dealing with the moral dilemma of crossing over from gospel. "To me gospel was very big; that was the epitome of show business," said Maxine Brown, a soul singer who started singing gospel with the Charles Taylor Singers at the Apollo. When she debuted as a professional soul singer, she had second thoughts. "I thought I was committing a sin. The church didn't approve and you can't imagine what happened, being out there as a single in rock and roll, as they would call it. My mother had passed away by the time I became a single. Had she lived she would never have come to see me. I really ripped myself for a long time. Even though I had a big record, I still whipped myself for being on the devil's side, as they call it. I still have some regrets. I still get that feeling."

Despite the conflict of conscience, more and more singers made the move from gospel to commercial soul music. By the early sixties, the gospel shows had lost their unique allure. Soul music took the gospel rhythm and feeling and secularized its message to create a broader appeal that attracted a far larger audience—both black and white. "The novelty wore off and they just weren't productive [financially]," Bobby Schiffman has said of the Apollo's gospel shows. But it was more than that: gospel had lost its soul to soul.

7

THE SIXTIES

. . . .

They had waited for hours on lines that stretched for blocks around the Apollo. On an October evening in 1962 there was no more exciting way for these freshly scrubbed black kids dressed in their finest apparel to spend an evening. At last they were inside, their eager faces turned toward the stage in anticipation, knowing they were to witness something spectacular. They cheered the band's instrumental warm-up numbers and the Hortense Allen dancers. Then the moment they had been waiting for arrived.

The master of ceremonies strode on stage and announced: "So now, ladies and gentlemen, it's *Startime*! Are you ready for *Startime*?" An explosive *"Yeah!"* greeted him. "Thank you kindly," replied the m.c. as he began his lengthy buildup. "It is indeed a great pleasure to present to you at this particular time, nationally and internationally known as the 'Hardest-Working Man in Show Business,' the man who sings 'I'll Go Crazy.' . . ." There was a flourish of trumpets, and the audience roared in recognition. " 'Try me' . . ." As each song was announced, the trumpets blared in crescendo, and the crowd screamed. Finally, after eight more titles, the m.c. bellowed, "Mr. Dynamite, the amazing Mr. 'Please, Please' himself—the star of the show, *James Brown and the Famous Flames!*"

Instantly the Flames launched into a rapid instrumental break, and the kids in the Apollo erupted as, seconds later, James Brown bounded on stage. When he grabbed the mike, the music abruptly stopped. "You know I feel alright," he moaned. "You know I feel alright, children." Then wailed, *"I feeeeeel aaalriiiiiiiight!!"*

As all twenty-two members of the band fell in behind him, James Brown reached out, grabbed the ecstatic kids in the Apollo audience, and lifted them out of the ghetto to a place where everything was alright.

For much of the sixties, James Brown owned the Apollo Theatre outright. With this devastating 1962 show, he made his down payment. He had been around since the mid-fifties when, as a down-and-out singer with a gospel background, he appeared on the theatre's Amateur Night. Gradually, from his destitute youth in rural Georgia, he worked his way up to a talented rhythm-and-blues attraction backing up Little Willie John, Etta James, and Hank Ballard and the Midnighters at the Apollo, then to a powerful entertainer who relentlessly rehearsed his outfit until it was the premier r-and-b show band on the chitlin' circuit of Southern and ghetto theatres. He earned the nickname "The Hardest-Working Man in Show Business" by playing over three hundred nights a year, doing spectacular shows.

"We started going to the Apollo Theatre regularly," said Danny Ray, who has been Brown's m.c. for over twenty years, "and the crowds started building, because they knew one thing. If you go, you know he's going to stay an hour and a half or two hours onstage. You will get your money's worth out of it. And this reputation began to build."

"He always worried about that," added St. Clair Pinckney, Brown's longtime band director. "Take less money and spend more time onstage. Because he said, 'If they don't see you, actually see you perform, give it all, then why go?' Get this type of feel onstage and you'll get the money later."

Sam Cooke had sex appeal, Jackie Wilson wowed crowds with his acrobatics, Screamin' Jay Hawkins knew how to shout, but nobody put it all together like James Brown. Dressed in one of his hundreds of self-designed outfits, hair piled high on his head, he would plead, "please, please, please," fall to his knees, then jump up, spin around, scream "aaahoo" into the mike, hydroplane to the left then the right, and finally crash to the floor in his trademark split, seemingly spent. Danny Ray would rush out and drape a royal cape of shimmering velvet over King James's shoulders, and he and a band member would attempt to help the

James Brown in the mid-1960s. ★ *Dressed in one of his hundreds of self-designed outfits, hair piled high on his head, he would plead, "please, please, please," fall to his knees, then jump up, spin around, scream "aaahoo" into the mike, hydroplane to the left then the right, and finally crash to the floor in his trademark split, seemingly spent.*

exhausted Brown up. But "Mr. Dynamite" would shake off the robe, wave his aides away, and bounce back for more.

"From the first note things would be jumping," said Ray. "He'd come out onstage with his red tails and white bucks and start dancing, and the crowd would go wild. The minute they'd see us in town they knew it was gonna be excitement."

It was precisely that excitement that Brown hoped to capture when he decided to record his October 1962 Apollo show. The idea of a live soul album was new at the time, but Brown believed it would be the best way to represent his sound—especially at the Apollo. "Sid Nathan, head of King Records, said, 'You gotta be crazy to do that,' " according to Danny Ray. "James replied, 'Sometimes it makes sense to do something crazy.' " Brown had to put up his own money to make the record.

The fans who packed the Apollo for this engagement were not notified that the event was being recorded, so the response was spontaneous. "[Brown] said, 'I guess you're wondering why you see all these mikes and stuff around,' " recalled St. Clair Pinckney. " 'In case you're wondering about it, we're recording, and ninety percent of it is over with already. So do whatever you want.' "

The audience response was so overwhelming that the engineer actually had problems minimizing certain reactions. "There were quite a few young ladies down front," said Pinckney. "They were naturally into the music. In this one tune this little girl kept saying over and over again, 'Sing it, shit! Goddamn it, sing it!' The engineer worked four days trying to minimize that little statement."

The resulting album, *The Apollo Theatre Presents James Brown*, was released early in 1963 and rocketed up the charts. Black radio stations played the record, all of it, over and over, for months. It remained on the *Billboard* charts for an unprecedented sixty-six weeks. From then on, James Brown and the Apollo Theatre were forever linked, and Brown became a superstar.

James Brown smashed all attendance records at the Apollo. "He's probably done more business there than anyone," said Scoey Mitchlll. "James told me once years ago he knew he'd never be a class act, but he said he was going to be the biggest rock-and-roller they ever had. And he was. You know how you talk to performers and you say, 'How's it going?' and they say, 'It rained all the fucking time we were at the Apollo.' I said, 'If they want to see you, there's no reason why they won't.' I saw them lined up around the block, in the cold driving rain, snow on the ground, to get in the Apollo to see James Brown."

Building on his success, James Brown did what few other black performers had ever done—gain complete control of his own career. He formed his own production company, demanded and got a percentage of all his shows, and controlled his stage presentation. No one could tell him what to do. Even at the Apollo where the Schiffman authority normally was unquestioned, Brown had his way.

In the early sixties he insisted upon and was grudgingly granted the right to use his own band instead of the Reuben Phillips house band for his shows, and his sets had to be just right. "James Brown always wanted to have a set that was very specially created for him," said Bobby Schiffman. "He came into Showman's Bar about eleven one evening and sat down with our production manager, Honi Coles, to discuss what he wanted for his show three or four weeks down the pike. Honi was three-quarters drunk, and he and Brown wrote it down on a matchbook cover. Later, we figured out what it said on the matchbook cover, and we put together this magnificent set that involved about four hundred different-colored platforms hung so as to form a backdrop of a seashell. It was a massive job and it involved a tremendous amount of time and money. It was breathtaking, and we couldn't wait for Brown to get there to see it. When Brown came in, it was not what he expected. He was fuming, and he proceeded to ream my ass out about the way the set had come out. I proceeded to try to tell him that we'd done the best we could with the illustration we had on the back of the matchbook cover. After ranting and raving and screaming and hollering, he said, 'Okay, you fucked up. Now I'm not gonna. I'm gonna go out there and do it good for these people.' Which he proceeded to do. He's got the biggest ego of any man I've ever met in my life, but you can never count him out."

James Brown not only helped define a new musical form—soul music—he also helped define a new role for blacks in the entertainment business. He showed others that they had the power to reach for self-determination in their lives and careers. He proved, through giant crossover hits like "Papa's Got a Brand New Bag," that purely black music which made no concessions to white tastes could be accepted and widely popular. And through songs like "Say It Loud I'm Black and I'm Proud" he celebrated the new surge of black pride and power—earning the title "Soul Brother Number One."

. . . . .

The success of James Brown helped set the stage for a new era at the Apollo. Its fourth decade as a black theatre became its most celebrated and successful. The sixties were an historic time for the black community—a time of sit-ins, demonstrations, Freedom Rides, boycotts, marches, bombings, riots, and assassinations, as well as the War on Poverty, voting rights, school desegregation, civil-rights legislation, Black Muslims, black nationalism, and Black Power.

On 125th Street, charges of white hegemony over Harlem's main commercial district reemerged with new force. In 1962 the city's Human Rights Commission was told that the owners of the Apollo Theatre had rented an adjacent storefront to a white steak-house operator in order to drive Lloyd's, the only black-owned steak house, out of business. Pickets marched in front of Lloyd's, claiming that a "gentlemen's agreement" still existed among the white owners of Harlem's main street to keep blacks out of the action. Two years later a local civic group claimed that twenty-nine stores on 125th Street employed not a single black, while others employed blacks only in menial positions. Reluctantly, the store owners agreed to sponsor an on-the-job training program for minorities. Meanwhile, resentment against whites increased. In a one-month period early in 1964, four white people were murdered in Harlem.

Whether out of true moral convictions or, as some claimed, out of a cynical sense of self-preservation, the Schiffmans did not behave like the other merchants on the street. As Percy Sutton, the black Manhattan borough president who would one day take over the Apollo, said in 1968, "The Schiffmans have traditionally involved themselves in Harlem community affairs. If all businessmen had done as much, community tension would be considerably lessened."

During the early sixties the Apollo began billing itself, somewhat wistfully, as "The World Famous Apollo—In the Heart of Friendly Harlem." The Schiffmans became more active in the community and in black causes. In 1964, they gave "Passes for Equality," allowing one free admission to anyone donating $2.50 to CORE. Martin Luther King, Jr., wrote Frank Schiffman to express his gratitude "for the dedicated aid you have given to us and to the civil rights movement" through personal donations and the use of the Apollo for benefits. Peter Long, the Apollo's public-relations director, said the theatre presented twenty to twenty-five "community activities" such as educational programs and local theatre productions from 1966 to 1971. And throughout the sixties the Apollo was the unofficial sponsor of scores of community activities. "If there were demonstrations in this community," Bobby Schiffman told newspaper columnist Pete Hamill, "the Apollo was often the focal point mainly

244

because they knew you could attract TV cameras at the Apollo when you couldn't get them elsewhere in Harlem."

. . . . .

The mood of the black community was reflected, as always, in the Apollo's presentations. The most dynamic new trend was the rise of the sound that became known as soul music. Early soul stars like James Brown, Ray Charles, Sam Cooke, and Jackie Wilson came out of rhythm and blues or pop. But the soul music they sang was patterned directly on the gospel music that was such an important part of their early lives. The word *soul* itself had religious and spiritual connotations, and soul music was, at its heart, a music with a message. The disappointments and frustrations of the early postwar years and the restrictions of segregation had led blacks to create an insular music—rhythm and blues—that was bound to remain within the confines of the ghetto. But the optimism and euphoria of the early sixties and the freedom of increasing integration produced a hopeful music—soul—that preached a message of love to the world years before the Beatles took up the cause.

The soul artists reflected the surge of black pride in America. Soul music was the first pure black form that truly celebrated blackness, and it reached out for and achieved popular acceptance without blatantly catering to white tastes. Partly because the essence of soul music was an expression of the feeling of being black, and partly because of an increased awareness on the part of whites toward the needs and aspirations of blacks, soul music was also the first black musical form that whites could never successfully steal. Some, like Tom Jones, the Young Rascals, even Van Morrison, imitated the sound, but their "blue-eyed soul" was heard and accepted as an imitation and form of homage rather than as a new idea that they themselves created. White rock-and-roll and pop singers admired the feeling and emotionalism the great soul artists conveyed and the bond they were able to create with their audience. They eagerly soaked up as much of the sensation as they could at the Apollo, which for them, as for blacks, had become the home of soul.

. . . . .

In 1960, the Apollo first used the word *soul* when it described Ray Charles as the "Soul Genius." The remarkable black, blind, heroin-addicted piano player whom the Schiffmans initially had presented as a complete unknown in the early fifties had gradually developed a style of

245

Ray Charles, late 1950s. ★ *In 1960, the Apollo first used the word* soul *when it described Ray Charles as the "Soul Genius."*

playing and singing that heralded soul. Ray had played rhythm and blues and jazz, but with the release of "I've Got a Woman" in 1955, he revealed something new. He sang the bluesy lusty lyrics in an uninhibited emotional way that was as close as possible to gospel music. The Apollo audience had never experienced anything like him before. Ray put everything he could into the song to churn up the raw emotionalism that only the great gospel artists could equal. Many in the black church were outraged, and some r-and-b artists also cried foul, but the crowd at the Apollo cried with delight.

The Ray Charles song that really propelled the sound of soul onto the American consciousness had come out in 1959. The moans and wails previously associated with people in the throes of spiritual ecstasy were now offered for public consumption by a demon screaming about secular love and pure lust. In "What'd I Say," Ray used every gospel device, including a call-and-response passage, and even played an electric piano to approximate more closely the churchly sounds of the organ. Many radio stations banned the record, but it became a giant hit—not only in the black community, but as a top-ten pop hit. It made Ray Charles a star, and America got its first taste of what would become soul music.

Jackie Wilson helped define the sound and look of soul. He could get down and slug out a rocking tune, but he also polished his act and style with a different kind of pop sensibility. Wilson left Billy Ward's Dominoes in 1957, and a Detroit music publisher named Nat Tarnopol became his manager, securing the singer a contract with Brunswick records. His first records, "Reet Petite" and the smash hit "Lonely Teardrops," were composed by a struggling Detroit songwriter named Berry Gordy, Jr., who, with his earnings from the songs, began a little homemade record company called Motown. After helping Berry launch Motown, Jackie's popularity grew, and in May 1963 Jackie Wilson became the Apollo's all-time box-office champ—until James Brown set another record the following year.

Beverly Lee of the Shirelles remembered Jackie Wilson at the Apollo: "He would always bring the house down when he sang 'To Be Loved' and they put the little red pinlight on him. He drove the women crazy. We were friends with him and *we* were drooling. But he was always a very warm and friendly person. He's magnetic. He had such drawing power. He loved to greet you with a nice kiss and a smile; always up and up, a lot of energy. He was like a very slinky powerful leopard onstage. There was nothing he couldn't do there. He was very sexy. When he would do his little shadowboxing as I call it—his little movements, and the way he handled the mike—he was just amazing."

Despite his remarkable stage presence and showmanship—he may have been James Brown's greatest influence—Wilson never achieved Brown's stature. And despite the fact that he indirectly helped Berry Gordy launch Motown, he stuck with Brunswick and never quite managed to cross into the pop field as did so many of Gordy's artists. In 1975 he suffered a massive heart attack onstage, which ended his career.

Like Ray Charles and Jackie Wilson, Sam Cooke provided a vital link between fifties rhythm and blues, gospel, pop, and sixties soul. His sleek good looks and sexy voice pushed the gospel sound to the limits of propriety. Cooke's first pop hit, "You Send Me," which came out in 1957, sold over two million copies worldwide. For the next six years he produced a string of hits, including: "I'll Come Running Back to You," "Wonderful World," "Chain Gang," "Twistin' the Night Away," and "Having a Party." His 1962 smash, "Bring It on Home to Me," a call-and-response opus on which Cooke, aided by Lou Rawls, successfully combined the gospel and r-and-b sounds, may have been the first true soul song. Cooke was also a groundbreaker in the white market, thanks to his clean-cut image, good looks, and smooth sound. Blacks loved his sound, admired him for his style, and idolized him as they had Duke Ellington, Billy Eckstine, and a few others.

Cooke's career, and his life, ended tragically, in violence, on December 10, 1964, in Los Angeles. A twenty-two-year-old black woman claimed he'd offered her a ride home, but drove her instead to a motel and molested her. She said she escaped with his clothes, and when he pursued her into the manager's apartment, the manager, a black woman, shot him three times and clubbed him to death. The black community canonized Sam Cooke, and worshiped him long after his death. In the early seventies, street vendors outside the Apollo sold memorial photographs of heroes Martin Luther King, Jr., JFK, RFK, . . . and Sam Cooke.

. . . . .

Two factors that helped make Sam Cooke a superstar—the wholesome image that endeared him to the Apollo audience and the unthreatening style that made him a big hit in the white market—also worked for a number of black women singers who started at the Apollo in the early sixties and went on to become widely popular with white audiences as well.

Jackie Wilson with manager Nat Tarnopol and deejay Alan Freed backstage at the Apollo, about 1960. ★ Beverly Lee: *"He was like a very slinky powerful leopard onstage. There was nothing he couldn't do there."*

Dionne Warwick, mid-1960s. ★ *"I turned around and looked in the wings and said, 'I can't sing this song here?' I told the audience, 'The man who runs this theatre told me I can't sing this song here. I'll sing it anywhere. I'm bringing downtown uptown!'"*

Dionne Warwick was a young, classically trained musician singing backup for the Drifters when she met Burt Bacharach and his partner Hal David. They wrote "Don't Make Me Over," the first of a string of hits for her. When she first came into the Apollo as a professional, Dionne recalled, "Reuben Phillips said the song could not be played. My music was probably the hardest music in the industry. It wasn't the regular I-IV-V-IV [chord] changes. I said, 'I will sit and play it for you, and then your band will play it.' That's exactly the way I did it, and they played it. I made them use their knowledge. Nobody else did that. They thought, 'Here is this kid from New Jersey with this goddamned music that nobody understood. What is she doing to us?'

"The first time I had a performance at the Apollo was with a Scepter Records package: the Shirelles, Chuck Jackson, Tommy Hunt, Maxine Brown, the Isley Brothers, and Dionne Warwick. And I opened the show. I was the baby in the business, the new kid on the block, and they really protected me. There were a lot of elements, so they kind of sheltered me from that 126th Street crowd.

"One time this guy came up to my room. This is just to show you how well they kept me away from the bullshit. He came in with a brown paper bag and said, 'I've got some really great stuff here.' My mind said diamonds, emeralds, and rubies and all kinds of goodies. I stuck my hand in this bag and pulled up all this ugly stuff that looked like tobacco and I said, 'Oh, this is tobacco.' It would have been priceless if I had gotten a photograph of that man's face. He said, 'Tobacco?' I said, 'Yeah.' And I threw it back into the bag. My friend was sitting in the chair across from me and he was hysterical, laughing. The man said, 'No, I don't think you want any tobacco.' The man ran down the steps and stopped at every dressing room and told them what happened on the third floor. I'm standing in the wings waiting to go on, and Spayne comes up to me and said, 'You want some tobacco?' I said, 'Why would you send someone up there with a bag of tobacco? You know I smoke Salems.' I went into this long dissertation and he just looked at me and said, 'I want you to stay as naïve as you are.' Do you know for almost three years after that I had no idea what that man had brought me? Tobacco. I was the tobacco kid."

Dionne was the darling of the Apollo, and thanks to Bacharach-David hits like "Anyone Who Had a Heart," "Say a Little Prayer," and "Do You Know the Way to San Jose," she gained a great following internationally and on the white nightclub scene. Dionne was more a pop singer than a soul singer, but she played the Apollo along with the top

250

soul stars. "I never had any problem relating to the people at the Apollo because that was my heritage," said Dionne. "But a lot of people tell me, 'I don't understand how you played the Apollo. They don't understand your music.' What do they mean they don't understand my music? Hal David wrote lyrics that spoke to your heart. Everybody's got one of those regardless of how rich or poor you are, or the color of your skin.

"When *Funny Girl* was just opening on Broadway, I was doing 'People' in my repertoire at the Copa. I just took my show up and did the same show at the Apollo. But Bobby Schiffman said to me at the rehearsal in the basement, 'You cannot sing this song here.' He was referring to 'People.' 'They'll boo you off the stage. They won't understand it.' I said, 'Bobby, I want you to stand in the wings tonight.' That particular evening especially, I think because I was so angry with him, even Streisand could have just packed the song away. She would never have topped that evening. It was the first standing ovation he had seen in the theatre since he was a kid. I turned around and looked in the wings and said, 'I can't sing this song here?' I told the audience, 'The man who runs this theatre told me I can't sing this song here. I'll sing it anywhere. I'm bringing downtown uptown!' "

Nancy Wilson was another popular song stylist who brought a sophisticated sound to the Apollo. Most young black singers who made the Apollo home in the sixties were singing soul, but Nancy's act was hard to categorize. As with Dionne, the is-she-or-isn't-she-a-soul-singer debate followed her throughout her career. "Most jazz buffs will say I'm not a jazz singer," she has said. "Most rhythm-and-blues buffs will say I'm not a r-and-b singer, and most pop buffs will say I'm not a pop singer."

Although she often headlined jazz shows at the Apollo, her forte was the blues ballad. Cannonball Adderley, the star alto sax player, saw her and helped her get a recording contract. She scored a great hit with the blues ballad "Guess Who I Saw Today" in 1960 and made her Apollo debut, also like Dionne, at the bottom of the bill.

"I had dressing room number eleven," she recalled, "on the top floor, and there were several other singers there. I only did three songs. By the time I got to the Apollo I was very well seasoned. I had had a television show at fifteen, and I had seven years under my belt as a professional. I was not an amateur by any means. The Apollo was a different thing, but it didn't bother me at all. It was just a matter of time. Most people who were in front of me deserved to be. I was not afraid of the Apollo, and it was wonderful to get the kind of reception I got there.

Nancy Wilson, mid-1960s. ★
*She played the Apollo in the
early 1970s immediately
following the sudden death
of her brother, Tony. "This is
the only place I can think of
where I'd want to play right
now," she tearfully told
the audience.*

The Shirelles in the early 1960s. Beverly Lee is on the lower
left. ★ *"The Apollo Theatre was our first professional
engagement."*

The next time I went back I was the headliner. It happened that fast."

Nancy Wilson, as did so many other performers, had a very special feeling about, and a deeply personal relationship with the Apollo, for she celebrated the joys of birth there as well as the sorrow of death. "One moment none of us there forgot was when I was seven months pregnant," she said. "I was working with Cannonball. We were doing 'Save Your Love for Me' and when we got to the bridge—the lyric 'save your love for me'—I could feel it. The baby had shifted, and it was so obvious: my whole dress shifted. I could feel it and I couldn't conceal it. It was, pow! Well, the band broke up. Cannon fell out. And the audience—it was quite obvious to them because they could see the baby move—well, the whole audience just went crazy. It was so funny. It was one of the most beautiful, marvelous feelings you'd ever want to get."

Nancy was after a similar feeling when she played the Apollo in the early seventies immediately following the sudden death of her brother, Tony. "This is the only place I can think of where I'd want to play right now," she tearfully told the audience. "I've come here when it would have been so easy not to, because I wanted to share my sorrow with you. Not only have you shared that sorrow, you've given me something to take to my parents. They wanted me to come here." A young man called to her from the audience, "You can come home anytime, Nancy." The audience cheered.

As the new black singers emerged from the Apollo in the late fifties and early sixties, popular music was going through one of its periodic times of change. Many of the great rhythm-and-blues artists were playing oldies shows at the Apollo—usually without a great deal of success. Elvis Presley had been sidetracked by the Army and the lure of Hollywood. Buddy Holly was dead. A slew of boy teen idols was churning out dozens of throwaway pop ditties that were really incidental to their gleaming smiles and neat pompadours. Luckily the girls came to the rescue, the so-called girl groups—the Chantels, the Angels, Rosie and the Originals, the Crystals, and especially the Shirelles. The girls were generally black, but the Svengalis behind them, the men who wrote their material, produced their records, and guided their careers—such as George Goldner and Phil Spector—were usually white. Their sound was a mix of rhythm-and-blues styles sung with girlish delight, but carefully crafted by the greatest pop record makers. While their genre was in vogue, from the late fifties until the mid-sixties, the girl groups were vastly popular among blacks and whites around the world.

"The Apollo Theatre was our first professional engagement," said

Beverly Lee of the Shirelles. "With our first record, 'I Met Him on a Sunday,' we went in with Jocko Henderson and the 'Rocket Ship Show' [1958]. The first time we went in we didn't have any arrangements, we didn't know we were supposed to. We got a record player and some of the guys in the Reuben Phillips band listened to the song. With them being so professional, they wrote a few notes and chords for it. The next time we came in, we were totally prepared. At first we didn't know we were supposed to be in the union. It was downstairs in the basement of the Apollo that we found out about AGVA and joined the union.

"We were the opening act, and were nervous as hell, not knowing how the audience was going to respond to us. As we went back to the Apollo through the years, we would play there several times a year. We developed a following. As a matter of fact, there were some young kids that would hang backstage, and we would baby-sit for them between shows."

While the Shirelles became worldwide stars, their record company chose the Apollo as the site to present the girls with their first gold record for "Soldier Boy," in 1962. It was an appropriate choice since the group had got their start there and introduced the song at the theatre. "We all felt, 'How are we going to go in there and sing this corny song for these people?'" said Beverly Lee. "Everybody else is doing all these heavy love songs, or blues. We said, 'They're not gonna like us. What can we do this time so they'll like us?' So we came up with a comedy act for 'Soldier Boy.' We would sing it, and we had a guy that worked with us. He and Doris Kenner would do a comedy act. He was the long-lost soldier coming back home, and he wanted to know why she stopped writing. We did a whole skit." Their fears were groundless, and the song was a great hit.

During one of their Apollo engagements Muhammad Ali came backstage and asked the girls to dedicate 'Soldier Boy' to him—ironically, just as he was going through his fight with draft officials to be declared a conscientious objector. "We often laugh about that," said Beverly.

Beverly has continued to be surprised and pleased with the reception the Shirelles received at the Apollo. "I always thought of our songs as very corny and very lollipopish," she said. "But the people there accepted them. They liked them. We thought they would want more rhythm and blues and soul. We were middle of the road, and we got airplay that most other black artists didn't get unless they had a top-ten song. Our songs were a little different from theirs. Whites could relate to them more. I couldn't understand it myself. We could work clubs that some of the biggest black acts couldn't work." Could it be because they were so innocent, and posed no threat? "It could be," said Beverly. "We were told we were called the Sweethearts of the Apollo or the Sweethearts of America. That could have had an effect."

· · · · ·

Indeed, America had become sweet on black music. At the beginning of the rhythm-and-blues era, there were almost no black-oriented radio stations. By 1967 there were a hundred stations primarily playing black music—even though only five of the stations were owned by blacks. Hundreds of other pop-oriented stations also included many black records on their playlists. As the restrictions of segregation began to crumble thanks to the civil-rights movement, black music recorded by black artists became big business.

However, it was usually the entrepreneurs—black and white—not the artists, who garnered the bulk of the profits. While the record companies made millions, artists were sometimes paid a royalty of less than 2 percent on records that listed for $3.98 or $4.98, minus recording costs. In the sixties, recording artists, especially black ones, relied upon personal appearances for the bulk of their income, while their records served as promotional vehicles that drove the fans in droves into the Apollo and other theatres.

The job that had once belonged to the Apollo's show producers, and later to the disc jockeys, was now usurped by the powerful record companies. They organized revues, or packages, for the Apollo that consisted entirely of their own recording artists. Two companies led the black record business during the sixties: black entrepreneur Berry Gordy's Motown and Ahmet Ertegun and Jerry Wexler's Atlantic.

"Eventually, what grew out of the rhythm and blues of the forties and fifties were two strains," Ahmet Ertegun explained. "There was an Atlantic type of style, which was Sam and Dave, Wilson Pickett, and Otis Redding. Then there was another kind of style that came out of Detroit, which was the Motown thing. It was more advanced, more sophisticated, hipper, and also less real and less authentic: not as close to what we tend to think of as authentic blues. But the Motown style was more adventuresome, more pop, and more representative of what the modern black person wanted to hear. At the time, we at Atlantic were developing a

255

Pictured in the mid-1960s, Wilson
Pickett (right, at the Apollo), and Otis
Redding (above) epitomized the
Atlantic style. ★ Ahmet Ertegun:
*"At the time, we at Atlantic were
developing a kind of modern r-and-b
sound with a more funky style."*

kind of modern r-and-b sound with a more funky style. We had a lot of white sales, as did Motown, [but] the kind of music Motown pioneered is really the music that became the pop music of America."

Motown soul did eventually sweep the country, but when Berry Gordy initially proposed a Motown Revue to Bobby Schiffman, the theatre owner had barely heard of the new company. "At first I thought it was Motortown," said Bobby. "As a matter of fact, when we finally played the show I had a sign made that said Motortown, and had to change it. They had a bunch of young people—never heard of them. Berry Gordy and his sister, Esther, came to see me and asked me to put on this show that included all their young potential stars. And we did the show in 'sixty-two—thirty-one shows over seven days—and it included Smokey Robinson and the Miracles, Diana Ross and the Supremes, the Temptations, Martha and the Vandellas, Marvin Gaye, Stevie Wonder, the Contours, and a singer called Marv Johnson. The show cost $7,000, and soon most of those people were getting $40,000 to $50,000 a night.

"The Motown operation became the major supplier of acts for the Apollo because they had so many. Nearly every one of those acts became headliners. They had a young fellow named Lou Zito who became the emissary and controlled the destinies of all the Motown acts. I remember once—my father was a very rigid man about how his theatre was run, and when you came to his office you had to be announced. Lou Zito and I became very friendly on the telephone; I was doing all the buying at the time. Lou walked into the Apollo—*I* knew he was coming—and asked, "Where's Bobby?' The girl at the reception desk told him upstairs. He started up the stairs as my father was coming down, and my father stopped him and said, 'Who are you? You can't go up there. You have to be announced.' I couldn't *wait* for Lou Zito. Evidently they got into some heated words about it, and almost blew Lou Zito and Motown out of there."

Sometimes the soon-to-be-superstars of Motown didn't get any respect either. "Diana Ross and the Supremes were on one show where I was the comic," said Scoey Mitchlll. "They were on in front of me, then I was to come on and do my act. One of the disc jockeys was the m.c. We used to shoot craps and play Tonk at the Apollo, [and one time] the disc jockey wasn't there to take the Supremes off the stage. So I went out and said, 'Ladies and gentlemen, the Supremes,' and then I went on and did my act. By then the disc jockey had come back, and took me off. The next show, the same thing happened. Diana Ross and the Supremes got through with their act and the disc jockey wasn't there to take them off. I

The Motown Revue, Live at the Apollo, 1962. ★ Bobby Schiffman: *"They had a bunch of young people—never heard of them. Berry Gordy and his sister, Esther, came to see me and asked me to put on this show that featured all their young potential stars. And we did the show—thirty-one shows over seven days. The show cost $7,000."*

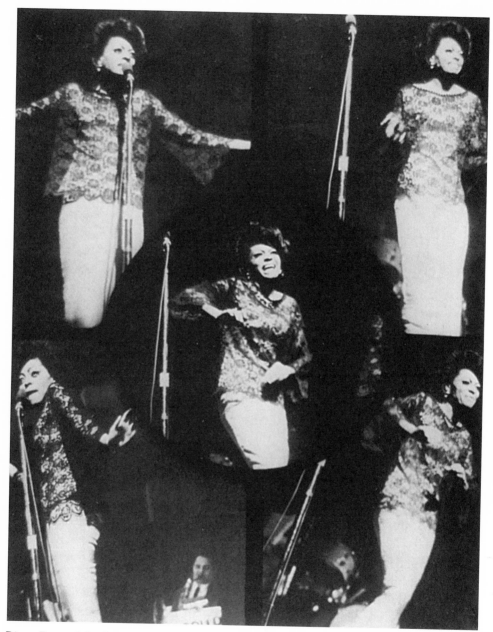

Diana Ross of the Supremes at the Apollo, late 1960s. ★ Scoey Mitchlll: "I said, 'I tell you what, little girl. You better stop fussing with me and go and try and get yourself a hit record.' They rolled off about twenty-eight of them right after. So every time I see her I say, 'You listen good!' "

didn't want to emcee, and just to keep a bad habit from starting, I didn't take them off. So they had to walk off, and then I walked on and introduced myself and did my act.

"After, when I came off, one of the guys backstage says, 'Miss Ross wants to see you upstairs.' So I went upstairs to their dressing room and Diana said, 'Where were you? Why weren't you there to take us off?' I said, 'Beg pardon?' She said, 'Why weren't you there to take us off?' I said, 'Oh, I see. No, I'm not the m.c. I'm the comic on the show.' She said, 'Comic, m.c., what difference does it make?' And I said, 'I tell you what, little girl. You better stop fussing with me and go and try and get yourself a hit record.' They rolled off about twenty-eight of them right after. So every time I see her I say, 'You listen good!' "

The Supremes became Motown's greatest commercial success. After hitting with "Where Did Our Love Go?" in 1964, they ran up twelve number-one pop hits in the next five years. They became such a powerful attraction at the Apollo that they broke James Brown's all-time theatre attendance record. But the Supremes were just one act in a stable of Motown stars that took the Apollo and America by storm. By the early seventies two other Motown stars, the Temptations and Gladys Knight and the Pips, had also set new Apollo house records.

Gordy dubbed his Detroit headquarters "Hitsville, U.S.A."—a particularly apt title for the greatest hit-making machine the record business has ever had. Gordy's shop had some of the assembly-line aspects of his powerful industrial neighbors in Detroit, but in many ways, Gordy and Motown did what Frank Schiffman and the Apollo had always done. The Apollo used a group of crack show producers who fit the best talent available into a formula—the Apollo variety revue format—that met its audience's expectations and stayed fresh and exciting by presenting the latest developments in entertainment. Likewise, the key to Motown's success was its reliance upon its talented producers and songwriters, among them Smokey Robinson, Norman Whitfield, Nick Ashford and Valerie Simpson, and especially Lamont Dozier and his partners Brian and Eddie Holland. They used Motown's artists to greatest advantage by employing a formula—the Motown sound—that consistently relied upon surefire hooks while always remaining inventive and fresh. Also, Gordy, like Frank Schiffman, was a benevolent despot paternalistically looking after his family, and keeping them completely within his control for as long as he could. Like the elder Schiffman, Gordy worked closely with his artists, nurturing them, training them, sometimes honing acts for months before releasing a record or sending them on the road.

In one case no amount of reassurance from Gordy nor a string of hit records—"Can I Get a Witness," "Ain't That Peculiar," and "What's Going On"—could instill enough confidence in the man known as the Prince of Motown, Marvin Gaye. Bobby Schiffman told of Gaye's insecurity: "He was very much affected by his feeling that he was lousy onstage. And, in truth, there was a lot to be desired in his offering. Yet he was extremely popular. The girls and guys absolutely adored him. But he knew he was a pretty piss-poor performer, in the beginning at least, and as a consequence of that was always very nervous about going on the stage.

"One time when he was scheduled to play the Apollo, I decided to go to the airport to meet him. He called me from the house in Detroit, told me what flight number and time and airport to meet him. When I went out to the airport—this was eleven on a Friday morning, opening day—I couldn't find him. We had a tremendous advertising campaign, and were expecting to sell out every show.

"When I got back to the theatre, I called him in Detroit and left a message. At three in the afternoon, he called me. I said, 'I went to the airport. Where are you?' He said, 'Bobby I couldn't do it. I came to New York, got off the plane, and was so scared I got on another plane and went back to Detroit.' I said, 'Marvin, we're sold out.' He said, 'I can't help it. I'm afraid.' So that engagement was canceled."

What really ignited the Motown revues at the Apollo was the slick sophisticated choreography of the great male groups like the Four Tops and especially the Temptations. "The Temps were known for that," said Gladys Knight, "and the Apollo Theatre perpetuated that style because it became popular with the audiences there, and they just ate it up." Gladys Knight and the Pips had been on the scene professionally for ten years before the Motown revues began, but didn't join the Motown caravan until the mid-sixties. The Pips' dancing ability, fine-tuned by Honi Coles's partner, Cholly Atkins, was a tremendous influence on the Temptations.

"Cholly Atkins was our everything," said Gladys. "He taught us how to walk onstage, how to walk offstage, how to move—for me, surprisingly, how to be feminine. He didn't want me to dance. 'You just be a lady,' he used to tell me. And the guys, he used to work them to death. We used to work from nine in the morning until nine in the evening, rehearsing.

"He would come right down the aisle at the Apollo if we weren't doing something right. We'd be right there onstage doing our thing, and he would tell us, 'Get over there, you're not supposed to be over *there*!' It was great. Then, after the show, Honi would come backstage and give us the same fit that Cholly had given us: 'Now you guys know you didn't do this and you didn't do that.' But when we got those standing ovations at the Apollo he was so proud of us. He'd just beam, and he and Honi would say, 'Hey, man, they're doing all right.'

"The Pips were doing their high-stepping choreography—I mean the class thing, without the acrobatics and the tumbling and that kind of thing—which they actually started in the business, before the Temps and all the other fast-stepping groups got to be popular. The Temps, when they were born as an act, they were watching us. They'll tell anybody. They used to stand in the wings and watch every move the Pips made. That's how Berry Gordy found out about us. His act was going back and telling him about us. Naturally, they wanted to be good in their own right—as good or maybe better than the Pips—but we had a certain camaraderie in those days that kept the competition healthy. Everybody should have a certain amount of competition to have pride in his act."

"Motown's roots," wrote Joe McEwen and Jim Miller in the *Rolling Stone Illustrated History of Rock and Roll*, "may have been in gospel and blues, but its image was purely one of upward mobility and clean, wholesome fun (Gordy's vision of 'Young America'). Motown's stars were groomed to offend no one; the songs they sang were equipped with romantic lyrics that could appeal to practically anyone; and the music itself was rarely demanding, or even aggressive in the tradition of Southern soul." The same could not be said of the music of the soul stars who created the Atlantic style in the Stax/Volt studios in Memphis and the Fame studios near Muscle Shoals, Alabama.

An example is Sam and Dave's tune "Hold On, I'm Coming," a hit in 1966. "When we first released that tune," said Dave Prater, the Dave of Sam and Dave, "the FCC banned it for about six months because of the title of the song. At that time those words were too suggestive. The disc jockeys on the radio were twisting it worse than what it was, and the FCC didn't like that. So we had to prune the tune back, and just put the title as 'Hold On.' We had to sing the tune on every show at the Apollo. That was the 'in' thing, man, like they were really into it. I tell you what, it made a lot of babies that year."

Sam and Dave at their best epitomized the earthy carnal power of fellow Atlantic male sex symbols such as "Wicked" Wilson Pickett and Otis Redding. At the Apollo, they conveyed exactly the type of virile

Marvin Gaye, mid-1960s. ★ Bobby Schiffman: *"He was very much affected by his feeling that he was lousy onstage. Yet he was extremely popular. The girls and guys absolutely adored him."*

Sam and Dave, late 1960s. Dave Prater is on the left, Sam Moore on the right. ★ *"We had to sing ['Hold On, I'm Coming'] on every show at the Apollo. That was the 'in' thing, man, like, they were really into it. I tell you what, it made a lot of babies that year."*

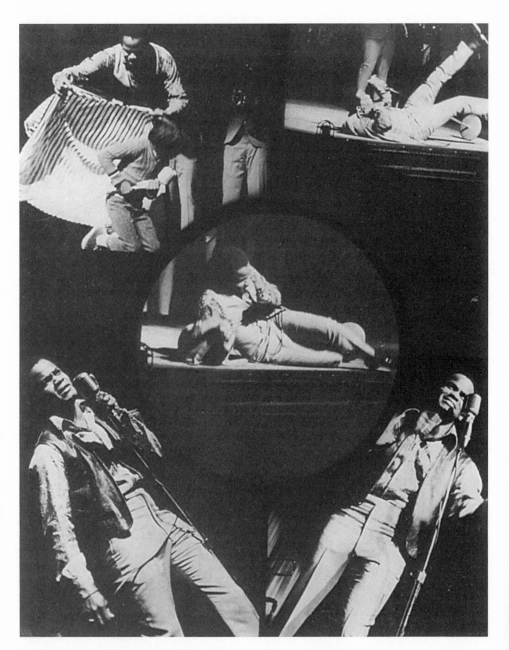

Joe Tex at the Apollo, about 1966. ★ *The showmanship of Joe Tex and the other top men of soul bordered on braggadocio, and often the microphone served as the phallic symbol of their sexual prowess.*

lusty allure the Motown acts avoided. When Sam and Dave cried about coming down a dusty road with a truckload of good loving in their smash hit "Soul Man," they expressed and defined the spirit and sensibility of the Atlantic style. If Motown celebrated the new opportunities of black people to establish themselves in modern urban America, then the Atlantic soulsters gloried in the proud heritage of black people whose roots were in the dusty roads of the South.

Relationships between men and women were the major concern. When Joe Tex performed his hit "Skinny Legs and All" at the Apollo, he would bring a member of the audience up onstage for a potentially humiliating, but humorous, mock auction that ended on an assuring note. "Who'll take the woman with the skinny legs?" he'd ask. And while there would be no takers he would dismiss her, singing "But don't you worry about a doggone thing at all. Because there's someone, somewhere who'll take you, woman, skinny legs and all." Again he would repeat the procedure for "the man with the raggedy clothes."

Joe, of course, never had problems finding women. The showmanship of Joe Tex and the other top men of soul bordered on braggadocio, and often the microphone served as the phallic symbol of their sexual prowess. "Joe used to do all sorts of tricks with the microphone," said Bobby Schiffman. "He would have it on this stand that was weighted on the bottom. He used to spin the microphone and stand across the stage and it would pirouette and be about to fall, and he would dive on it. He had all sorts of amazing gimmicks he did with it."

Solomon Burke, another Atlantic recording artist, was one of the most influential soul artists. His 1961 hit "Just Out of Reach (Of My Two Open Arms)" was fundamental to the emergence of soul music, and his gospel-imbued sound influenced other soul artists as well as white rock singers including Mick Jagger. From an early age, Solomon sang in church as a soloist. Before he was twelve, his parents discovered he had a natural talent for inspirational speaking, and he began preaching. Known as the "Wonder-Boy Preacher," he led his own church, Solomon's Temple, in Philadelphia. Many Apollo performers relied on a subtle preacher-congregation relationship with their audience; in Solomon's case, it was much more pronounced. So were Solomon's entrepreneurial tendencies.

"Solomon always had special ideas to capitalize on what he did, in other ways than just singing," said Ahmet Ertegun. "He decided to make up his own popcorn and sell it as Professor Solomon Burke or Doctor

Solomon Burke, or whatever he wanted to call himself. You know, special popcorn with a large photograph of himself on the front of the box. He went into the Apollo as the star of the show, and between the first and second shows on the first day, he put on an apron and he went up and down the aisles selling this popcorn himself."

Bobby Schiffman recalled, "I said to him, 'Go fuck yourself. You're not selling any popcorn here, 'cause I sell popcorn.' After a long harangue, he said, 'Hey, Bobby, what am I gonna do with my popcorn?' I said, 'Take it out and sell it on the street. Give it away at the playgrounds. Do something.' He had a huge tandem trailer full of popcorn. The next day, he had his truck at a local school playground giving away free popcorn, courtesy of Solomon Burke." The trailer contained so much, they had trouble giving it all away. "There was one little boy standing by the side of the truck," Bobby continued, "and the fellow who was giving the popcorn out said, 'Here you go, fella, take a bag of popcorn.' The little guy said, 'Listen, you greasy motherfucker, if you make me eat one more bag of that stale popcorn I'm gonna puncture your tires.' "

"Schiffman called me up," said Ahmet Ertegun, "and said they had a franchise and would I please explain it to Solomon. So I explained to him that they already sold the rights to other people to sell popcorn and colas and hot dogs and so forth. He said to me, 'Does that franchise include fried pork-chop sandwiches?' I said, 'No, it doesn't.' So he got a little electric cooker, a little gas range, and he started making up these sandwiches. It stunk the place up, and they were going to fire him for the week, but they didn't have another act."

Aretha Franklin, perhaps the greatest female soul artist, who signed with Atlantic after her career was launched by John Hammond at Columbia, also came from a religious background, albeit a more traditional one than Solomon Burke's. When Hammond first heard her he called her "an untutored genius" and said she had "the best voice I've heard since Billie Holiday." But she was insecure about her abilities and not comfortable with the pop market strategy Columbia's top a-and-r man, Mitch Miller, had mapped out for her. She ran away from recording sessions. "When I first recorded Aretha in 1960," said John Hammond, "I twisted Frank Schiffman's arm and he hired her because she had a couple of successful records. She didn't show up until the third day. He held me personally responsible."

After her shaky start, Aretha's natural talent became apparent to

Solomon Burke, about 1963. ★
Ahmet Ertegun: *"He said to me,
'Does that franchise include fried
pork-chop sandwiches?' I said,
'No, it doesn't.'"*

Aretha Franklin, about 1962. ★
John Hammond: *"When I first
recorded Aretha in 1960, I twisted
Frank Schiffman's arm and he
hired her because she had a couple
of successful records. She didn't
show up until the third day."*

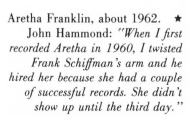

the Schiffmans. She gained confidence. Cholly Atkins taught her dance steps to improve her showmanship. By the end of 1966 she was with Atlantic, and ace producer Jerry Wexler eased her career into high gear with gold records that included: "Chain of Fools," "I Never Loved a Man (The Way I Love You)," and her magnum opus, Otis Redding's "Respect." In 1971 when she appeared at the Apollo, the marquee bannered: "She's Home—ARETHA FRANKLIN."

Aretha's 1971 Apollo appearance was treated as a major cultural event, and the two opening-night shows could not accommodate the throngs who waited out on 125th Street. Celebrities such as the Reverend Jesse Jackson and Zulu chief Gatsha Buthelezi from South Africa paid homage. "It is the most overwhelming thing we have ever had in the theatre," said Peter Long, the Apollo's public-relations director. "The thousands of black people who saw and heard Miss Franklin," wrote C. Gerald Fraser in *The New York Times*, "were more than an audience. They were part of a black interaction—they came not only to see and hear 'Lady Soul,' 'Soul Sister Number 1,' 'The Queen of Soul' and all those other labels she bears, but also to participate with her in an exultation of her blackness."

· · · · ·

On the flip side of the early soul and pop scene at the Apollo was the remarkable and intense jazz scene. During the late fifties and early sixties, as r and b fizzled and soul began to sizzle, the Schiffmans bolstered the Apollo roster with shows featuring the top names in jazz.

This was one of the most important and innovative periods for jazz, almost equal to the bebop revolution of the early forties and the great Jazz Age of the 1920s. Yet the great jazz artists were creating a less accessible, more intellectually demanding music. Some, like trumpeter Miles Davis, one of the most important figures in the history of jazz, so scorned the idea of his music being mere entertainment that he usually played most of his performance with his back turned to the audience.

The more melodic or surgingly rhythmic players were the most popular jazz artists at the Apollo: pianist Horace Silver and drummer Art Blakey were always crowd pleasers. So, too, were many of the white jazzmen who were especially fine attractions in the fifties: Dave Brubeck, Herbie Mann, Gerry Mulligan, Stan Getz, and Maynard Ferguson. Buddy Rich, the pugnacious little drummer, was an Apollo favorite. He once thrilled the Apollo audience, and won their hearts, by playing a furiously lively engagement with one broken arm in a cast.

Even with the greatest jazzmen on the bill, the Schiffmans found that the jazz shows needed help to make them commercially successful. "No jazz show was successful unless it had a major female artist headlining," said Bobby Schiffman. "If you had Sarah Vaughan, you had a successful jazz show. You had Nancy Wilson, then you could have Cannonball Adderley and any number of major attractions there. But you better have that vocalist, who is gonna express what they had to say in words—rather than on the horn—as the main attraction of the show. I have had some great pure-jazz shows with Miles Davis, Mongo Santamaria, Charlie Parker, Thelonious Monk, Errol Garner, or Dave Brubeck. But if you don't have Ella Fitzgerald, Sarah Vaughan, or Dinah Washington as the headliner, you can forget it. I can never explain why the great jazz talents of our day—almost all of whom were black, and if they were not black they played the Apollo anyhow—just couldn't make it unless they had a major female vocalist. If you had Betty 'Bebop' Carter and you had Miles Davis as the headliner, it was no good. She had to be the headliner. At least that was the pattern."

The great innovators in jazz during the late fifties and early sixties were not concerned with popular tastes. They were artistic pioneers searching for new means of expression, new sounds that would have a lasting impact. John Coltrane, the most significant improviser since Charlie Parker, was renowned for his lengthy solos of breathtaking originality and emotional intensity—which were nevertheless scorned by many critics and members of the jazz establishment.

"I'm still primarily looking into certain sounds, certain scales," Coltrane told writer Nat Hentoff. "Not that I'm sure of what I'm looking for, except that it'll be something that hasn't been played before. I don't know what it is. I know I'll have that feeling when I get it. And in the process of looking, continual looking, the result in any given performance can be long or short. I never know."

Unfortunately, the crowd at the Apollo wasn't always willing to follow Trane on his journey. "I saw Coltrane play the Apollo one time," said Lionel Hampton. "The place was packed when he went in there. When he left, there wasn't but a handful of people in there. He was playing his piece 'My Favorite Things,' and he played that piece for about half an hour. He was just giving vent to his feelings. Coltrane figured his music wasn't being accepted by everybody. Then it was the

Ruth Brown headlines a late-1950s jazz bill featuring two of the most important jazz musicians of all time, Miles Davis and Thelonious Monk. ★ Bobby Schiffman: *"No jazz show was successful unless it had a major female artist headlining."*

The classic John Coltrane quartet, 1962. From left to right: McCoy Tyner, Coltrane, Jimmy Garrison, and Elvin Jones. ★ *Trane was a soloist of breathtaking originality and emotional intensity who was constantly searching for new sounds. Unfortunately, the crowd at the Apollo wasn't always willing to follow him on his journey.*

sixties when there was a lot of trouble in the air. Racism. The black man hollering for freedom. Coltrane got caught up into it. He was taking his feeling out that he had against the happenings of the time, taking it out on his horn. One of the things somebody told me a long time ago was, 'When you get on that stage, you're in show business. You be kind to your audience. Try to make communication with them. Give them what they want.' "

Leslie Uggams remembers a time at the Apollo when another jazz master failed to communicate with her father. "My father used to go to the Apollo a lot," she recalled. "He went to see Miles Davis, and he was sitting there, and across from him was another man about his age, about sixty. Miles started off with a melody, then he began embellishing it. My father lost the tune Miles was playing. At the same time, he and the other guy turned and looked at each other. And the other guy leaned over and said, 'What are we doing here? We're too old for this.' And they both got up and left."

When Thelonious Monk, the continually inventive pianist and one of the jazz world's great eccentrics, played the Apollo in the late fifties, he wore a pink sequined necktie—his one concession to the demands of show business. And as he was wont to do when his sidemen took solos, he got up and danced around his piano. Monk was the epitome of the far-out jazz musician, and he lived in his own little world. "Monk was scheduled to play the Apollo," said Bobby Schiffman, "and at noon on Friday we couldn't find him. It was time for him to go onstage, and I'm running around frantically trying to find him. I see him standing up on the fire escape backstage, outside the building in the middle of winter with an overcoat on and his hat pulled down over his head. Just standing there peering at a tenement house. Everybody else has a case of nervous disorder, and he's standing out on the fire escape."

· · · · ·

Like the jazz artists, comedians in the sixties often found that the Apollo could not provide them with enough time to adequately express themselves and did not always accord them the respect they felt they deserved. According to comedian Scoey Mitchlll, "We were just handymen for the show. Ben E. King, Chuck Jackson, Jackie Wilson, Solomon Burke—that's what they came to see. The only comedian who might mean something was when a Redd Foxx came in, because he was going to talk dirty, and he was going to talk about everybody. Or Nipsey

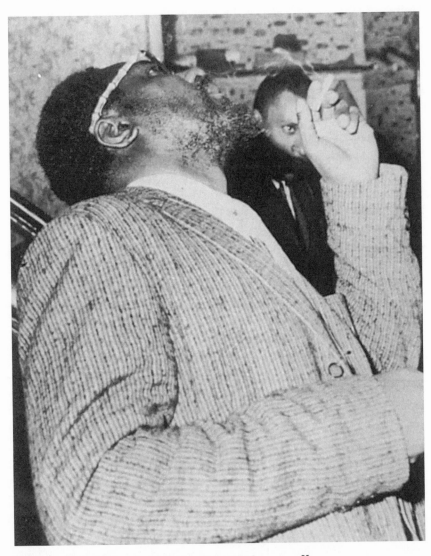

Thelonious Monk, backstage in the early 1960s. ★ *He lived in his own little world.*

Russell, because he was very popular in New York. But I don't think the talking acts really meant anything. I remember when Bill Cosby came to the Apollo. Nobody even knew he was a comic. They just knew he was the guy from 'I Spy.' But they could tell you who had the hit record that week."

"Apollo comedians," Bill Cosby told Vincent Canby of *The New York Times*, "usually get small billing and seven minutes to do their thing." That was one reason why Cosby had stayed away from the Apollo until his only engagement at the theatre, in 1968. But another reason, as Scoey said, was the fact that Harlemites knew him only as Alexander Scott, secret agent, from television, and had no idea what he was doing at the Apollo. Not many first-time Apollo performers ride uptown to their debuts with one of the *The Times*'s top critics, but Cosby did. Yet until word of mouth began packing the theatre after the first couple of days, Cos sometimes played to audiences of only a few hundred people. "I am not one of the black performers who had to or even necessarily wanted to play the Apollo," said Cosby in an interview for this book. "I played there once and by the time I got finished paying everybody off, I ended up with about one twelfth of what I would ordinarily get."

Although he only played the Apollo for one week, people in Harlem still remember the engagement fondly because Bill Cosby is a very funny man and because his star quality shone through as he handled the affair with aplomb. Canby reported that early in his first show the audience cheered Cosby when he silenced a heckler by calmly telling the lady, "Now we aren't going to trade talk back and forth. I got some routines to do and I'm going to do them." He also knew just the right strings to pull to tug at the heart of the Apollo crowd. Along with now-familiar Cosby routines about his childhood and his friend Fat Albert, he gained their respect and sympathy with the problems of affluence. His $24,000 Rolls-Royce "always ran so quiet, man," he said, "I didn't know it had broken down. But the trees weren't moving, so I figured it had. Then I figured for $24,000 the place I was going to would come to me." Finally, he told of his introduction to the Apollo's dour stagehands: "Is that him?" one asked. "Yeah, that's the cat," said another. "What's he going to do?" asked the first. "I don't know," said the other, "maybe shoot some cats."

Most of the Apollo's comics during this period were only locally known. "There was a group of us at the time," said Scoey Mitchlll: "Stu Gilliam, Flip Wilson, myself, Erwin C. Watson, Jimmy Pelham, and Clay Tyson. We were just a level below the Redd Foxxes and Nipsey Russells or George Kirby and Slappy White. We were as good as any of them, but when we went in they'd pay us $300 or $400 a week, and they'd have to pay Nipsey $2,500. Just pure economics had them turning to us for a while. The Apollo was the only place most of us worked in New York, prior to us breaking in downtown in the Village and places like that."

This new breed of black comics often was not content to play an ancillary role in show business, and as new venues opened up to them—especially television—they abandoned the Apollo. "I used to fight with Bobby Schiffman all the time," said Scoey Mitchlll. "I used to tell him, 'Hey, man, I'm not an m.c. Get one of them disc jockeys to emcee. I just want to come out and do a spot.' See, he wanted an m.c. to introduce the other acts and so forth. I was difficult. I just wanted to be a comic, and the rest of the guys they'd go in and do the emceeing and so forth, and after the first few times that I went in, I refused to emcee."

"I used to do a lot of stuff about marijuana," Scoey said. "My act dealt with the seamy side of life and race problems. We used to do a lot of dope material and it used to be funny. Like 'Cuckoo Clock'—you remember that? That's an old joke. Everybody was sitting around smoking some weed and all of a sudden came a knock on the door. 'Who is it?' 'Police.' Everybody's looking around trying to find out where they're going to throw their roaches. Just then the cuckoo came out of the clock. So everybody took their roaches and threw them into the cuckoo clock. The cops came in and searched the place, couldn't find anything, and left. Everybody's sitting there waiting for the cuckoo to bring the roaches out. It's 8:30, no cuckoo . . . 9:00, still no cuckoo . . . 9:30 . . . 10:00—still the cuckoo doesn't show. So round about 10:30 one cat says, 'If that cuckoo isn't out of that clock at 10:30, I'm gonna tear that clock apart.' So 10:30 comes, and the little door eased open, and the cuckoo came out and says, 'Say, man, what time is it?' "

Flip Wilson got forty dollars a week for years as an Apollo m.c. and comic. "I have a thing with the Apollo audience," Flip has said. "Maybe I feel they know me better. I tell the same stories at other places and the reception is just as good, but at the Apollo *I* feel different. Maybe it's because I know they need to laugh more—it's nothing but a jive dollar to get in there, but when *they* pay that bread they got to laugh. I know I'll never come to a point where I lose contact with them."

It's not exactly what Flip had in mind, but there is a story about one particular way Flip kept in contact with the Apollo even after he had become a television star. "There was a girl that used to work for me, Angela Aguiar," said Bobby Schiffman. "She was my secretary, and she

Bill Cosby and friend at the Apollo, 1968 ★ *"I am not one of the black performers who had to or even necessarily wanted to play the Apollo."*

Scoey Mitchlll at the Apollo, early 1960s. ★ *"The Apollo was the only place most of us worked in New York, prior to us breaking in downtown in the Village and places like that."*

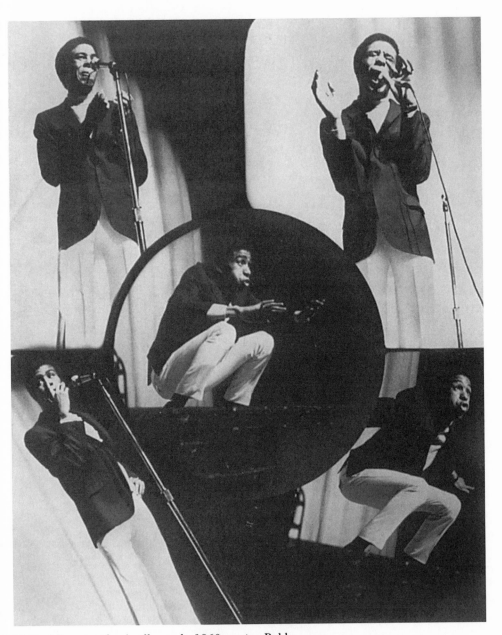

Richard Pryor at the Apollo, early 1960s. ★ Bobby
Schiffman: *"He was dirty, and there were possibly a lot of
people who walked. But Richie was before his time."*

was a dynamite lady, very talented. Flip Wilson was crazy about her. Angela was a professional virgin. She was not going to go to bed with anybody till she had that gold ring on her finger, and that was it. She was raised in a very strong Catholic-Spanish upbringing, and that was her thing. Well, Flip tried to get her to go out with him a thousand different times. He went out to California and spent a couple of years doing the TV show. When he came back to New York, he stopped in at the Apollo. Of course, she was thrilled to see him, and he was thrilled to see her. They were right up in my office, and he got down on his knees and begged her to go out with him. She said no. He sat down, and she came to the door and in a very saucy way said, 'Listen, Mr. Wilson, you went to California. I never heard from you. I never got anything from you, and I'm not interested in going out with you.' He got so crazy that he took a hundred-dollar bill out of his pocket. She had never seen a hundred-dollar bill. He wrote 'Flip Wilson' across it, dropped it on her desk, and left. She was hell-bent on giving it back to him."

Another fledgling comedian who helped make his mark at the Apollo was Richard Pryor. "The first time he played the Apollo," recalled Bobby Schiffman, "was with Count Basie, Billy Eckstine, Coles and Atkins, and Freda Payne. We paid Richard $350 and he was outrageous. The highlight of the show was the finale. Everybody in the cast would come out and they would do something together to close the show out. You know the old adage about black folks having rhythm? Well, the finale was a musical number, and everything Richard did was out of sync. Everything—intentionally out of sync. Well, the audience went into hysteria because Richie could not get into sync with anything. He was in the wrong key. He was tapping his foot at the wrong beat. The rest onstage kept mugging with him, and it was really very, very funny. He's a brilliant comic."

It is said the Pryor's routine was so dirty that he was actually booed off the Apollo stage, though Bobby doesn't remember that ever happening. "He was dirty, and there were possibly a lot of people who walked. But Richie was before his time. He was a coming thing. His comedy routines were very street-oriented and very unique and fresh. The people just loved him. Off the stage he's a very softspoken, easy to talk to, quiet, unassuming person. As opposed to Redd Foxx, who is onstage all the time. Foxx is Foxx all the time. What you see is what you get."

Redd Foxx and Bobby Schiffman were close friends. Both are avid hunters, and once appeared together on television on "American Sportsman." Both are natural pranksters, too, and sometimes the situation at the Apollo threatened to get out of hand. On one such occasion Bobby tried to get Redd to clean up his notoriously dirty act. "We used to have a good deal of control over what performers did onstage," said Bobby. "I used to review the opening show on Friday. Then I would go backstage and make corrections. I went into Redd's dressing room and he was slouched down on a couch, and he had his hands in the pockets of his bathrobe. I said to him, 'Foxx, you're going to have to take out the blue shit. You're just gonna have to.' He said, 'I'm not gonna do it.' I said, 'Please don't fuck me over, this is a family theatre. I can't have you joking about assholes in the middle of the afternoon with a guy sitting there with his seventeen-year-old daughter.' He said, 'I'm not gonna take it out.' Now he's joking and I'm joking at this point. I used to wear a sidearm when I took money to the bank. I said, 'I'm gonna put a hole in you.' He said, 'You're gonna do what?' I said, 'I tell you, take it out or I'm gonna put a hole in you.' He said, 'Bobby, before you get to that thing you're wearing on your hip, I'll put my knife through your chest.' He's still lying there on the couch. I pushed my hand across my chest to open my coat like Jesse James would do to uncover my pistol. When I did that, his hand came out of his pocket and he had a knife. It was open, and he threw it across the room. It whistled past my ear, stuck in the wall, and went, 'booiiing!' So I said, 'Okay, what are you going to do now?' He said, 'You don't know what's in my other hand.' "

Redd was also involved with "gunplay" on another occasion at the Apollo. "I used to do a gunfighter thing," recalled Sammy Davis, Jr. "We were starring at the Apollo, and Redd Foxx was the comedy star. Redd used to do an Indian thing. He'd say the famous last words of Custer. He'd put a cowboy hat on: 'Hot damn, I ain't never seen this many Indians in my life.' I had done a couple of Westerns by that time. So I'm doing my fast-draw thing. I did the impressions of all the cowboys walking—Wayne and all those—the brothers and sisters uptown loved that. I had one piece at the end where I'd say, 'Let's see if I can get a couple of fast ones off.' The closing show I went, 'Let me see if I can get two off,' and I went, 'Pow!' Redd fell down and sacked out in the middle of the stage, and about ninety people fell out of the wings. All the stagehands were falling out of the wings. He put them up to it."

Redd began his career in comedy in the late forties with his partner, Slappy White. But his career really took off when he began interjecting "blue" material into his act, and made a series of dirty party records that were very popular in the black community. When Bobby Schiffman

Redd Foxx, a real hep cat, with the Buddy Johnson band at the Apollo, 1944. ★ Bobby Schiffman: *"I said, 'Please don't fuck me over, this is a family theatre. I can't have you joking about assholes in the middle of the afternoon with a guy sitting there with his seventeen-year-old daughter.' He said, 'I'm not gonna take [the dirty language] out.'"*

Bobby Schiffman with Miriam Makeba, about 1967. ★ *"The Apollo responded as it always had in trying to get things it thought the black community was interested in."*

alerted him to the possibilities for comedians on television, he did clean up his act; and Bobby helped Foxx break into the medium that would make him a nationwide star. "Redd was sitting in my office one day," recalled Bobby. "I said, 'TV is the thing, and you're eliminating that marketplace from your possible work area because you're so dirty. Why don't you cut it out and make some inroads into TV?' He said, 'My reputation precedes me. If I decided tomorrow that I would never say anything vulgar again, they would still not want to go near me because they would be fearful that I would.' I said, 'Well, you are making a mistake.' He said, 'You can't get me a TV show.' I said, 'If you give me your word that you won't do anything to embarrass me, I'll get you a TV show.' He said, 'Okay, you got my word.'

"So while we sat there, I got on the phone and called 'The Tonight Show.' Just as a matter of coincidence, Skitch Henderson got on the phone, and he knew my father. I introduced myself and he asked about my father, and I asked, 'Would you be interested in Redd Foxx?' He said, 'Oh, definitely, but I'm a little tied up. I'll call you back in twenty minutes.' He hung up, but I didn't tell Redd. Instead, I stayed on the phone and said, 'He won't do anything dirty. I can guarantee it.' And I waited a few seconds and said, 'I give you my personal guarantee, the guy won't do anything dirty.' Then I hung up and said, 'You can't do anything to embarrass me.' He said, 'Okay,' and he left. I called Skitch up and we got Redd on the 'Today' show the next day, and 'The Tonight Show' the same night. Redd killed them, and he didn't do anything dirty, and that was the start of his whole involvement with TV and movies and Vegas. His price went from $2,500 to $15,000 a week or something like that."

. . . . .

By the late sixties, as the optimism of the early civil-rights movement gradually gave way to more militant and nationalistic sentiments, the black community grew increasingly impatient and cynical about the promise of integration and turned instead to a greater appreciation of its African heritage.

The Apollo responded by spicing the steady diet of soul music with attractions like the Nigerian musician Babatunde Olatunji and his dancers and the South African singer Miriam Makeba. "Although these shows were not outrageously successful, financially," said Bobby Schiffman, "they did have a great deal of artistic merit. And they satisfied

280

some of the root-seeking on the part of the intellectuals of the community. Also, the shows were really exciting, and if you had some sort of appreciation for it, it only nurtured that and developed it. The Apollo responded as it always had in trying to get things it thought the black community was interested in."

Though the objective was to give Harlem a taste of Africa, inevitably Africa—or at least the Africans who played the Apollo—was influenced by Harlem, too. "When the African Ballet was offered to us, we snapped it up," said Bobby Schiffman. "It had all French-speaking people in it; nobody in the company spoke English. So we hired an interpreter. Now, the African Ballet created a great deal of excitement in the press, and ABC or NBC covered the first performance. They had cameras set up in the theatre, and they had their own independent lights that they would turn on whenever they would shoot, because the normal theatre setting didn't have enough light. There was a very key blackout in the show—that's when all the lights go out at one time, and it's usually part of the crescendo of the number.

"We had been struggling with this lack of communication because they all spoke French. And the TV guys were up in the box on the left side of the theatre, and every once in a while they would turn their lights on and shoot a segment of the show. Well, this key blackout was coming up, and just as this blackout was about to occur, everybody on the technical side of the theatre realized that the TV guys were going to blow the blackout by turning on their lights. Suddenly, this non–English-speaking technician with the African Ballet stepped out of the wings, pointed up to the TV booth, and said, 'Out the motherfuckin' light!' They had been there one day and they picked up 'motherfucker' right away."

Despite the Schiffmans' attempt to stay in tune with the black community, the bitterness of the time put a great deal of pressure on the Apollo's white owners. Tensions nearly boiled over in a dispute over a show called the Jewel Box Revue—a transvestite spectacle that billed itself as "25 Boys and One Girl." The Jewel Box Revue had been a prime attraction at the Apollo throughout the sixties. "It was a very productive show," said Bobby Schiffman, "because we used to play it for the month of February every year for the whole month, a time of year when major performers didn't want to come to New York because they were fearful of the weather, especially if they were on percentages. The Jewel Box Revue enabled us to keep everybody employed for a whole month. It also produced a very good profit, so we used to look forward to having that show and doing it three times a day."

The show consisted of the standard female-impersonator fare. As the *Variety* reviewer wrote of the 1968 show: "In past years it was easy to spot the femme. She was the one with the mustache. Now that it's off, she's still recognizable by her baritone voice. Most of the others are sopranos. . . . It's an even better show in the audience. Many partisans of the femme impersonators onstage came to pay respect and reverence for what they regard as the apex of any art form, as was evidenced by their applause and rapture." Bobby said, "The weirdest thing was to go backstage between shows—and some of these guys had gone so far as to have silicone shots, so they had tits—so you would walk backstage and you'd see these big burly creatures walking around with huge bosoms. The show was very good, and the people were very much into it. Some people used to come back ten to twelve times to see it.

"The shows came to an end because a local nationalist group menaced the theatre in a most violent way, saying they would blow up the theatre if we put on the show. They said that it glorified the homosexual, and that was a threat to black life and the black family. They threatened to blow the theatre up, and kill me and kill everybody that worked for me if we opened the doors with that show, and they were going to drop violence on us. Originally, we had a couple of picket lines around the theatre, and the people who came to patronize the show didn't give one good hoot about the picket lines. They just told the pickets to get the fuck out of their way. But when it came to my life, you could take that show and stick it. I wasn't going to play it."

Racial violence was becoming more of an everyday occurrence in the streets of Harlem, but even in the midst of hostilities, there could be a time out for laughter. "I remember during the [civil-rights] movement," said Scoey Mitchlll, "there was a bomb threat in the Apollo. They cleared the Apollo, and they had the street blocked off in front of it. Honi Coles, Reuben Phillips, myself, and someone else, it might have been Sandman, were standing in front of the Apollo talking. There was a junkie lying against the door. All of a sudden, eight squad cars come screaming up to the front of the Apollo. And the junkie looks up, you know, and he sees all these cops and takes off down the street. So the cops come in and check out the theatre and leave, and we're still standing there talking. The junkie comes back and comes over to us and he says, 'That sure wasn't funny, man.' He thought we'd called all those cops just for him."

Throughout the sixties, though, the Apollo was protected from direct harm, even when the rest of the community was devastated. In

Members of the Jewel Box Revue backstage at the
Apollo in the early 1960s. ★ Bobby Schiffman: *"A
local nationalist group said it glorified the homosexual,
and that was a threat to black life and the black family.
They threatened to blow the theatre up."*

July 1964, the worst riot in Harlem in more than two decades broke out when an off-duty cop shot and killed a Harlem teenager. There was one death, 140 were injured and 500 arrested, and the violence spread to the black neighborhoods of Brooklyn. Sporadic trouble continued throughout the sixties, culminating in more rioting in the aftermath of the assassination of Martin Luther King, Jr., in 1968. The violence and tension effectively sealed off Harlem to whites. "Whites don't come up here anymore," said Honi Coles in 1967, "because they are afraid to. All of this racial stuff and the riots has them scared."

Nevertheless, the Apollo continued in the show-business tradition of "the show must go on," and blacks and some adventuresome whites continued to fill the theatre. "I played there during a riot," said singer Maxine Brown. "I saw people beaten in the streets, shootings, and so on. The shows still went on. The Apollo had their own security, and of course there was the police, but you see—no one touched the Apollo Theatre. I was looking out the window backstage and I saw this poor white boy coming down the street. They had stripped him down to his underwear, and, without realizing it, I just screamed from the window, 'Leave him alone.' But you still did your shows. The crowds were still out there. People were running everywhere, but the shows still went on."

Maxine Brown in the mid-1960s. ★ *"I played there during a riot. I saw people beaten in the streets, shootings, and so on. The shows still went on."*

8

THE STRUGGLING
SEVENTIES
··········

The Apollo was standing room only—all 1,700 seats were filled and hundreds more people were packed in the aisles and in the back behind the orchestra section. It was a Friday night in December 1975. The big stars no longer appeared quite so regularly at the Apollo, and when they did, they performed only two shows a day. So when word went out that Smokey Robinson was going to be at the theatre, people began lining up early. Smokey delighted the opening-night crowd with a sampling of his early hits with the Miracles as well as his new solo material.

In the upper-right-hand box, eighteen-year-old Darryl Scullack of West 148th Street and his friends sat enjoying the show. Scullack had had a tough time lately. He was out on $500 bail after being arrested for robbing a bar on Eighth Avenue, and the previous Saturday he had been shot at, near his home. The word out on the street was that Darryl Scullack's days were numbered.

As Smokey began his final tune, a gunman entered Scullack's box and began firing wildly, killing the youth and wounding one bystander in the thigh and another in the arm. At first Smokey thought the shots were firecrackers lit by kids fooling around. For several seconds afterward, the Apollo was silent. Then people began screaming and shouting and a number of people rushed from the theatre, apparently including the gunman and Darryl's friends. Smokey Robinson walked offstage.

Darryl Scullack probably felt safe in the Apollo, for it had been a place that was respected and revered; to hurt it would be to hurt oneself, to commit violence there would be to commit violence in one's own home. The gunman obviously didn't feel that way.

The violence and crime that plagued the black community could no longer be kept out of the Apollo as dreams of the Great Society crumbled in the burned-out tenements of Harlem in the seventies. By the mid-seventies the theatre was frequently the scene of dressing-room rip-offs—Ray Charles and Gladys Knight were among those victimized. And the Apollo had become a favorite place to transact drug deals. The darkened theatre that had for generations provided the requisite atmosphere for joyful fantasy now was reduced to providing cover for furtive exchanges that led to other illicit and dangerous forms of escapism.

The day after the Scullack shooting, the crowds returned to the Apollo; and Smokey Robinson finished out a successful week. But the singer said he would never come back. Within a month the Apollo Theatre had closed its doors.

· · · · ·

Since 1934 the Apollo had shared a special relationship with its community, withstanding hard times, enjoying good times. But it could not overcome the array of problems that brought it all to an end. When the end came, it came quickly; however, the Apollo went out at the peak. "In all the years that the Apollo was in business," Bobby Schiffman remarked, "the years from 1970 to 1974 were the banner years financially"—thanks to the loyalty of many big stars and to another talented crop of newcomers.

In the early seventies, the initial wave of soul music had crested, artistically, but its biggest stars began to achieve their greatest commercial success. The Motown hitmakers, many of whom would soon abandon Motown for more attractive deals, were riding particularly high. Gladys Knight, whose career really took off after she left Motown and moved in a more pop-oriented direction, became the first performer to sell out an entire week at the Apollo in advance. It was a heady time. "I get goose pimples thinking about it now," said Gladys.

Just as thousands of other hopeful amateurs, like Gladys Knight and the Pips, had before them, the group that became Motown's premier attraction in the seventies, the Jackson 5, came to the Apollo to try to

RIGHT: Smokey Robinson (left) and the Miracles, mid-1960s. ★ *As Smokey began his final tune, a gunman entered the box and began firing wildly.* BELOW: Gladys Knight and the Pips in the 1970s. ★ *She became the first performer to sell out an entire week at the Apollo in advance.*

break into show business. Nine-year-old Michael Jackson, his brothers, and father first went to see James Brown, who was in New York at the Americana Hotel, about hiring the young group for his stage show. "James wouldn't do it," said Dave Prater of Sam and Dave. So the Jackson family went to the Apollo and approached Sam and Dave in their dressing room.

"We couldn't handle them as an act on the show with us. We didn't have the money because we had just started making money ourselves, and had just bought a big ole bus and all that shit. But we talked to Honi Coles, and he put them on the amateur show." The response to their first song was so enthusiastic that they were brought back for an encore of two more songs, and easily won the contest. Yet their big break didn't come until later. "The next thing I heard about them," said Prater, "Diana Ross had them. She took them to Berry Gordy at Motown. About six months later, Berry Gordy had a hit out by them. Goddamn!"

In 1971 James Brown was the highest-paid black entertainer in the world. Between 1969 and 1971 he had seventeen Top Ten hits on the rhythm-and-blues charts. The media called him "the Black Messiah" and "the most powerful black man in America." He was a business tycoon who owned three radio stations at a time when only five in the country were owned by blacks. He launched a host of business ventures, and his empire was overseen by a staff of eighty-five with an annual payroll of one million dollars. He was a superstar who had filled Yankee Stadium for a concert; yet he never forgot the Apollo, and made a point of playing there once or twice a year in the early seventies.

His visibility and power attracted him to major politicians of both parties. When Hubert Humphrey lost the Democratic nomination to George McGovern in 1972, Brown came out in favor of Richard Nixon, and one of the strangest political alliances of the seventies was created. The effect of the Nixon endorsement on Brown's career was catastrophic. At his first Apollo show after the election, in May 1973, he was met by pickets carrying signs that read: "James Brown, Nixon's Clown" and "Get the Clown Outta Town."

"After the Nixon thing: boom!" said Danny Ray, Brown's m.c. "It was like a big bomb. We was catching hell." St. Clair Pinckney, his band director, agreed: "It hurt. It hurt. Our engagements, every location on the circuit instantly became booked, no open dates. Everything was booked because this man had such a reputation." At the Apollo, one of Brown's entourage appeared onstage at the opening show to defend the singer. Yet even with all the controversy, the usual lines of James Brown fans thronged 125th Street all week for his Apollo engagement. But Brown had been truly shaken by the Nixon incident. He has had a difficult time trying to regain his footing as a musical innovator and businessman ever since.

As some established stars prospered and others declined in the early seventies, a new breed emerged and began dominating the boards at the Apollo. Whereas Detroit had been the town that produced many of the great black singers of the sixties, Philadelphia became the starmaker of the seventies—especially an independent record company called Philadelphia International. Philly was started in 1971 by ace producers Kenny Gamble and Leon Huff, and they were soon joined by another top arranger-songwriter-producer, Thom Bell. Among them they controlled the destinies of many of the top chartmakers of the seventies, and they scored big on the burgeoning disco scene in the middle of the decade. Thom Bell produced eleven hit singles in 1974 and the team of Gamble and Huff ten. The records that came out of their Sigma Sound studios were smoother and more lush than the soul music of the sixties, and the throbbing beat behind them would soon be echoed in every disco in the world. The Philadelphia groups such as the Delfonics, the O'Jays, the Stylistics, First Choice, the Spinners, and the Three Degrees created what became known as the Sound of Philadelphia.

Perhaps the most important of the Philadelphia International groups was Harold Melvin and the Blue Notes, featuring Teddy Pendergrass. Melvin's group began in the fifties. They first played the Apollo in 1960 after achieving a minor hit with a song called "My Hero." In the sixties they became a bow-tie-and-tuxedo nightclub act that made a good steady living playing to the white double-knit set in Vegas, Miami, and Puerto Rico. Things began to change in 1969 when, as group member Lawrence Brown has said, "We heard our drummer, Theodore Pendergrass, sing something and we thought, 'There's a voice the Blue Notes need.' "

Pendergrass played the hard-luck sexpot, and with his deep raspy vocals moaned his way through seventies hits such as "If You Don't Know Me By Now," "Yesterday I Had the Blues," "Where Are All My Friends," and "Bad Luck (Part I)." "Teddy had become the sweetheart of the Harold Melvin fans," recalled Bobby Schiffman. "He was the key to the act. Although Harold always had quality acts, he had nurtured and developed Pendergrass as a lead singer to the point where Teddy was as much of an attraction as Harold Melvin."

Pendergrass ultimately decided that he could make it as a single. He

The Jackson Five, about 1970 (Michael is wearing the hat). ★
Dave Prater: *"We talked to Honi Coles, and he put them on the amateur show. The next thing I heard about them, Diana Ross had them. She took them to Berry Gordy at Motown. About six months later, Berry Gordy had a hit out by them. Goddamn!"*

Leon Huff (left) and Kenny Gamble (right), early 1970s. ★
They controlled the destinies of many of the top chartmakers of the 1970s, and they scored big on the burgeoning disco scene in the middle of the decade.

made his move in 1975. "We had Harold Melvin and the Blue Notes in the Apollo when the breakup occurred," Bobby said. "We had done outrageous business on that Friday and Saturday. On Sunday, Pendergrass didn't show up. He got into an argument with Harold, and their involvement together terminated. The Apollo carried the brunt of that situation when Pendergrass didn't show up. We were looking for him all day and couldn't find him. Finally we had to announce to everybody that Pendergrass would not be there, and of course the show fell flat on its face after that." Teddy Pendergrass went on to become one of the top black idols of the decade, but Harold Melvin and the Blue Notes continued as a hot act without him.

. . . . .

Until Bobby Schiffman closed the Apollo in 1976, he actively wooed the top black stars with a pitch that urged them to return to their roots. As Bobby said, "It was always an ancillary part of the Apollo Theatre's buying that it was asking acts to work at a great financial sacrifice. The Apollo didn't have the ability to entice people with money. The Apollo hinged its pursuit of major performers on the tack of, 'You have to play for the people of Harlem because they have no other place to see you.' Almost one hundred percent of the people who played the Apollo, who were noted people, played it at great financial sacrifice. There was a basic desire on the part of performers to play for Harlemites. There was an uncomfortable feeling for people from our community going downtown. They didn't feel welcome down there. So if you wanted to play for the mass of black people, you had to play the Apollo."

"I practically paid money to go in and do it the way I wanted to do it," said Dionne Warwick of her gala return engagement in October 1970. "I put a lot of money into my own show. And they made an awful lot of money, which is good, because it kept the doors open. They were getting ready to close the Apollo the year I went back in there. The doors were literally slammed, probably broke. I was approached, and I said, 'You will never close the Apollo. Not as long as I live.' That's when I took my choir in with me. We had twenty strings. The theatre was gorgeous. They built scenery for me. We did lighting. The sound has always been impeccable in that theatre. The best in the world. They even painted my dressing room and recarpeted it for me. It was a wonderful, wonderful week, and it gave them the leverage that they needed. The week after I closed was when Lou Rawls went back in, and Nancy Wilson went back in, the Temptations, who were burning up. I brought everybody back to the Apollo."

Nancy Wilson explains why she went back: "The Apollo needed me and I needed it, and it was a wonderful coming together. I talked with Pop Schiffman and Bobby and I said, 'How in the world can you keep the Apollo going? It's needed.' I know it sounds strange to say it needed me, but it did. I played there because I felt I should. I played there because the Schiffmans were the kind of people you should go places for. The audience and the people, the community needed us performers. I played there because it made them feel good. I played there because I knew they wanted me there.

"When I came back, when I came in to work that night, I was greeted at the stage door by the doorman in a tux. The light man had a tux on. The sound man had a tux on. Every person backstage who worked the Apollo, including the Schiffmans, had a tux on. That was quite a night. I think it was the only time it ever happened. The complete staff dressed black-tie—Baby was back and we're going to let her know how we feel about her."

Sammy Davis, Jr., summed it up: "Everybody said, 'You didn't have to go back.' But, yeah, I had to go back to prove to myself that I'm still worthy of that audience. They showed me how much they appreciated my being there. Boy from Harlem who made good, coming back to the Mecca of show business. It always had that kind of a taste to me. It wasn't money, certainly. You could get more money downtown. There was a need. It's the mere fact that you've got to be around your own. And if you're an entertainer, you want to entertain your own."

But after a while, the Schiffmans' pleas began to wear a bit thin. In December 1975, a year after his father's death, Bobby tried to persuade Nancy Wilson to come back one more time, but the Apollo was already doomed. He wrote:

Dear Nancy:
How to begin a plea to someone like you who has been so cooperative and so much involved in the good fortunes of the Apollo Theatre without sounding like an absolute ass is difficult. So instead of beating around the bush with a lot of hogwash, I'll just lay it on the line. . . .

You are a key show business personality to the Apollo, for you stand alone the elegant Queen of Beauty and Love. Very frankly, I need you desperately. I must have one performer who can truthfully say they don't need the Apollo, they can survive without a New York engagement.

John [Levy, Wilson's manager] tells me that you feel that you have done your bit for the Apollo, and God knows I cannot argue with that. John says you feel it is not a good career move for you to come at this time. But I say that people like you whose cooperation can be counted on make the whole damn thing worthwhile so that in addition to the wonderful week's business that you always generate, you create inspiration for the management of this theatre and give a gift of love to Harlem. Please do not turn your back on us now. . . .

. . . . .

By the mid-seventies, the Apollo was having great difficulty booking effective stage presentations, and it was operating at less than half its potential—producing only twenty-two weeks of live entertainment a year. To fill in the off weeks, the Apollo sought to present films that would appeal to the black community. At the height of Hollywood's brief enchantment with black films, the theatre found that the only films it could book were cheap B-grade quickies or long-since played-out major motion pictures. So Bobby Schiffman and Walter Brecher, son of Apollo co-owner Leo Brecher, launched a vigorous campaign to secure for the Apollo first-run major motion pictures of particular interest to the black community.

At one time or another, the Brechers owned a number of downtown movie theatres, including the Little Carnegie, the Plaza, and the 68th Street Playhouse. They knew that successful movies made the bulk of their money in the first few months of release. Second- and third-run houses—which appeared to be the fate of the Apollo—got only the leftovers. The pattern in New York had been for black-oriented films to open at one of the big theatres on Broadway, in Times Square, and simultaneously at one of the Yorkville movie palaces on East 86th Street. These places were deemed accessible to the black community as well as to whites. The Broadway and Yorkville exhibitors feared that an additional first-run showing uptown at the Apollo could siphon off a part of their business. Distributors felt blacks would buy in greater numbers downtown, and therefore there was no reason to open at the Apollo. The filmmakers feared that even though the films in question were black-oriented, an Apollo opening would scare away any potential white audience.

293

But the Apollo disagreed and took them all on. Only two films had opened at the Apollo, Bill Cosby's *Man and Boy* and Oscar Williams's *The Final Comedown*, both small independent productions. The Apollo wanted a motion picture from one of the major studios. In September 1973 it got Paramount's *Save the Children*, a film of a 1972 Operation PUSH concert. The Apollo run yielded about the same as a simultaneous run at the Criterion on Broadway. Still, it was not a major film. When, in the summer of 1974, a suitable film came along, Sidney Poitier's *Uptown Saturday Night*, produced by Warners and starring Bill Cosby, the Apollo tried to secure it, to no avail. The film opened on Broadway, and everyone attending the premiere was shuttled up to Harlem for a party afterward. An ad for the film boasted: "You can still go uptown without getting your head beat in by going downtown to see *Uptown Saturday Night*." That was too much for the Apollo to bear.

Bobby Schiffman complained bitterly about the implications of the ad. National Urban League leader Vernon Jordan pledged his support for the Apollo's film struggle. And Congressman Charles Rangel wrote Schiffman: "I am glad that the management of the Apollo Theatre reacted quickly and vociferously in protesting this ad." And he noted in a handwritten addition to the letter that he was glad that Cosby apologized to the people of Harlem.

The Apollo had just begun to fight. Bobby Schiffman charged that the film industry was "bigoted and narrow-minded, downright unfair, downright selfish." He told *The New York Times*, "We get black-oriented films when all the meat is off the bones." The Apollo filed a suit against a number of major studios, film distributors, and exhibitors seeking to prevent the defendants from allegedly "conspiring in restraint of trade and to monopolize" first-run movie exhibition in Manhattan. The suit asked $2.5 million in damages.

Perhaps spurred by the suit, Warner Brothers relented and agreed to open the "blaxploitation" flick *Cleopatra Jones and the Casino of Gold* in July 1975 simultaneously at the Apollo and at a Broadway and Yorkville theatre. A recorded telephone message at the Apollo gushed: "A great victory for the people of this community." But as the front-page headline on the August 6, 1975, *Variety* blared: "BLACKS SHUN PIC AT HARLEM SITE—'Apollo Experiment' Fails to Pull Locals."

The bulk of the business was done by the Broadway theatre, and the Apollo barely reached its break-even point. "I don't know what happened," admitted Bobby Schiffman. "The box-office pattern set by

The Apollo wanted a motion picture from one of the major studios. In September 1973 it got Paramount's Save the Children, a film of a 1972 Operation PUSH concert.

125th STREET APOLLO THEATRE
JOINS IN WELCOMING YOU UPTOWN AFTER THE
EXCLUSIVELY DOWNTOWN PREMIERE OF THE MOVIE.
WONDER WHY UPTOWNERS CAN'T SEE IT UPTOWN
NOW ?
BECAUSE JIM CROW LIVES!
125th STREET IS STILL THE BACK OF THE BUS,
MOVIEWISE THAT IS.

Handbill distributed on 125th Street by the Apollo in protest of the downtown premiere of the 1974 film Uptown Saturday Night. ★ An ad for the film boasted: "You can still go uptown without getting your head beat in by going downtown to see Uptown Saturday Night."

Cleopatra," the *Variety* article stated, "bolsters the traditional contention of major distribution companies that there's no economic justification for including the Apollo (or any other Harlem house) in first run playoff tracks in Manhattan."

In a letter to the editor of *Variety*, Walter Brecher replied that the film really hadn't done worse at the Apollo than in Yorkville, and that the Apollo needed more time to build a film audience. "Harlem is unique in its creativity and dynamism," he wrote. "These gifts have enriched the city and the nation. But if Harlem gets nothing in return, they may well dry up along with the theatres and businesses and services that are vital to a living community." The issues were never settled, for the Apollo could no longer hold on.

• • • • •

The business of show business changed drastically in the seventies, and while this represented the major breakthrough for black artists that the Apollo family had always hoped for, ironically it spelled doom for "Harlem's High Spot." Previously, performers had made most of their money from personal appearances, and the record companies kept the bulk of the profits from their recordings. Only the biggest stars considered records to be much more than promotional vehicles for their live shows. Most acts toured constantly, as the best way to increase their income. But as performers grew into superstars, they began to demand a larger slice of the pie from recordings. Then they could afford to relax their touring schedules.

"The business started changing a lot," explained Leslie Uggams. "A lot of people felt, 'I'm at the point where I don't have to do four or five shows a day'—and that had always been the policy of the Apollo. And then the record business—black performers started getting played on white stations and the careers and the money started growing. . . ." It was a far cry from the golden era of the independent record companies in the fifties. Deborah Chessler, the Orioles' manager, mused, "The money that they make today, nobody ever dreamed of in those days."

"It was in the early seventies or the late sixties," said Bobby Schiffman, "when the record industry started to pay the kind of money that became the dominant force in the earning power of acts; acts could then afford to be very selective in the engagements that they worked, because they had so much other income from record royalties, and later on television shows, and further on even motion-picture production. Of course most of the acts of real substance also create music, and the music-publishing end of the business is very productive. So acts decided to work less and less. Well, when they decide to work less and less, they are not going to work 125th Street."

By the mid-seventies, even new and untried acts could demand star salaries—if they had a hit record. "There's a record playing across the street now called 'Love to Love You Baby,' " Bobby Schiffman told Steve Tomashefsky of *Living Blues* magazine in 1975. "It's a girl by the name of Donna Summer. Nobody's ever seen her, she doesn't have an act, she hasn't performed anywhere. It's a smash record that will undoubtedly be one of the top records of the year, as far as sales is concerned. Nobody's ever seen her perform, and they're already asking five or six thousand dollars a night for her." Bobby was right; the record was a smash, the first superhit of the disco era. Donna Summer became a superstar, the Queen of Disco. And disco—an entertainment form based solely on records—became the logical outgrowth of the dominance of the record companies.

The Apollo got priced out of the market. "Toward the end in the seventies," lamented Bobby Schiffman, "an act who was in demand—and you need acts who are in demand—could make more money in one night in a bigger and better location than they could make in the Apollo in a whole week. The Apollo, in its management, had the additional chore of trying to keep the prices at a level that the people could afford to pay. If you had an act in the Apollo for $6, that act could sell tickets for $16 downtown, or $20 or $50. You have entertainment facilities in New York with many multiples of the number of seats that you have in the Apollo. When I left, the Apollo had 1,683 seats. The Felt Forum has 4,500. Madison Square Garden has 20,000. The Nassau Coliseum has 19,000. Now the Byrne Arena has 22,000. Carnegie Hall has 2,800. Lincoln Center 4,500. Well, the dollar potential in those areas is a lot greater."

Everyone, it seemed, had given up on Harlem. Visitors were frightened off. The media rarely covered uptown events—except for heinous crimes. Entertainers and entertainment executives wanted nothing to do with the area. In 1975, seven black Broadway shows, including *Bubbling Brown Sugar* and *The Wiz* lured Harlemites downtown. And the city government had left Harlem to deteriorate. The Apollo had been a bright spot in Harlem for more than forty years, but the problems of the new times made it impossible for the show to go on.

"Towards the end, in the seventies, 125th Street turned into a very

297

much deprived street," said Bobby Schiffman. "The streets were dirty. Crime on the streets ran rampant. The discomfort in coming to the theatre was multiplied. After the rioting, all the storekeepers on 125th Street had felt impelled to put in those steel doors that closed over the windows, so the street was unattractive. You drive through 125th Street after seven o'clock and it was like a fortress. That does not lend itself to encouraging people to come.

"The City of New York fell very short in its obligations to provide customer services as it did in other areas of the city. For example, let's take the parking problem, which is a major problem. In every area of the city, there are municipal parking facilities and private facilities that can absorb most of the parking needs of that area. In the Harlem area there is not a single parking facility of merit. There is not a single one where you can park on a municipal base.

"In addition to that, the ancillary things to going to the theatre are not there. If you and your girlfriend or wife decide to go to the theatre, you want to be able to go into a nice cocktail bar or restaurant for a sandwich or what have you. You want to be able to go into a nice clean facility where you know you'll be comfortable—and that stuff doesn't exist uptown. It's unfortunate that customer services that are ancillary to going to the Apollo are not there. Geographically, 125th Street is in a very favorable situation. All of the major highways cross there. You got all the major subway lines. All the major bus lines. It should have developed. But obviously the city fathers took the position that there are just black folks up there, we'll do them last. It was with the greatest heartache that I relinquished my involvement with that community."

Yet the time had clearly come for Schiffman to leave. "What happened is that with the advent of Malcolm X and the strong growth of nationalistic pride in the black community, which was a very valid and worthwhile force," said Bobby, "there came the feeling that the black community should own and operate their own institutions. And the Apollo was a major institution in the black community, and for years the aim of [our] management of the Apollo was to sell it to a black entrepreneur. We had several offers from white businessmen who wanted to buy the Apollo, but we always turned them down. We were waiting for a black organization to come along that had the knowledge, wisdom, and money to buy the Apollo."

The Apollo had been quietly up for sale as early as the mid-sixties. By the early seventies, reports of imminent deals for the theatre began appearing occasionally in the press. In the fall of 1972 it was announced

Donna Summer, 1975. ★ Bobby Schiffman: *"Nobody's ever seen her perform, and they're already asking five or six thousand dollars a night for her."*

Percy Sutton with Moms Mabley at a party in the newly remodeled Apollo lobby, early 1970s. ★ *The initial deal with Sutton "fell through" in 1974, but in 1981 Sutton realized his dream to own the Apollo.*

that a $3 million deal for the Apollo and "several buildings along 125th Street" was near. The prospective buyer was Clarence Jones, the publisher of Harlem's newspaper, the *Amsterdam News*, and the AMNEWS Corporation, which also owned radio station WLIB. Percy Sutton, then Manhattan borough president, was the second largest stockholder in the parent company, but Bobby Schiffman announced that Sutton had not taken part in the negotiations that had been under way for several months. A year later the sale was still "pending" to the same principals, now under the banner of a new corporation, Inner City Communications, Inc.

By early 1974 plans for the Apollo had blossomed into what Schiffman said would be a "gorgeous, luxurious, and funky" entertainment and commercial complex. The old Apollo would be razed and a new 3,000-seat theatre would be the centerpiece of a development that would encompass a 400-room hotel, two radio stations, and the offices of the *Amsterdam News*. It was envisioned that Bobby would remain as manager of the theatre for its new black owners. But, as Schiffman has said, this grandiose scheme "fell through" when "the national interest rates went up."

In 1975, ads appeared in the classified sections of the *Wall Street Journal*, *The New York Times*, and the *Village Voice* reading: "For Sale: Harlem's World Famous Apollo Theatre." *The Times* said the asking price was $2 million for the Apollo and "an office building." In April, Eugene Giscombe of the brokers Webb, Brooks and Brooker said that they received inquiries every day and that the Apollo would be sold "in the not too distant future." But there was no future for Bobby Schiffman's tenure at the theatre that had been in his family for so long, and he was forced to close the Apollo in January 1976.

He took a job with the top black booking agency, Universal Attractions, and the task of reopening the theatre under black ownership continued. Several black promoters were contacted about promoting occasional shows in the vacant Apollo. An effort by promoter Clarence Brown to produce a Christmas 1976 show failed. A June 1977 benefit was held. Detroit promoter Eddie Phelps was able to put together a Christmas show in 1977. Not coincidentally, this show package included all Universal Attractions acts: Millie Jackson, the Manhattans, and Harold Melvin and the Blue Notes. The show was a financial and critical success, but people connected with the show were upset by the badly deteriorated condition of the theatre. "It looks like a rathole," one person reported.

Finally, a deal was struck for the sale of the Apollo. *Billboard* announced in March 1978 that the theatre "has been purchased by an unnamed group of individuals. The new owners are reported to be from the Harlem area." The Apollo's lawyer, Marshall Gluck, said the magazine, "declined further comment, saying the new owners would make their plans and identities known shortly."

The Harlem grapevine was ripe with rumors. Although the general consensus uptown was that the new owners were black, the *Village Voice* reported: "There have been rumors circulating that whites are in control behind the scenes, primarily for two reasons (beyond normal paranoia): one, the 253 Realty Corporation, which is listed as the new ownership together with Elmer T. Morris, is made up of 'private investors,' and in such a public operation everyone wants to know why; and two, certain businesses, such as one well-known black-owned and -operated enterprise to which the Apollo owed outstanding debts of many thousand dollars, claim that the new owners have not paid up. 'How can you take over a business and not be aware of its past debts?' said one creditor who wished anonymity. 'Something's fishy.' "

Some even suggested that the "individual investors" were Nicky Barnes, the notorious Harlem drug dealer, and his mob. It was whispered that Barnes kept an office in the Apollo, until he was busted for dealing heroin in 1978 and sentenced to life without parole, and that his organization merely planned to use the theatre as a front to launder drug money. Elmer T. Morris was the only person publicly associated with the Apollo during 253 Realty Corporation's tenure at the theatre, and in the subsequent court documents.*

Before Morris could open the Apollo, the deteriorated theatre had to be completely overhauled at a reported cost of $350,000. The stage had been ruined when water pipes froze and burst, and it was replaced along

---

*Five years after he bought the Apollo, the alleged link between Morris and the Harlem mob was made public by none other than Leroy "Nicky" Barnes himself—who decided to sing to the authorities in the hope of gaining presidential clemency. The police then arrested nine men, accusing six of being members of a "council" that, according to the *Daily News* of March 11, 1983, "divided the city's drug customers and planned and executed murders of informants and others who gave the gang trouble." Three others were accused of participating in the distribution of narcotics, including one Elmer T. "Coco" Morris, Jr., who was described as a former Tuckahoe, New York, police officer.

According to *The New York Times* of the same date: "The arrest complaint quoted Mr. Barnes as saying that Mr. Morris, the former policeman, had acted as 'an instructor to provide firearms and martial arts training to members of the council and their subordinates.' Mr. Barnes also said that Mr. Morris had used law-enforcement contacts to find out that certain individuals were informers, the complaint continued, and that the informers were subsequently killed."

Patrons line up to enter the newly reopened Apollo on May 5,
1978. ★ *Dozens of celebrities strolled through the lobby to
their seats in the VIP boxes.*

with the lighting and sound systems. The entire theatre was painted, new floor tiles and carpeting were laid, drop ceilings added in the lobby and foyer, the dressing rooms were redone, and all the seats reupholstered. Ticket prices were raised to a $10 top, and for the first time they would be sold only on a reserved-seat basis.

The Apollo marquee was relit on May 5, 1978. A huge red, white, and blue banner stretching across 125th Street proclaimed: "The All New Apollo Grand Opening." And it was a gala affair. Maintaining the Apollo tradition of presenting the latest in black music, the headliner was Ralph MacDonald, a Harlem-born Afro-Latin percussionist whose rollicking "Calypso Breakdown" was heating up both the disco and jazz scenes. Dozens of celebrities strolled through the lobby to their seats in the VIP boxes.

Apollo personnel, not used to the new reserved-seating system, had trouble coping with the crowd. Lines grew as ticketholders were met in the lobby and let in a few at a time so that they could be led by ushers, with a bit of confusion, to their seats. Unlike at the Apollo of old, the show began fifty minutes late—without the usual greeting, "Ladies and gentlemen, it's showtime at the Apollo!" As MacDonald began his second number, two banks of speakers on the stage failed, and sound problems marred the entire show, even after a fifteen-minute intermission stretched to forty-five minutes as technicians frantically attempted to fix the system. But the great skill of MacDonald's troupe, which included top musicians Michael Brecher and Toots Thielman, flutist-singer Bobbi Humphrey, and a dance troupe from Soweto, saved the night. The enthusiastic, good-natured crowd was just delighted that the Apollo was back.

After a strong start in 1978, aided by the draw of top disco acts like War, the T-Connection, and Sister Sledge, the Apollo's new owners ran into trouble. Manager David McCarthy and talent-coordinator Sparky Martin complained that black artists, controlled by greedy white managers, were shunning the Apollo. "We're offering them top dollar for a house our size," Martin told the *Amsterdam News* in the summer of 1978, "for them to play here anywhere from three to five days. The O'Jays coldly rejected our $40,000 offer. We tentatively had Teddy Pendergrass about to sign for an August appearance. What happened? His William Morris agency shafted us and booked him instead at Jones Beach." The next summer McCarthy claimed that Sister Sledge's management refused to consider a return engagement even though the Sisters wanted to come home to the Apollo to perform their hit "We Are Family."

Some of the acts may have been scared off by unfamiliarity with and uncertainty about the new owners, and by the rumor that the Internal Revenue Service might attach the Apollo's box-office receipts at any time for failure to pay back taxes. The IRS did make its move in November 1979 after successful concerts by reggae star Bob Marley and Parliament-/Funkadelic. It closed the theatre for failure to turn over payroll taxes for 1978 and 1979. The IRS charged that the taxes, duly withheld from employee paychecks, were used to keep the theatre going. Plagued with more financial problems than it could cope with, the 253 Realty Corporation was forced to declare bankruptcy on May 6, 1981. Although it sought to reorganize under Chapter 11 of the Bankruptcy Act, it listed $585,000 in debts to sixty-two different creditors. All attempts by the corporation to resuscitate the Apollo were doomed to fail.

· · · · ·

Some artists stuck by the Apollo until the bitter end. James Brown, despite his rocky relationship with the black community in the early seventies, appeared in 1978, saying he would rather play for "his folks" at the Apollo than at the White House. And George Clinton, leader of Parliament/Funkadelic, bypassed Madison Square Garden to help keep the Apollo going. Clinton and "P-Funk" were heroes in the ghettos of America, the leading proponents of the wild style and loose philosophy known as funk. Their shows, over the weekend of March 1, 1980, the last live shows at the Apollo, were spectacles of abandon perfectly in keeping with the theatre's grand tradition.

It was 1980, but it could have been 1960 or 1940. The Apollo was all lit up on an icy early March Saturday night. Despite the bitter cold, 125th Street was thronged with people. There was a sense of anticipation in the air. Black teenagers, passing each other on the street, yelled, "Hey, we gonna see Funkadelic!" and gave each other the funk sign: a "U" formed by clenching the fist and extending the pinky and index finger. It stood for Clinton's motto: "One Nation, United, Under Groove."

Inside, the Apollo was packed to the rafters with an almost-all-black crowd made up mainly of teenagers, but with contingents of all ages. A foursome in their mid-thirties sat impassively, perhaps a bit annoyed by the antics of the young energy-packed audience. A little girl in a fluffy red dress danced atop the back of a seat with her father's burly arm holding her tightly around the waist. Spirits were high, literally so, since—a jarring note for those used to Frank Schiffman's Apollo—marijuana

Sister Sledge, late 1970s. ★ *The Apollo's manager claimed that Sister Sledge's management refused to consider a return engagement, even though the Sisters wanted to come home to the Apollo to perform their hit "We Are Family."*

Parliament-Funkadelic, mid-1970s. ★ *"One Nation, United, Under Groove."*

smoke permeated the air. Joints were openly smoked, no furtive cupped-hand tokes as in the Fillmore East; one dude blithely sat puffing on a two-foot-high water pipe.

The m.c. introduced the opening act, the Brides of Funkenstein, and the Apollo's new gold curtain parted, to the cheers of the crowd. Three gorgeous women, provocatively dressed in tight revealing costumes, lured the teenagers to the edge of the stage, and the kids met the Brides with a forest of outstretched hands that the performers grabbed whenever possible. The lead singer, in a shiny, skintight, green leotard, drenched with dangling corn-row braids of hair, elicited squeals of delight and whistles, when, as she danced, the fullness of her breasts was revealed. There was a new addition to the Apollo: a tongue projecting from stage center about eight or ten feet into the orchestra section. As in the old days, each performer worked to outdo the others. Each of the Brides took her turn wriggling and wailing down this appendage, doing her damnedest to outdo her sister. Flashbulbs popped everywhere as people snapped souvenir photos. A young black man dressed in regulation blue polyester bell-bottoms, Adidas shoes, and red stocking cap jumped onstage and began dancing with the lady in green. He was gently eased offstage by a couple of stagehands, and the Brides exited, to the cheers of the audience.

The curtain closed, but the music continued, and the young man with the stocking cap jumped back onstage. The light operator threw the spotlight on him and he shimmied away to the music. The audience cheered him on, and he cheered himself, too. He became a star. He waved his arms in the air and crashed to the floor in a split. The audience squealed its appreciation. There wasn't a kid in the house who didn't envy him. He was a star; he was the show. It was Saturday night at the Apollo Theatre.

Next came a gangly young black comic. He was no fool. He knew enough to direct his first joke to the kids in the Buzzard's Roost, way up in the second balcony. "I just wanted to say hello to you folks up in the second balcony," he said. "I know not all of us could afford reefer, and that's the only way you could get high!" He worked the crowd well with a routine of scatological jokes, and others about dope, getting high, and nodding out—these kids knew well of what he spoke. After he left, to cheers and applause, there was a five-minute break, unlike the seamless shows of the past.

But soon it was startime. Suddenly, the music blasted from speakers powered by P-Funk's huge multimegawatt sound system. The curtain parted to reveal the Parliament/Funkadelic lineup. They looked like a cross between Kiss and the Sun Ra Arkestra. The four guitarists were dressed in superhero garb: winged shoulders, flashy vestments emblazoned with strange insignias, knee-high multicolored boots with six-inch thick soles. George Clinton wore a tan leather jump suit with dangling beads and feathers, a baggy sheepskin cap that hung down his back, and huge white sunglasses. Another character, sporting a close-cropped zebra-striped Afro, wore an old lady's hat and black veil that completely covered his face. There were two percussionists flailing away at an assortment of drums and other noisemakers, and the keyboardist was surrounded by six different keyboards that produced an orchestra's-worth of sound. People outfitted as cartoon characters—a snowman, a gas can with a long snout, a dwarf—cavorted around the brass section. It was controlled pandemonium. The audience went wild. It was Saturday night at the Apollo.

As the band launched into its anthem, "One Nation, United, Under A Groove," the audience stood. Everyone sang along and stomped their feet. Hands folded into the funk sign punctured the air. The band stopped singing, but the audience continued: "One Nation, United, Under A Groove!" Suddenly, two smudge pots on stage exploded in a flash. Pow! Pow!

It was a Saturday night in 1943, and as Porto Rico detonated an explosive charge, Lionel Hampton leaped atop his tom-tom, drumsticks in hand, dancing wildly, as his big band wailed away behind him and the crowd erupted with delight. . . .

"ONE NATION, UNITED, UNDER A GROOVE."

Parliament/Funkadelic changed constantly as group members left the stage and returned wearing different costumes and playing different instruments. Clinton returned in superhero gear and his trademark long black wig.

"ONE NATION, UNITED, UNDER A GROOVE."

Changing pace, a singer named Felipe took center stage. He sang in a style securely in the soul tradition. George Clinton wanted these kids to know that they had a past. Felipe did imitations of soul immortals Sam Cooke, Billy Stewart, Al Green, and Otis Redding. Great grins broke out on the faces of the foursome of older folks who had been trying gamely to get into the P-Funk groove.

"ONE NATION, UNITED, UNDER A GROOVE."

The finale began. The band started to chant, "Do you want to ride on the mothership?" The kids screamed as a ramp, similar to those used to disembark passengers from airplanes, was wheeled onstage. The band screamed chorus after chorus of "Do you want to ride on the mothership?" The funk signs flew, and the band traded choruses, interspersing "One nation, united, under groove" with "Do you want to ride on the mothership?" A giant ten-foot egg was slowly lowered onstage and stopped on top of the ramp. There was another explosion. Pow!

It was a Saturday night in 1937, and as the egg cracked open little Chick Webb emerged and hobbled up to his massive drum set to join the rest of his Chicks. . . .

"ONE NATION, UNITED, UNDER A GROOVE."

No!

It was a Saturday night in 1948, and the huge bubble carrying Dinah Washington stopped too short, jamming the door, while Dinah cussed up a storm inside. . . .

"ONE NATION, UNITED, UNDER A GROOVE."

No!

It was a Saturday night in 1961, and as deejay Jocko Henderson's rocket ship landed on stage, Jocko stepped out to introduce his first act with a "well all roother. . . ."

"ONE NATION, UNITED, UNDER A GROOVE."

No!

It was a Saturday night in 1980, and as the giant egg landed on the ramp, it cracked open, and out popped the lunatic with the zebra-striped Afro wearing nothing but a diaper and sucking away at a baby bottle filled with milk. . . .

"ONE NATION, UNITED, UNDER A GROOVE."

As the Apollo will always be.

"ONE NATION, UNITED, UNDER A GROOVE."

The Apollo got two multi-million dollar renovations in twenty years.

Chris Rock shocked and slayed the Apollo crowd on his 1999 HBO special.

AFTERWORD: How the Apollo Got Its Groove Back

· · · · · · · · · · ·

Just when it seemed that George Clinton's hopeful words would ring hollow down The Block, a long time friend of the Apollo stepped in to try to get the theatre's groove back after 253 Realty's bankruptcy. Percy Sutton finally realized his dream of owning the Apollo when his Inner City Broadcasting Corporation took over in 1981. With a $3.5 million loan from the New York State Urban Development Corporation in May 1983, work began on a total overhaul of the dowdy old theatre that would ultimately cost $16 million.

On June 29, 1983 the Apollo was designated a cultural landmark.

However, in a skeptical community that had been disappointed by the many missteps and false starts at the Apollo it would take some effort to win back the people of Harlem. Billy Mitchell, today the Apollo's Group Tour Director and premier guide, was a newly hired usher in 1984 as Sutton sought to breath new life into the Apollo. "It was so disheartening," he recalled. "It was cold as hell and we were walking around the neighborhood with stacks and stacks of tickets. Going to bars, restaurants, saying, 'The Apollo's opening back up.' We couldn't get people to go through the doors the first few months. The theatre had been closed for quite a while. They'd seen so much going on here, opening, closing. The economy was screwed up. The music changed and didn't appeal to older folks. It took a lot to get people back. Then people started trickling in. Young folks started coming in, and it was something new to a new generation. And, before you knew it this was the place to be again. It was a real party."

As it had throughout its history, in the eighties the theatre presented the latest black sound: rap music, Sutton's WBLS and WLIB radio stations helped promote several contemporary urban shows a month. Amateur Night was triumphantly revived on Christmas Eve, 1985—once again emceed by originator Ralph Cooper. Also, in May of that year, NBC aired *Motown Returns To The Apollo*, a three-hour prime-time special featuring performances by Stevie Wonder, Smokey Robinson, The Temptations and many other Motown stars. It received an unprecedented 11 Emmy nominations and won for best music-variety show. The *Hollywood Reporter* called it "the perfect combination of celebration and commemoration."

As the community came back to the Apollo, 125th Street showed signs of blossoming and regaining vitality. By the late eighties the theatre even became a popular stop again for busloads of European tourists.

But the biggest changes at the theatre in the eighties were largely invisible to its patrons. Most of the renovation costs went into the construction of a television and audio recording facility, much of it in a new building connected to the theatre. A 4,000 square foot television sound stage was built with a control room capable of handling up to eight studio cameras. The most noticeable results were the television programs *It's Showtime at the Apollo*, and another show, *The Apollo Comedy Hour*. But the theatre also did shows for NBC, Nickelodeon, and others, plus numerous commercials. About two dozen music videos were shot at the Apollo in the 1980s for acts such as Stevie Wonder, Whitney Houston, U2, and even Barbara Streisand. Its satellite link up enabled the Apollo to do live broadcasts for Japanese and Italian television. A 24-track audio recording studio with a computerized console attracted work from the likes of Run DMC and Boogie Down Productions. Patti LaBelle and B.B. King recorded live albums.

Nevertheless, Sutton soon ran into many of the same problems the small theatre experienced in the 1970s, as well as new ones. The Apollo still found it difficult to compete for talent and box office with larger venues such as Radio City. Costs of production at the Apollo were about the same as for doing shows at theatres two or three times its size. The Reagan and Bush administrations drastically cut arts, cultural and educational funding. As their trickle down policies failed to reach the cities, New York found itself in a deep recession. Audio and video outfits all over the city went out of business. The Apollo's production business dried up.

All along, Sutton had been pumping his own money into his beloved Apollo trying to keep it going. The annual shortfall made up by Sutton personally and by Inner City Broadcasting was said to reach $2 million. While downtown non-profit venues such as Carnegie Hall and Lincoln Center had high-powered corporate benefactors such as Mobil and Philip Morris to help out, the Apollo had none.

The nineties began on a heavy downbeat for the theatre, but would end on an uplifting high note that carried into the 21st century.

In June 1991, Sutton, unable to continue by himself, asked the state to step in. Working with Congressman Charles Rangel, they established the Apollo Theater Foundation, and Rangel became its Chairman. New York's Empire State Development Corporation took over the theatre and leased the Apollo to the Foundation for 99 years.

On August 4, 1992, sadly and symbolically, the Apollo lost it's greatest link to its storied past when Ralph Cooper died. His wake and funeral were held at the theatre on August 10 and 11 and were described in a *New York Times* obituary headlined "One Final Curtain Call For Apollo's Star-Maker:"

"Through the haze of an oppressively humid day, thousands of people, some dressed in their Sunday finery, filed into the lobby of the Apollo Theater. . . . Elegantly dressed in a gray suit, red tie and matching pocket handkerchief, Ralph W. Cooper, the soul of the theater for 50 years, lay in state in an open coffin surrounded by flowers. 'People were out here long before we opened the doors at 3 o'clock,' said Ozzie Thompson, director of community affairs for the Apollo, 'People know what he's meant.' In a stutter-step, people walked slowly up to Mr. Cooper's body. Theater staff and a police honor guard in white gloves stood in silence. There was no music during the wake, only the bluesy murmurings of people saying under their breath how much Ralph Cooper was going to be missed. Outside, black bunting hung from the theater's marquee, which read: 'Ralph Cooper Sr. We Love and Miss You.' "

Carrying on was a struggle in the early and mid-nineties. Amateur Night, even without its founder, kept bringing people into the Apollo, and in 1992 the Foundation awarded Sutton a five year contract to continue producing and distributing the *It's Showtime at the Apollo* TV show. Performances at the theatre included a VH1 concert by the artist formerly known as Prince in 1993, and *Swing into Spring: A Harlem Tribute to Lionel Hampton* in 1996. But the great showplace once again began to physically deteriorate as revenues shrunk. Sutton and Rangel reached out to a corporate angel that would ultimately become the Apollo's savior, initiating discussions with Time Warner in 1997.

Finger pointing became nearly as common as foot tapping at the Apollo in the late nineties. Some said Sutton's Inner City Broadcasting had a sweetheart deal with the Apollo Theater Foundation for the TV show. Others said he was doing the best he could for the theatre and that he had invested and lost millions. In April 1998 the *Daily News* initiated a series of hard-hitting articles and editorials criticizing the Apollo's financial dealings and decrying the dilapidated condition of the theatre. This catalytic reportage won the newspaper a Pulitzer Prize in 1999—if not the love of the community. Under pressure from the media, Sutton and his associates settled a state lawsuit, paying the Foundation $1 million (with Time Warner kicking in half), and Congressman Rangel resigned as Chairman of the Apollo Board. The people of Harlem seethed as powers beyond their control seemed to be targeting their leaders and jeopardizing their theatre.

Time Warner's involvement was the key to straightening out the mess. Its president, Richard D. Parsons, who later became CEO of Time Warner, was not only one of the most powerful black executives in the world, he was also chairman of the Upper Manhattan Empowerment Zone. For Parsons, helping the Apollo was a way to help his company and Harlem. Time Warner could use the Apollo for its HBO, CNN, movie, television and music divisions in exchange for "adopting" the theatre by providing business advice, technical assistance, equipment and funds.

It also was able to lure new high-powered Foundation board members like Beverly Sills, former chairwoman of Lincoln Center; George Weissman, her predecessor at Lincoln Center and a former chairman of Philip Morris (both of whom left the Board in 2002); producer Quincy Jones; Howard Dodson, director of Harlem's Schomburg Center; Val Azzoli, co-chairman of Warner Music's Atlantic Group; the actor Ossie Davis (Chairman Emeritus); and entertainment lawyer, Jonelle Procope, who joined the Board in 1999 and became its President and CEO in 2003. Parsons was named Chairman of the Board.

In June 2001 a $53 million multi-year renovation got underway, led by Derek Q. Johnson, a Harlem-bred Time Warner senior vice president who became President of the Apollo Theater Foundation. A makeover that will keep the theatre out front well into the 21st Century, it includes computerized enhancements to the famed Apollo marquee, a state-of-the-art sound and lighting system, a new lobby and dressing rooms, and major cosmetic improvements. However, an even more ambitious plan, championed by Johnson, to combine the original Apollo with the adjacent Victoria Theatre (which is also owned by the state) into a $250 million entertainment complex was put on hold as the general economic climate slowed in August 2002, and Johnson resigned.

Even throughout the fractious days of the late nineties and early 21st century, the Apollo continued to maintain and even expand it's innovative and broad based presentations. The rock group Korn became the first of their genre to perform at the Apollo in 1999 and the performance was heard worldwide via satellite, radio and webcast. In the next few years they would be followed into the theatre by other rockers such as David Byrne, The Strokes and Annie Lennox.

A seasoned theater management executive and arts director, David D. Rodriguez, became Executive Director of the Apollo Theater Foundation in 2002. He guided the theatre to an increasingly energetic schedule of musical and other theatrical presentations, and pushed to capitalize upon the Apollo's reputation beyond Harlem. "Urban music and the urban lifestyle is huge all over the world," he says, "and the Apollo is one of the greatest urban brand names with an 80 percent recognition factor internationally. People are buying urban culture in Duluth, and we want the Apollo to go beyond its walls and reach them."

Surely the Apollo enjoys its greatest reach through the hit syndicated television show *Showtime at the Apollo* which is seen in over a hundred markets nationwide. After a successful, if sometimes controversial, run of more than fifteen years, Percy Sutton's Inner City Broadcasting lost the rights to produce the show. For a time he continued with a similar show of his own, but after a legal challenge Sutton backed off and since 2002 *Showtime at the Apollo* has been produced by Suzanne de Passe, a former head of Motown Productions who had won an Emmy in 1985 for *Motown Returns to the Apollo*.

The lure of the Apollo legend regularly reels in high profile events and top stars.

Solidifying its stature as one of the nation's highest profile venues—and with great symbolic importance on the part of the Democratic Party—the Apollo hosted a presidential debate between Democratic contenders Vice President Al Gore and former Senator Bill Bradley on February 21, 2000. Former President Bill Clinton made a point of opening his post-presidential office just down 125th Street from the Apollo in the summer of 2001. In April 2002, Clinton appeared at a fundraiser at the theatre that featured performances by Michael Jackson, Tony Bennett, Reuben Blades and k.d. lang, raising about $3 million for the Democratic National Committee.

Dance, film, and particularly legitimate theater has returned to an even more prominent place in the Apollo's lineup.

The Dance Theatre of Harlem, for the first time, performed its season at the Apollo in 2001. Two years later The Alvin Ailey American Dance Theater's *Ailey at the Apollo!* showed off the talents of Ailey II and The Ailey School's top students. On February 24, 2003 the Apollo presented the Imagenation Independent Film & Music Festival with honorees that included Erykah Badu and Chuck D, and a screening of Stanley Nelson's film *The Murder of Emmett Till*. Important theatrical events at the Apollo in recent years have included, on March 30, 2002, a special presentation of Eve Ensler's *Vagina Monologues*, and The Royal Shakespeare Company's production of Salman Rushdie's *Midnight's Children* which opened in March 2003.

Perhaps the most memorable and important theatrical production was *Harlem Song*. Tony-award winning director George C. Wolfe—the man behind hits such as *Bring in da Noise, Bring in da Funk*, and *Jelly's Last Jam*, and the producer of the Joseph Papp Public Theater—previewed the $4 million production in July 2002. The 90-minute production used dialog, song, dance, slides and film to tell the artistic and social history of Harlem in the 20th Century. It was the first-ever show with an open-ended run to play the Apollo. But the end came sooner than anyone hoped when, in the autumn of 2002, disappointing ticket sales resulted in perilously tight production funds. An infusion of capital kept the show going for a while longer, but it was forced to close at the end of the year.

The community eagerly looks on as the new Apollo recreates itself. "In Harlem it's always 'watch and see,' " says Billy Mitchell. "But I'll tell you what. In all the years I've worked here I truly think now we're on the right road with all the right people in place and the right organization, and I'm so proud. And as this theatre thrives, so does the community."

"Our new vision is to become the epicenter for urban perform-

315

ing arts and culture," says Foundation President and CEO, Jonelle Procope. "Walking around Harlem, you can feel the energy and see the commerce. The Apollo is the economic engine for much of this activity. We've gotten the Apollo on firm footing and now the fun part starts. . . . to build on the Apollo's legacy and take it in new directions. Today, African-American performers can perform pretty much anywhere in the world. But Harlem will always be home to the African-American community and the Apollo home to black performers. Harlem is becoming much more ethnically diverse. Because of what the Apollo represented historically we must preserve its cultural heritage but at the same time offer programming that appeals to a wide range of people."

The Apollo Theatre remains at the heart of the African-American community—the place that legends still call home—as it's been since 1934. . . . James Brown, Smokey Robinson and George Clinton come back. . . . Top black pop stars including Mary J. Blige and P. Diddy, trod the Apollo stage, following in the footsteps of Nat King Cole, Johnny Mathis and Dionne Warwick. . . . Hip-hop group, The Roots, bring the sounds of the street into the theatre like the Orioles in their day. . . . The Apollo's "Latin Nites" series continues the vibrant tradition of Tito Puente and Mongo Santamaria. . . . Wynton Marsalis carries the jazz standard of Dizzy Gillespie. . . . On his 1999 HBO special, Chris Rock shocked and slayed the Apollo crowd summoning memories of Redd Foxx. . . . Debuting her first tour in a decade at the theatre, Whoopi Goldberg, after enjoying mass stardom, paid homage to the Apollo much as Bill Cosby once did. . . . Anxious neophytes continue flocking to Amateur Night in hopes of making it big by touching The Tree of Hope. . . . Through good times and bad, changes in time, taste and technologies, it will always be Showtime at the Apollo.

Index

··········

Note: Page numbers in boldface indicate illustrations.
The Afterword is not indexed.

Abrahamson, Herb, 174
Adams, Joey, 23, 72
Adderley, Cannonball, 251, 253, 269
African Ballet, 281
Aguiar, Angela, 274, 277
Alexander, Willard, 86
Alhambra Theatre, 40, 49, 55, 57, 95
Ali, Bardu, 89
Ali, Muhammad, 7, 254
Allen, Lewis, 145
Allman Brothers, 4
Amateur Night at the Apollo, 18–19, 104–31, **148**, 187, 288
    audience at, 117–31
    "blow-offs" at, 109–12
    careers launched by, 104–05, 112–17
    influence of, 71–72, 82, 107, 109
    origin of, 63, 64, 107
"Amazing Grace," 234
American Federation of Musicians, 133
American Guild of Variety Artists (AGVA), 78
Ammons, Albert, 174
Ammons, Gene, 140

Amsterdam News, 69, 78, 97–98, 157, 300, 303
Anderson, Ernestine, 83
Anderson, Gordon, **76**, **147**, **164**
Anderson, Jervis, 177
Anderson, Maceo, 100
Andrews, Inez, 232
Apollo Burlesque, 60
Apollo Entertainment Television, **309**, 310
Apollo Theatre, **2**, **68**, **127**
    admission charge at, 37, 69, 75, 137, 274, 297
    African music at, 280–81
    Amateur Night at, *see* Amateur Night at the Apollo
    arrangements with other theatres, 29– 30, 53, **54**, 55, 96, 98, 206
    audience at, 74, 117–31, 161, 206–07
    backstage at, 7–12
    balconies at, **127**, 130–31, 153, 180, 229
    basketball at, 10
    bebop at, 132–33, 137–44

317

Apollo Theatre (*cont'd*)
blackballing by, 29, 55, 57
black experience and, 13, 24–25, 123
child entertainers at, 185–88
chorus girls at, 77–78, **79**
closing of, 286, 300
comedy at, 91–97, 165–66, 177–84,
    271–80
as communications center, 7
competition at, 120–22, 262
conditions at, 10, 157
crime at, 8, 10, 285–86
disc jockeys at, 175–76, 195–98, **199**
doubling and, 70–71
dressing rooms at, **5**, **9**, 10, **11**, 12,
    14, 150, **283**
drugs at, 7, 203–04, 250, 286, 304,
    306
during the 1930s, 67–103
during the 1940s, 132–66
during the 1950s, 166–213, **266**
during the 1960s, 239–84
during the 1970s, 285–308
early years of, 60–66
as the establishment, 13, 17
fall reopenings at, 149
as a family, 7, 12, 22
flexibility of, 17
in the future, **309**, 310
gambling at, 8, 10
gangsters and, 37
girl groups at, 253–55
gospel music at, 117, 214–15, 224–38
Harlem community and, 34, 37–38,
    69–70, 74, 117–31, 137, 244–45,
    282, 284, 286, 291–304
heroes of, 13
holdovers at, 146, 157, 168
holiday shows at, 69–70
house band at, 194–97
inaugural show of, 61
influence of, 71–72
jam sessions at, 132–33, 138
jazz at, 268–71
kids and, 128–31
last shows at, 304–08
last years of, 286–308
latest talent and, 17, 18–19
Latin shows at, 178, **179**
lobby of, 3, **126**
management of, 17–22
masters of ceremonies at, 78, **79**, 80,
    196, 274

Motown at, 255–62, 286, 288
movies at, 128, 293–96
mythology of, 13
as only theatre to hire blacks, 27
original name of, 39, **50**, 57, **58–59**,
    60
producers for, 75, **76**, 77, 78, 260
programs at, **20**, **21**, **118**, **134**, **182**
pure blues at, 214, 215–22
record companies and, 255–68
reopening of, **302**, 303–08, 310
revues at, 75–78, 175–76, 260
rhythm and blues at, 167–78, 195,
    210, 219, 227
rhythm-and-blues revues, 176–77
sale of, 298, 300–303
Schiffmans and, *see* Schiffman, Bobby;
    Schiffman, Frank
show-business policy at, 18
significance of, 4, 7, 13, 17, 22
songpluggers at, 173
soul music at, 237–48, 255–68
stagehands at, 12, **15**, 161–62, 185,
    187, 210, 273
swing era and, 80–91, 132–35
talent agents at, 19, 22
tap dancers at, 97–103, 162–63, 177
transvestites and, 131
ushers at, 128
variety of shows at, 17–18
vaudeville at, 19
vocalists at, 144–52
white audience at, 123
white performers at, 22–24, 72, 74,
    206–07, 268–69
Apus and Estrellita, 29, **164**
Arlen, Harold, 44
Armstrong, Louis, 10, **11**, 24, 44, 52, 57,
    69, 141, 187
"Around the World" circuit, 55, 98, 206
Arrington, Joe, Jr., 105–06
    see also Tex, Joe
Ashford, Nicolas, 260
Atkins, Cholly, **16**, 98, **99**, 261–62, 268,
    277
Atlantic Records, 255, 257, 262–67
Auerbach, Larry, 236

Baby Grand bar, 169, 178
Bacharach, Burt, 250
Bailey, Pearl, 3, 24, 105, 112–13, **147**,
    160, 177
popularity of, 146

Baker, Josephine, 188–89, **190**
Balanchine, George, 101
Ballard, Hank, 240
Band Box Club, 44
Banks, Ristina, 77, 78
Baraka, Imamu Amiri, 72, 215
Barbeque, The, 44
Barnes, Nicky, 301*n*
Barnet, Charlie, 24, 72, 74, **76**, 88
Barr, Fred, **196**, 234
Barris, Chuck, 112
Bart, Ben, 201
Basie, Count, 3, 8, 80, 82, **84**, 88, 89, 131, 133, 174, 195, 277
   popularity of, 83
Baskette, Jimmy, 92
Bates, Peg Leg, **164**
Beatles, 4, 22, 23, 245
Bebop, 132–33, 137–44
Bechet, Sidney, 174
Belafonte, Harry, 23
Bell, Arthur, 192
Bell, Thom, 289
Bentley, Gladys, 46
Benton, Brook, 237
Berigan, Bunny, 24, 72, 132
Berle, Milton, 23, 72, **73**
Berry Brothers, 100–101
Billboard, 145, 170, 242, 300–301
Blackman, Teddy, 77
Black Panthers, 192
Blaine, Jerry, 169
Blakey, Art, 140, 268
Bland, Bobby "Blue," 215, 221
Blue Notes, Harold Melvin and the, 289, 291, 300
Blues, city, 219
Blues, pure, 214, 215–22
Bolden, Bunny, 41
Braddock Hotel, 136, 143, 175
Bradford, Alex, 231, 232
Bradford, Perry, 40
Bradley, Oscar, 141
Bradshaw, Tiny, 64
Brecher, Leo, 25–27, 49, 61–66, 293
Brecher, Michael, 303
Brecher, Walter, 293, 296
Brice, Fanny, 57
Briggs, Bunny, 163, **164**, 175
Brooks, Apus, 29, **164**, 165–66
Brooks-Morse, Estrellita, 29, 30, 57, 60, 77, **164**, 165–66
Broonzy, Big Bill, 216

Brown, Clarence, 300
Brown, James, 3, 10, 19, 105, **115**, 156, 170, 200, 201, 237, **241**, 245, 288, 304, 310
   Nixon and, 288–89
   popularity of, 116–17, 128, **129**, 239–43, 247, 248, 260
Brown, Lawrence, 289
Brown, Les, 133
Brown, Maxine, 238, 250, **284**
Brown, Ruth, 7, 12, 105, 112, 113, **114**, 116, 119, 131, 150, 170, 175, 197, 203, 205, **270**
Brown, Troy, 61
Brubeck, Dave, 24, 268, 269
Bryant, Willie, 13, 27, 78, **79**, 80, 135
Bubbles, John, 29, 52–53, 70, 101, **102**, 103
Buck and Bubbles, 52–53, 70, **102**, 103
Burden, Eric, 23
Burke, Solomon, 265, **267**, 271
Burlesque, 57, 60
Burns, Sandy, 92
Buthelezi, Gatsha, 268
Butterbeans and Susie, 92, **93**, **108**
Byas, Don, 46

Caesar, Shirley, 232
Café Society, 145
Calloway, Blanche, 57
Calloway, Cab, 3, **32**, 43, 44, 57, 70, 82, 95, 98, 135, 137, 140, 146, 156, 225
Calvin (cabdriver), 71
Cambridge, Godfrey, **20**
Canby, Vincent, 273
Cantor, Eddie, 100, 101
Capone, Al, 43
Caravans, 232
Cardinals, 143
Carey, Addison, 53, 77
Carpenter, Thelma, **111**
Carson, Johnny, 181
Carter, Benny, 61, **62**, 133
Carter, Betty "Bebop," 269
Carter, Carol, 77
Charles, Ray, 4, 8, 19, 245, **246**, 247, 248, 286
Charleston, Yellow, 46
Chase, Bill, 158
Chessler, Deborah, 162, 168–70, 173–74, 175, 187, 296
Child entertainers, 185–88

319

Childs Restaurant, 49
Chords (rock group), 205
Christian, Charlie, 138
Civil-rights movement, 24–25, 37–38, 244
Clam House, 46
Clapton, Eric, 4
Clark, Dick, 23
Clark, William E., 165
Clarke, Kenny "Klook," 138, 141, 227
Cleopatra Jones and the Casino of Gold, 294
Clinton, George, 304, 307
Clouds of Joy, **85**, 87–88
Clovers, 19
Coasters, 200
Cobb, Arnett, 153
Cochran, Wayne, 23, 206
Coconut Grove, 57, 105
Cohen, Oscar, 19
Cohen, Sidney, 39, 57, 60–66, 78
Cole, Clay, 197
Cole, Nat "King," 144, 145, 146, **148**
Coles, Honi, 31, 33, 72, 77, 97–98, **99**, 103, 243, 261, 262, 277, 282, 284, 288
Collins, Bob, 110
Coltrane, John, 269, **270**, 271
Comedy, black, 91–97, 165–66, 177
  "blackface" makeup and, 92, **94**, 165, 180
  new breed of, 178–84
  in the 1960s, 271–80
Como, Perry, 145, 168
Connie's Inn, 43, 44, 47, **51**, 55, 78, 96
Consumers' Protective Committee, 157–58
Contours, 257
Cook and Brown, 150, 152
Cooke, Sam, **14**, 234–37, 240, 245, 248
Cooper, Ralph, 61, 63, 64, 71, 75, 78, **79**, 80, 82, 87, 96, 107, 132
Cosby, Bill, 3, 273, **275**, 294
Cotton Club, 26, 43–44, **45**, 47, 71, 77, 78, 88, 95, 101, 225
Covering, 198, 205–06, 221
Cox, Ida, 40
"Crazy Blues," 40–41, **42**
Crescent Theatre, 49
Crewcuts, 205
Crickets, 206–07, **208**
Crocker, Frankie, **196**, 197

Cromer, Harold, 19, 22, 27, 69–71, 72, 80, 119, 128, 130, 177, 181, **182**, 183, 192, 194, 195
Crosby, Bing, 113, 168
Cross, Jimmy, 69–71, 78, 177, 181, **182**, 183
Crows, 116
Crudup, Arthur "Big Boy," 3
"Crying in the Chapel," 173–74
Curtis, King, 105, 117

Dameron, Tadd, 140
Dance, Stanley, 81
Dance, 97–103, 160, 162–63
Dancing Feet, **48**
Darin, Bobby, 24, 206
"Darktown Follies," 52
Davenport, John, see Little Willie John
David, Hal, 250
Davidson, John, 187
Davis, Charlie, 77
Davis, Miles, 140, 268, 269, **270**
Davis, Sammy, Jr., 3, **5**, 7, 8, 24, 95, 153, **159**, 163, 278
  on the Apollo audience, 119–20, 124–25, 292
  popularity of, 160–62
Davis, Sammy, Sr., **159**, 160, 161
Day, Doris, 168
De Koenigswarter, Baroness, 144
Delfonics, 289
Dells, 122
Demange, George "Big Frenchy," 47
Dickenson, Vic, 174
Diddley, Bo, 1, 3, 207, **208**, 209
Disc jockeys, 175–76, 195–98, **199**
Disco, 297, 303
Dixie Hummingbirds, 225, 232, 233
Doggett, Bill "Honky Tonk," 1
Domino, Fats, **15**, 17, 23, 198
Dominoes, 116, 210, 213, 234, 247
"Don't Make Me Over," 250
"Don't Mean a Thing If It Ain't Got That Swing," 82
Dorham, Kenny, 140
Dorsey, Jimmy, 4, **5**, 82
Dorsey, Thomas A., 224
Dorsey, Tommy, 4, **5**, 82, 132, 133
Douglas Theatre, 26
Downbeat, 82
Dozier, Lamont, 260
Draper, Paul, 103
Drifters, 116, 210, **212**, 213, 234

Drinkard Sisters, 229
Dr. Jive (Tommy Smalls), 1, 2, **115**, 175–76, **196**, 197
Duchin, Eddy, 43
Dymally, Mervyn, 171

Eagle Band, 41
Earle Theatre, 29, 53
Eckstine, Billy, 3, 98, 113, 135, **139**, 140, 144, 160, 168, 277
  popularity of, 145, 149
Edwards, Susie, 92, **93**, **108**
Eldridge, Roy, 140
Elks' Rendezvous, 156
Ellington, Duke, 3, 24, 41–42, 44, 46, 80, **84**, 100, 101, 163
  popularity of, 82–83, 146
Ertegun, Ahmet, 4, 13, 17, 23, 174–75, 203, 210, 213, 255, 265–66
Esquires, 116

Fabian's Seafood Shop, 49
Famous Flames, James Brown and the, 239–40
Ferguson, Maynard, 268
Fields, Al, 180, 181
Fields, Dorothy, 44
Finton, Nick, 138
First Choice, 289
Fitzgerald, Ella, 3, 10, 12, 30, 87, **90**, 120, 135, 146, 187, 269
  popularity of, 89, 91, 112–13
Five Blind Boys, 227
Five Crowns, 213
Flamingoes, 1, 122
Fletcher, Dusty, 23, 92, 96, **99**
Fletcher Henderson Orchestra, 43
"Flyin' Home," 153
Fosse, Bob, 100
Foster, George "Pops," 227
Four Aces, 206
Four Bobs, 75
Four Jacks, 1
Four Seasons, 24
Four Step Brothers, 100
Four Tops, 261
Foxx, Inez and Charlie, 117
Foxx, Redd, 3, 8, **9**, 19, 37, 146, 178, 271, 273, 277–80
Franklin, Aretha, 4, **16**, 233, 266, **267**
  popularity of, 268
Franklin, Reverend C. L., 233
Frank's Restaurant, 37, 49

Fraser, Gerald, 268
Freed, Alan, 176, 197, 209, **249**
Freedom National Bank, 38
Fulson, Lowell, 219

Gale, Moe, 64
Gale Agency, 169
Gamble, Kenny, 289, **290**
Garland, Phyl, 123, 222
Garner, Errol, 269
Garrison, Jimmy, **270**
Gaye, Marvin, 22, 257, 261, **263**
"Gee," 116
George, Cassietta, 232
Gershwin, George, 103
Getz, Stan, 268
Gibbs, Georgia, 205, 206
Gillespie, John Birks "Dizzy," **9**, 137–41, 149, 152
Gilliam, Stu, 273
Girl groups, 253–55
Giscombe, Eugene, 300
Glaser, Joe, 19, 151
Glenn, Darrell, 173
Glover, Henry, 106
Gluck, Marshall, 301
Godfrey, Arthur, 169
Golden Gate Quartet, 225, **226**
Goldner, George, 116, 253
Goldrosen, John, 207
Goodman, Benny, 74, 82, 89, 91, 133, 152, 153, 204
Gordon, Dexter, 140, 153
Gordy, Berry, Jr., 247, 248, 255–62, 288
Gosdorfer, Milton, 49, 55, 57
Gospel music, 117, 210, 214–15, 224–38, 245, 247
  reaction to, 229, 231
Gourdine, Anthony (Little Anthony), 12, 106–07, **108**, 122, 201–02, 237
Grable, Betty, 70
Green, Al, 19
Greenwood, Lil, 83
Grimes, Tiny, 113
Groundhog (dancer), 163
Guy, Joe, 138

Hale, Teddy, 13, 162–63
Haley, Bill, 206
Hall, Bob, 152, 210
Hamill, Pete, 244
Hamilton, Roy, 106
Hammerstein's Music Hall, 60

Hammond, John, 29–30, 49, 55, 57, 64, **65**, 66, 74, 77, 86, 87, 145, 146, 174, 216, 218, 266
Hampton, Gladys, 153, 156
Hampton, Lionel, 3, 128, 131, 141, 150, 152–53, **155**, 156, 170, 269, 271
Handy, W. C., 47
Harding, Ann, 26
Harlem:
  black comedy and, 91–92
  black community in, 25, 63
  black entertainers in, 158, 160
  during the Depression, 27, 40, 63
  during the 1950s, 177
  during the 1960s, 243–45, 280–84
  125th Street boycott in, 157–58
  as part of the Apollo, 34, 37–38, 69–70, 74, 117–31, 137, 244–45, 282, 284, 286, 291–304
  riots in, 136–37, 282, 284
  segregation in, 49, 52
  swing era and, 91
  white infatuation with, 40, 43–52, 123, 135–37, 177, 284
Harlem Hit Parade, 145
Harlem Opera House, 26, 27, 39, 60, **62**, 63–66, 82, 89, 107, 112
Harlem Renaissance, 39–40, 96
Harper, Leonard, 53, 55, 77
Harper, Toni, 185
Harptones, 1, 116
Harris, Little Benny, 138, 140
Harris, R. H., 234, 236
Harris, Wynonie "Mr. Blues," 152, **154**
Hartman, Eddie, 71
Hawkins, Coleman, 46, **134**
Hawkins, Erskine, **6**, 112, 133, 163
Hawkins, Screamin' Jay, 105, 125, 209–10, **211**, 240
Hayes, Edgar, 64, 146
Heart Beats, 1
Henderson, Douglas "Jocko," **196**, 197–98, **199**, 254
Henderson, Fletcher, **42**, 43, 82
Henderson, Skitch, 280
Henning, Pat, 189
Hentoff, Nat, 269
Herman, Woody, 72, 133, 140
Hill, Teddy, 138, 140
Hines, Earl, 81, 113, 131, 135, **139**, 140, 149
Hite, Les, 140–41
Hodges, Johnny, 175

"Hold On, I'm Coming," 262
Holiday, Billie, 3, 23, **85**, 88, 125, 135, **147**, 160
  popularity of, 87, 145–46
Holiday, Clarence, 87
Holland, Brian and Eddie, 260
Holly, Buddy, 24, 206–07, **208**, 253
Hooker, John Lee, 221
Hope, Bob, 80
Hopkins, Claude, 43, 80
Horne, Lena, 3, 44, 78, **90**, 136
  popularity of, 88–89
"Hot Mallets," 141, 152
House, Son, 216
Howard Theatre, 29, 53, **54**
Howell, Bert, 98
Howlin' Wolf, 1, 219
Hudson, George, 141, **196**
Huff, Leon, 289, **290**
Humphrey, Bobbi, 303
Hunt, Tommy, 250
Hunter, Crackshot, 165
Hurtig, Benjamin, 57, 60
Hurtig and Seamon's Burlesque, 39, 57, **58–59**, 60
Hutton, Ina Ray, 133

"I'm All Right," 237
"I May Be Wrong (But I Think You're Wonderful)," 75, 86, 120
Immerman, Connie and George, 44, 47
Imperials, Little Anthony and the, **108**, 122
Ink Spots, 18, 71, 136, 146, **148**, 160, 169
"I Put a Spell on You," 209–10
Isley Brothers, 19, 237, 250
"It's Not for Me to Say," 192
"It's Too Soon to Know," 169
"I've Got a Woman," 247
"I Want a Hot Dog for My Roll," 92

Jackson, Chuck, 24, 250, 271
Jackson, Jesse, 268
Jackson, Mahalia, 225
Jackson, Michael, 288, **290**
Jackson, Millie, 300
Jackson, Willis, 1
Jackson Five, 286, 288, **290**
Jack Storm Company, 75
Jacquet, Illinois, 152, 153
Jagger, Mick, 23, 265
James, Etta, 1, 206, 240

James, Harry, 24, 72, 132, 133
Jam sessions, 132–33, 137–40
Jazz, 40–52, 268–71
Jefferson, Blind Lemon, 216
Jenny, Jack, 132
Jessel, George, 57
Jeter, Reverend Claude, 232
Jewel Box Revue, 281–82, **283**
Johns, Vere E., 165
Johnson, Buddy, 133, 140, **279**
Johnson, David "Pop," 110
Johnson, Jack, 43
Johnson, James P., 40
Johnson, James Weldon, 52
Johnson, Marv, 257
Johnson, Mary, 3
Johnson, Myra, 75
Johnson, Pete, 174
Jolson, Al, 26
Jones, Clarence, 300
Jones, Elvin, **270**
Jones, Jo, 86
Jones, Junkie, 110
Jones, Tom, 23–24, 245
Joplin, Janis, 23
Jordan, Louis, 152, **159**, 160, 195
  popularity of, 156–57
Jordan, Vernon, 294
Josephson, Barney, 145
Jukeboxes, 144–45, 158, 195
"Jungle Alley," 46

Keith, B. F., 98
Kelly, Ted, 141
Kenny, Bill, 18, 105, 146, **148**, 169
Kentucky Club, 43
Keppard, Freddie, 41
Kersey, Ken, 138
Kilgallen, Dorothy, 70
King, B. B., 215, 216, 221–22, **223**
King, Ben E., 210, 213, 271
King, Martin Luther, Jr., **36**, 38, 192,
  244, 284
Kirby, George, 274
Kirby, John, 133
Kirk, Andy, 4, 29, 80–81, 82, **85**, 92,
  146, 195
  popularity of, 87–88
Kitt, Eartha, 189, **191**, 192
Knight, Gladys, 3, 8, 10, 19, 22, 105,
  117, **118**, 122, 131, 261, 286, **287**
  popularity of, 260, 286
Kohler, Ted, 44

Kongo Knights, 78
Krupa, Gene, 133

Lafayette Theatre, 25–26, 27, 40, 44, 49,
  51, 52–57, 61, 63, 82, 86, 89, 107,
  218
La Guardia, Fiorello, **28**, 60, 136
La Rue, John "Ashcan," **94**, 95
Laughton, Charles, 57
Laurence, Babe "Baby," 163
Lawson's Auditorium, 234
Ledbetter, George "Huddie" (Leadbelly),
  216, **217**, 218, 221
Lee, Beverly, 4, 7, 229, 247, **252**, 253–
  55
Lee, Peggy, 145, 168, 198
Leiber, Jerry, 213
Lennon, John, 22–23, 38
Lenox Club, 44, 46
Lenox Theatre, 26
Leroy and Edith, 75
Leslie, Lew, 29, 44, 101
Levine, Lawerence, 97
Levy, John, 293
Lewis, Jerry, 181, 183
Lewis, Jerry Lee, 206
Lewis, Meade Lux, 174
Lewis, Willie, 8
Lincoln Theatre, 26, 40, 49, 86
Little Anthony and the Imperials, 12,
  106–07, **108**, 122, 201–02, 237
Little Willie John (John Davenport), 13,
  19, 116, **199**, 240
  popularity of, 198–201
Lloyd's steak house, 244
Loco, Joe, **179**
Loew's Seventh Avenue, 26, 89
Loft's Candy Shop, 49
Long, Johnny Lee, 75, 92
Long, Peter, 244, 268
Louis, Joe, 17, **182**, 183–84
Lucky Seven Trio, 98
Lunceford, Jimmie, 80, 82
Lymon, Frankie, 105, **115**, 116, 201–02

Mabley, Jackie "Moms," 3, **15**, **99**, **299**
  popularity of, 96–97
McCarthy, David, 303
McDonald, Bill, 189
MacDonald, Ralph, 303
McEwen, Joe, 262
McGhee, Brownie, 215
McHugh, Jimmy, 44

323

McLean, Jackie, 143–44
McPhatter, Clyde, 116, 170, 210, **212**, 213
McShann, Jay, 143
Madden, Owney, 43, 44, 47, 88
Major, Addington, 44
Makeba, Miriam, **279**, 280
Malachi, John, 140
Malcolm X, 135, 136–37
Mambo Aces, **179**
"Mammy o' Mine," 52–53
Mann, Herbie, 268
Markham, Dewey "Pigmeat," 23, 72, 75, 87, 92, **94**, 95–96, 132, 165
Marley, Bob, 304
Marsala, Joe, 133
Marshall, Jimmy, 27, 31
Martha and the Vandellas, 257
Martin, Dean, 181, 183
Martin, Sally, 224
Martin, Sparky, 303
Martinez, Cliff, 116
Marx Brothers, 26
Mason, John "Spider Bruce," 92, **94**, 165
Mastin, Will, 153, **159**, 160, 161
Mastren, Carmen, 132
Mathis, Johnny, 192, **193**, 194
Melvin, Harold, 289, 291, 300
Meredith, Burgess, 70
Metronome, 146, 149
Mexico's (club), 46
Mezzrow, Milton "Mezz," 46
Micheaux, Oscar, 37
Milhaud, Darius, 43
Miller, Jim, 262
Miller, Mitch, 266
Miller, Norman, *see* Porto Rico
Millinder, Lucius "Lucky," 133, 135, 152, 187, 194–95, 225
Mills, Herbert, 70
Mills, Irving, 83
Mills Brothers, 52, 70, 146
Minsky, Herbert Kay, 60
Minsky's Burlesque, 60
Minton, Henry, 138
Minton's Playhouse, 44, 138, 140
Miracles, Smokey Robinson and the, 257, **287**
Mitchell, Loften, 78, 80, 130
Mitchlll, Scoey, 7, 125, 180, 242, 257, 260, 271, 273–74, **275**, 282

Monk, Thelonious, 138, 269, **270**, 271, **272**
Monroe, Marilyn, 161–62
Monroe's Uptown House, 44, 138, 140
Moore, Sam, 7, **263**
　　see also Sam and Dave"
Moore, Tim "Kingfish," 92
Morales, Noro, 167
Morris, Elmer T., 301
Morrison, Van, 245
Moten, Bennie, 86
Motown, 247, 248, 255–62, 265, 286, 288
　choreography, 261–62
Mound City Blue Blowers, 41
Mount Lebanon Singers, 116
Mulligan, Gerry, 268

NAACP, 92, 133
Nathan, Sid, 242
Navarro, Fats, 140
Nazarro, Nat, 162
Newman, Joe, 153
New York Age, 24, 27, 47, 61, 74, 78, 137, 158, 160, 165, 167*n*, 218
New York Daily News, 44, 46
New York Times, 91–92, 222, 268, 273, 294
New York World-Telegram, 67, 69
Nicholas Brothers, 44, 80, 100–101
Nixon, Richard, 288–89
Norton and Margot, 61
Norwood, Dorothy, 232
"No Time for Squares" (comedy routine), 180–81
Number One Chorus, 77

O'Brien, Joe, 107
Odeon Theatre, 26
Odetta, 215
O'Dwyer, William, 157–58
O'Jays, 289, 303
Olatunji, Babatunde, 280
Oliver, Joseph "King," 40
Oliver, Sy, 175
Olympians, 41
125th Street, **50**, **129**, 157–58, 244, 297–98
Ono, Yoko, 38
"Open the Door, Richard" (comedy routine), 96
Original Creole Band, 41

Original Dixieland Jazz Band, 41
Orioles, 13, 17, 143, 162, **172**, 175, 187, 210
  popularity of, 167–70, 173–74
  see also Vibranaires
Ory, Kid, 41
Otis, Johnny, 4, 17, 30–31, 120, **134**, 135, 171, 173, 175, 198, 202, 203, 219
  on racism, 204–05, 206
Owens, Frankie, 105

Pack, Vivian, 66
Page, Hot Lips, 86
Page, Patti, 205
Page, Walter, 86
Palace Theatre, 52
Paramount Theatre, 70–71, **73**, 162
Parker, Charlie "Bird," 3, 138, 140, 141–44, 149, 162, 175, 269
Parker, Junior, 3
Parker, Leo, 140
Parliament/Funkadelic, 304–08
Passman, Arnold, 197
Patton, Charley, 216
Payne, Benny, 70–71
Payne, Freda, 277
Payola, 197
Pelham, Jimmy, 273
Pendergrass, Teddy, 289, 291, 303
"People," 251
Petite, Joseph, 41
Phelps, Eddie, 300
Philadelphia International, 289
Phillips, Little Esther, 22–23, 171, 175, 185, **186**, 187, 202–03
Phillips, Reuben, 3, 4, 194, 195, 243, 250, 254, 282
Pickett, Wilson, 105, 255, **256**, 262
Pilgrim Travelers, 227
Pinckney, St. Clair, 200, 201, 240, 242, 288
Pips, Gladys Knight and the, 117, 131, 260, 261–62, 286, **287**
Pod's & Jerry's, 46
Poitier, Sidney, 24, 294
Police (rock group), 23
Pomus, Doc, 213
Pops and Louie, 100
"Porgy," 119
Porto Rico (Norman Miller), 27, 104, 106, 109–10, **111**, 185, 187

Potter, Tommy, 140
Powell, Reverend Adam Clayton, Jr., 157
Powell, Adam Clayton, Sr., 136
Prater, Dave, 7, 262, **263**, 288
  see also Sam and Dave
Presley, Elvis, 1–4, **5**, 170, 204, 209, 221, 253
Prima, Louis, 160
Pryor, Richard, **276**, 277
Public Theatre, 77
Puente, Tito, **179**

Racism, 37–38, 49, 52, 157–58, 160, 204–05, 244, 271, 280, 282–83
Radio City Music Hall, 101
Raft, George, 43
Ramey, Gene, 143
Rangel, Charles, 294
Ravens, 168
Rawls, Lou, 248, 291
Ray, Charlie, 95
Ray, Danny, 200, 240, 242, 282
Raye, Martha, 72
Razaf, Andy, 44
Rector, Eddie, 55, **56**, 78
Redding, Otis, 23, 255, **256**, 262
Redman, Don, 64, 75
Reed, Jimmy, 221
Reed, Leonard, 27, 29, 31, 53, 55, 64, 75, 77, 80, 106, 116–17, 176, **182**, 183–84, 206, 231
Reeve, Martha, 257
Rent parties, 47, **48**
Rhythm and blues, 13, 17, 116, 152, 167–78, 195, 210, 219, 227, 234, 236, 245
  reaction to, 170–71
Rhythm Club, 70
Rich, Buddy, 24, 175, 268–69
Richardson, "Jazz Lips," 75
Richmond, June, 72
Rico, Porto, see Porto Rico
Riley, Clayton, 91, 225
River, The, 128
Roberts, Lucky, 40, 163
Robeson, Paul, 24
Robins, 143
Robinson, Bill "Bojangles," 3, 44, 52, 81, 101, **102**, 103, 135, 160
Robinson, Bobby, 198
Robinson, Clarence, 53, 61, 75, **76**, 77

Robinson, Smokey, 3, 22, 257, 260, 285–86, **287**
Robinson, Sugar Chile, **108**, 185, 187–88
Robinson, Sugar Ray, 7
Rock and roll, 176, 177, 206, 236, 238
Rocky G, **196**, 197
Rogers, Timmie, 89, 165, **179**, 180–81
Rolling Stones, 4
Ronettes, 117
Roosevelt Theatre, 26
Roseland Ballroom, 43, 86
Ross, Diana, 3, 257, **259**, 260, 288
Royal Theatre, 29, 53
Runyon, Damon, 70
Rushing, Jimmy, 86, 87, 174
Russell, Nipsey, 178, 180, 271, 273–74
Ruth, Thurman, 225–37

Sam and Dave, 7, 255, 262, **263**, 265, 288
San Domingans, 78
Santamaria, Mongo, **179**, 269
"Save the Children," 294, **295**
Savoy Ballroom, 82, 89, 136
Schiffman, Bobby, **35**, 123, 131, 146, 150, 152, 161, 184, 187, 188, 244, 251, **279**
    on African music, 280–81
    Amateur Night and, 105–12, 117–20
    comedians and, 274, 277–80
    on covering, 205
    described, 33, 34
    disc jockeys and, 197, 198
    economic realities and, 17–18
    father and, 31, 33
    on gospel music, 229, 231, 238
    as head of the Apollo, 34, 37–38
    on jazz, 269, 271
    on the Jewel Box Revue, 281, 282
    last years of the Apollo and, 286, 289–300
    Motown and, 257, 261, 265–66
    new talent and, 17
    opening acts and, 19
    on pure blues, 215, 221
    revues and, 175–76
    rhythm and blues and, 167–69, 175–78
    various performers and, 22, 83, 189, 192, 194, 198, 200–201, 209, 236, 243, 292–93

Schiffman, Frank, **28**, **32**, **54**, 75, **79**, 91, 100, **108**, 123, 145, 149, 160, 162, 173, 180, 187, 206–07, 243, 257, 266
    Apollo and, 17, 27–34, 66, 71, 120, 128, 156
    bebop and, 137, 138, 140
    Brecher and, 25–27, 49, 61–66
    buffers for, 31, 33
    children of, 33–34
    civil rights and, 37–38, 244
    "color line" and, 72, 74
    competition and, 29, 39, 53–57, 61–66
    death of, 34, 292
    described, 27–34, 157, 292
    gospel music and, 225–28, 234, 237
    new talent and, 19, 87, 169
    pure blues and, 216, 218, 221
    retirement of, 34
    swing music and, 82
    talent agents and, 22
Schiffman, Jack, 19, 30, 33–34, 91 145–46, 163, 187
Scott, Mabel, 61
Scullack, Darryl, 285–86
Selah Jubilee Singers, 225, **226**, 227
Shad, Bob, 205
"Shake, Rattle and Roll," 175, 206
Shaw, Arnold, 19, 170, 195
Shaw, Artie, 82
Shaw, Billy, 169
"Sh-boom," 205
Sherman, Joe, 150
Shirelles, 229, 247, 250, **252**
    popularity of, 253–55
Short, Bobby, 185
Shuman, Mort, 213
Silver, Horace, 268
Simon, Paul, 232
Simone, Nina, 119, **121**
Simpson, Valerie, 260
Sims, Howard "Sandman," 8, 12, 19, 31, 37, 98, 100, 110, **111**, 112, 116, 130, 163
Sinatra, Frank, 145, 149
Sissle, Noble, 88–89, 146
Sister Sledge, 303, **305**
"Skinny Legs and All," 265
Skyliners, 206
Smalls, Ed, 46
Smalls, Tommy (Dr. Jive), 1, 2, **115**, 175–76, **196**, 197

Small's Paradise, 43, **45**, 46
Smith, Bessie, 3, 23, 31, **32**, 40, 52, 57, 150
Smith, Buster, 86
Smith, Mamie, 40–41, 216
Smith, Willie, "the Lion," 40, 46, 47
"Soldier Boy," 254
Son and Sonny, 100
Soul music, 234, 236–48, 255–68
   "blue-eyed," 245
Soul Stirrers, 225, 231, 234, **235**, 236
Sound of Philadelphia, the, see Philadelphia International
Spayne, William, 12, **15**, 187, 202, 250
Spector, Phil, 23, 253
Spector, Ronnie, 117
Spellman, A. B., 144
Spinners, 19, **21**, 289
Spo-Dee-O-Dee, 92
Staple, Mavis **230**, 233
Staple Singers, **230**, 232–33
Starr, Jackie, 181
Staton, Dakota, 1
Stearns, Marshall and Jean, 41, 98, 103, 162
Stewart, Billy, 117
Stoller, Mike, 213
Stone, Jessie, 175
"Strange Fruit," 145–46
Strayhorn, Billy, 83
Stump and Stumpy, 19, 22 69–71, 181, **182**, 183
Stylistics, 289
Sublett, John "Bubbles," 52
Sulieman, Idrees, 138
Sullivan, Ed, 23
Sullivan, Niki, 207
Summer, Donna, 297, **299**
Sunset Royal Band, 146
Sunshine Orchestra, 41
Sun Time theatrical circuit, 98
Supremes, Diana Ross and the, 257, 260
Sussman, Morris, 61–66, 78
Sutton, Percy, 244, **299**, 300, 310
Swanee Quintet, 232
Swan Silvertone Singers, 231, 232
Swing era, 80–91, 132–35, 137
Sydenham Hospital, 136
Symphony Sid Torin, **196**, 197

Tap dancers, 97–103, 162–63, 177
Tarnopol, Nat, 247, **249**
Taylor, Yak, 77

T-Connection, 303
Teagarden, Jack, 133
Teenagers, Frankie Lymon and the, 116, 201
Temple, Shirley, 101
Temptations, 257, 260, 261, 262, 292
Terry, Clark, 141
Terry, Sonny, 215
Tex, Joe, 105–06, 117, **264**, 265
Tharp, Sister Rosetta, 225, 227, **230**
Theatre Owners' Booking Association (T.O.B.A.), 53, 55, 96
Thielman, Toots, 303
Thigpen, Ben, 88
Thomas, Francis "Doll," 26, 27, 37, 49, 55, 57, 66, 128, 188
Thompson, Lucky, 140
Thornton, Willie Mae "Big Mama," 219, 221, **223**
Three Chocolateers, 181
Three Degrees, 289
Three Little Words, 100
Three Palmer Brothers, 61
Three Rhythm Kings, 61
Til, Sonny, 168, 169, **172**
Tillie's Chicken Shack, 46
Time, 83
Tip, Tap and Toe, 100
T.O.B.A., see Theatre Owners' Booking Association
Tomashefsky, Steve, 297
Tone, Franchot, 70
Tonk, 8
Tree of Hope, **51**, 105–06
"Truckin' " (comedy routine), 95
Tucker, Ira, 232, 233
Tucker, Sophie, 40
Turner, Big Joe, 4, **172**, 174–75, 206
Turner's Arcadians, 64
253 Realty Corporation, 301, 304
Tyner, McCoy, **270**
Tyson, Clay, 273

Ubangi Club, 163
Uggams, Leslie, 10, 33–34, 105, 175, 185, **186**, 187, 201, 203, 207, 271, 296
Ulanov, Barry, 146, 149
Universal Attractions, 300
"Uptown Saturday Night," 294, **295**

Valentine, Jerry, 131, 140
Vanderbilt, Emily, 43

Variety, 282, 294, 296
Vaughan, Sarah, 3, 17, 18–19, 105, **114**, 140, 144, 269
  popularity of, 113, 123, 149–50
Vibranaires, 168, 169
  see also Orioles
Vigal, John, **94**, 95
Village Voice, 301
Vinson, Eddie "Cleanhead," 113, 133, 135, 152, **154**

Walker, Aaron "T-Bone," 215, 219, **220**
Walker, Albertina, 232
Walker, Jimmy, 43
Waller, Fats, 40, 44, 49, 86, 132
War (disco group), 303
Ward, Aida, 61
Ward, Billy, 105, 116, 210, 247
Ward, Clara, 233, **235**
Ward, Joe, 57, 105
Ward Singers, 233
Warwick, Dionne, 3, 10, 23–24, 33, 105, 117, 120, 122, 229, **249**, 291–92
  popularity of, 250–51
Washington, Baby, **199**
Washington, Dinah, **14**, 17, **151**, 168, 169, 170, 185, 187, 202, 203, 269
  popularity of, 150, 152
Washington, Ford Lee "Buck," 52, 53, **102**, 103, 181
Waters, Ethel, 44, 52, 53, 69, 88, 101, **108**
Waters, Muddy, 207, 221
Watson, Erwin C., 273
Watts, Isaac, 224
Webb, Chick, 30, 82, 89, **90**, 91, 156
Webster, Ben, 46
Weinstock, Joseph, 60
Weissmuller, Johnny, 184
Weldon, Casey Bill, 216

Wexler, Jerry, 255, 268
Whaley, Tom, 27
"What'd I Say," 247
Wheeler, Doc, 113, 116, **196**, 197, 234
White, George, 100
White, Slappy, 274, 278
Whiteman, Paul, 41, 204
Whitfield, Norman, 260
Wilkins, Barron, 43, 46
William Morris Agency, 161, 189, 236, 303
Williams, Bert, 52
Williams, Cootie, 113, 133, 146, 152
Williams, Mary Lou, **85**, 88
Williams, Midge, 218
Willis, Lorraine, 140
Will Mastin Trio, 153, **159**, 160–61
Wilson, Dick, 88
Wilson, Edith, 95
Wilson, Flip, 19, 273, 274, 277
Wilson, Jackie, 17, 110, 112, 213, 237, 240, 245, 247–48, **249**, 271
Wilson, Nancy, 17, 125, **252**, 269, 291–93
  popularity of, 251, 253
Winchell, Walter, 70
Witherspoon, Jimmy, 215, 221
Wonder, Stevie, **129**, 257
Woods, Bertie-Lou, 77
Woods, Maceo, 233–34
World War II era, 135–37, 144

"You Done Lost Your Good Thing Now," 222
"You'll Never Walk Alone," 106
Young, Lester, 86
Young Rascals, 245

Ziegfeld Follies, 52, 101
Zito, Lou, 257